D0878094

Redesigning Women

FEMINIST STUDIES AND MEDIA CULTURE

Series Editor
Andrea Press, University of Illinois at Urbana-Champaign

A list of books in the series appears at the end of this book.

Redesigning Women

Television after the Network Era

AMANDA D. LOTZ

University of Illinois Press

URBANA AND CHICAGO

© 2006 by Amanda D. Lotz
All rights reserved
Manufactured in the United States of America
∞ This book is printed on acid-free paper.
1 2 3 4 5 C P 5 4 3 2 1

Library of Congress Cataloging-in-Publication Data

Lotz, Amanda D., 1974–
Television after the network era / Amanda D. Lotz.
    p.   cm. — (Feminist studies and media culture)
Includes bibliographical references and index.
ISBN-13: 978-0-252-03067-3 (cloth : alk. paper)
ISBN-10: 0-252-03067-2 (cloth : alk. paper)
ISBN-13: 978-0-252-07310-6 (pbk. : alk. paper)
ISBN-10: 0-252-07310-X (pbk. : alk. paper)
1. Women on television. 2. Television programs for women—United
States. 3. Television and women—United States. 4. Television broad-
casting—Social aspects—United States. I. Title. II. Series.
PN1992.8.W65L68   2006
791.45′6522—dc22   2005022122

For Wes and Sharon
and in memory of Jake

Contents

Acknowledgments

This work has survived a long journey, and as my first book, it requires the acknowledgment of many generous souls and influences.

This project began as dissertation research at the University of Texas at Austin, where I was fortunate to be surrounded by a community of mentors who challenged and inspired me and part of a cohort of students whom I valued for their intellectual engagement and friendship. Horace Newcomb and Janet Staiger helped me develop the craft of research and writing, and Gigi Durham, Mary Celeste Kearney, and S. Craig Watkins offered rigorous yet cordial reviews of my work. Horace, Janet, and Mary remain founts of advice. Sharon Ross, Mary Beltran, Susan McLeland, Kelly Kessler, Yeidy Rivero, and Fran Guilfoyle shared discussions of feminism, the shows, and pitchers of margaritas.

I composed the first draft of the manuscript during a Mellon postdoctoral fellowship at Washington University in St. Louis, where my colleagues Jeff Smith, Bill Paul, Wayne Fields, and Lori Turner helped protect my research time and offered valuable guidance in the transition from graduate school. Revisions continued after beginning a job at Denison University, where I shared my days with the most collegial and respectful group I can imagine. Tim Anderson, John Arthos, Jeff Bennett, Suzanne Condray, Amanda Gunn, Jeff Kurtz, Lisbeth Lipari, and David Winterstein have generously answered questions and helped me find time to write amidst an intense teaching environment and during some difficult years.

I would never have found my way to Texas without the wise counsel and encouragement of Chris Anderson and Herb Terry at Indiana University, and without advice and motivation from Robert Dawson, Kent Menzel, and

Meryl Altman I may have ended up a very unhappy lawyer. My graduate career and the media studies conference circuit have provided intellectual com-
patriots whose work I admire and enjoy. Tim Havens, Jonathan Nichols-
Pethick, Vicky Johnson, Elana Levine, Jason Mittell, Derek Kompare, Cynthia
Chris, Ron Becker, Vicki Mayer, and Jennifer Fuller have shared academic
pursuits, friendship, and fantastic conversations about television.

   I thank Andrea Press for identifying potential in my project. Bonnie J. Dow
offered a rigorous review of an earlier draft, and I am thankful for her willingness to engage a project that was still rough in many places with such precise and deliberate suggestions. Kerry Callahan at the University of Illinois
Press diligently matched my pace, and if any of the shows are still on the air
by the time this book reaches print, she is the one responsible.

   Interviews with Tim Brooks and Tricia Melton at Lifetime, Deborah Beece
and Sarah Barasch at Oxygen, and Lee Heffernan at Women's Entertainment
added valuable depth to my understanding of female-targeted cable networks. I appreciate their generosity with their time and data. Also, I may not
have pursued the institutional research if my first research experience with
Nancy Miller and Gary Randall had not been so fruitful.

   I have been blessed with uncommonly generous family and friends throughout my life. Although I'm still not sure that I have adequately explained what
it is that I do, Robert, Linda, and Nicholas Lotz have accepted and supported
my career choices and always shown up to help us move. Pam, Rick, and Clay
Huffstutter have also offered support over the long and continuing journey. I
am thankful that Horace continues to be a munificent mentor and wise counsel, offering quick response to my occasionally profuse e-mails.

   I dedicate the book to my husband, Wes Huffstutter, and my partner in
most things academic, Sharon Ross, in thanks for the many ways they helped
this book materialize. The nomadic years of early academia have challenged
Wes's career, and he has patiently accompanied me across the country and
back and has been a willing and able partner in this journey. He has also endured more than his fair share of female-centered dramas and unbegrudg-
ingly gave up control of the remote long ago. Sharon has juggled the hats of
co-author, therapist, critic, and friend with exceptional grace and always offered whatever assurance or critique was needed.

   I am sorry that I wasn't able to complete this project in time to share it
with a dear friend and kindred spirit. His courage, perseverance, and devotion remain an inspiration, and he is missed dearly.

Redesigning Women

Introduction:
Female-Centered Dramas after the
Network Era

In the fall of 1997, the prime-time television season began much like every other year. September arrived, and audiences greeted a range of new series amidst hype and fanfare, although most of these programs disappeared from the screen in less than a year. One member of the 1997 class surpassed the competition in popular accounts of the new television offerings. *Ally McBeal* initially mesmerized critics. Its playful form, quirky lead character, and some quality that no one could quite pinpoint—was it the tone, the actress, the digital graphics?—earned it a place on many "must see" lists. But as her audience grew to know her, fascination with the title character turned to debate. Due largely to the singular yet complexly contradictory voice that the writer and executive producer, David E. Kelley, gave to her and the rest of the cast, Ally and her real-life counterpart, the actor Calista Flockhart, found themselves at the center of cultural debates about feminism, femininity, and womanhood.

McBeal and Flockhart—as many popular accounts conflated the two—were initially praised for embodying a curious mixture of success and vulnerability. Described as "imperfection idealized" and "quirky, contradictory, and wonderful," Ally appeared to rewrite popular definitions of the "new woman" character type, with many critics comparing her to television's original new woman, Mary Richards of *The Mary Tyler Moore Show*.[1] Ally appeared as a sort of "new" new woman—she came of age amidst contradictory messages about female success and assumed the career gains that women of Mary's era fought hard to secure. When we first meet Ally, however, she has only partially achieved the utopian destiny supposedly afforded by second-wave feminism. Despite graduating from Harvard Law School and working for a Boston law firm, the lack of a romantic partner imbalances her and leaves her constantly pining for Mr. Right.

And so the debate began. A range of popular and academic feminist critics queried what kind of new new woman Ally was. Her soulful longing over lost and yet-to-be-found love earned her the status of a pariah in many feminist assessments, yet audiences continued tuning in. The high-water mark of the Ally debate came during the summer of 1998, between the first and second seasons of the series, when a *Time* magazine cover story on the status of feminism in contemporary U.S. society included Ally in a timeline of feminist figures.[2] Ghoulishly disembodied black-and-white head shots of the feminist thinkers Susan B. Anthony, Betty Friedan, and Gloria Steinem begin the progression, which is concluded by Flockhart as Ally in vivid color. Below the heads, the title caption asks, "Is Feminism Dead?" What had to this point been a random trickle of popular journalism considering Ally and her series now escalated into a tidal wave, with pundits in and out of the United States debating the significance of the series for popular understandings of feminism.

This "Ally mania" followed two years of other noteworthy gains in atypical depictions of female television characters that had yielded a similar renewed attention to the relationships between fictional television characters and the status of women and feminism. The appearance of "warrior women" began two years earlier with *Xena: Warrior Princess* in 1995 and *La Femme Nikita* and *Buffy the Vampire Slayer* in the spring of 1997.[3] Less than a year after the debut of *Ally McBeal, Sex and the City*, a series about the dating experiences of four women living in New York, appeared on HBO. Subsequent television seasons inaugurated further changes, as an unprecedented proliferation of dramatic series with women protagonists debuted: *Any Day Now, Charmed, Providence, Judging Amy, Once and Again, Strong Medicine, That's Life, The Huntress, Dark Angel, Gilmore Girls, The Division, Kate Brasher, Witchblade, Crossing Jordan, Philly, Alias, The American Embassy, The Court, Birds of Prey, Presidio Med, Girls Club, MISSING, Wildcard, Joan of Arcadia, Tru Calling, Cold Case, Karen Sisco, Wonderfalls, The L Word, Veronica Mars, Desperate Housewives, Medium, Grey's Anatomy, The Inside,* and *The Closer.*[4] All of these focus on one or more female character, and networks promote them in ways that are designed particularly to draw female audiences.

The significance of the concurrent appearance and success of so many female-centered dramas is noteworthy in relation to the historical lack of female-centered dramas. Prior to the late 1990s, U.S. network television primarily had confined complex representations of women to situation comedies (*I Love Lucy, That Girl, The Mary Tyler Moore Show, Roseanne, Murphy Brown*) and to individual characters placed in male-dominated dramatic settings (Captain Janeway in *Star Trek: Voyager,* for example). Female characters first achieved central roles in dramatic narratives that included an emphasis on adventure, such as in *Honey West, The Avengers, Police Woman,* and *Get Christie Love.* These characters were central to the narrative, but they were often partnered with a man. By the late 1970s, a trickle of dramas starring women without male partners appeared: *Charlie's Angels, Wonder Woman,* and *The Bionic Woman.* They expanded the previous adventure/dramatic roles of female characters, but like their predecessors, they often relied on the sexual appeal of their heroines in promotion while simultaneously trading on the differentiation provided by featuring women in "empowered" roles. A significant shift occurred with the arrival of *Cagney and Lacey* in 1982. This dramatic representation of able female cops led to *Murder, She Wrote* (1984–96), *China Beach* (1988–91), *Sisters* (1991–96), *Dr. Quinn, Medicine Woman* (1993–98), and *Touched by an Angel* (1994–2003), as a greater diversity of female-centered dramatic series appeared and succeeded in drawing sizable audiences to their stories. These series anticipated the watershed of female-centered dramas that emerged in the mid 1990s, an environment in which more than twenty dramatic series with female protagonists competed for the attention of audiences. As table 1 indicates, female-centered dramas date to television's early years, but many of these series were commercial failures (lasting one season or less), and it was unusual for a plurality of these series to air coterminously until the mid 1990s.

The arrival of all these dramatic series—with their empowered and fantastic action heroines, depictions of single career women, flawed yet authentic professionals struggling with family commitments and occupational demands, and even the continued success of characters depicting a more traditional femininity—indicates unprecedented possibilities for female characters and audiences, as these diverse series exist and succeed contemporaneously. Cable networks specifically addressing women expanded programming targeted to female audiences during this same period. Some of the dramatic series appear on Lifetime, a cable-television network that brands itself as "Television for Women." Lifetime began promoting its female focus in 1994 and has become one of the most profitable U.S. cable networks, ranking as the most watched cable network from the beginning of 2001 through the end of the first quarter of 2003.[5] The value of the female niche has not gone unnoticed; Oxygen Media joined the competition in 2000 as an integrated Web and cable media brand targeted to women with an edgier, more irreverent sensibility; and Rainbow Media relaunched their female-skewing Romance Classics Network as the Women's Entertainment Network (WE) in 2001. Lifetime also repackages its films on a second cable network, the Lifetime Movie Network (LMN), and it launched Lifetime Real Women (LRW) in 2001, a channel designed to specialize in reality programming.

In addition to these cable networks, which explicitly announce themselves as destinations for women, others target female audiences more subtly by programming genres and forms that traditionally have attracted female audiences. ABC debuted SoapNet in 2000 as a forum for a second airing of its daily soap operas as well as off-net, syndicated prime-time soaps such as *Falcon Crest* and *Sisters*. As part of the expanded packages available with sub-

Table 1. Relevant Female-Centered Dramatic Series

Multiple Seasons	One Season or Less
1945–54	
The Loretta Young Show (Anth: NBC, 1953–61)	*The Gallery of Mme. Lui-Tsong* (DUM, Sep.–Nov. 1951)
1955–64	
The Nurses (CBS, 1962–65)	*Decoy* (Syn., 1957–?)
1965–74	
The Avengers (ABC, 1966–69) *Police Woman* (NBC, 1974–78)	*Honey West* (ABC, Sept. 1965–Sept. 1966) *The Snoop Sisters* (NBC, Dec. 1973–Aug. 1974) *Get Christie Love* (ABC, Nov. 1974–July 1975)
1975–84	
Charlie's Angels (ABC, 1976–81) *Wonder Woman* (ABC, 1976–77; CBS, 1977–79) *The Bionic Woman* (ABC, Jan. 1976–May 1977; NBC, July 1977–Sept. 1978) *Cagney & Lacey* (CBS, 1982–88) *Murder, She Wrote* (CBS, 1984–96)	*Kate McShane* (CBS, Sept.–Nov. 1975) *Sara* (CBS, Feb.–July 1976) *Partners in Crime* (NBC, Sept.–Dec. 1984)
1985–94	
The Days and Nights of Molly Dodd (NBC, May 1987–June 1988; Lifetime, 1988–91) *China Beach* (ABC, Apr. 1988–91) *The Trials of Rosie O'Neill* (CBS, 1990–92) *The Hidden Room* (Lifetime, 1991–93) *Sisters* (NBC, 1991–96) *Dr. Quinn, Medicine Woman* (CBS, 1993–98) *Touched by an Angel* (CBS, 1994–2003)	*Lady Blue* (ABC, Sept. 1985–Jan. 1986) *Kay O'Brien* (CBS, Sept.–Nov. 1986) *Heartbeat* (ABC, Mar. 1988–Apr. 1989) *Brewster Place* (ABC, May–July 1990) *Veronica Clare* (Lifetime, 1991, 9 episodes) *Christy* (CBS, Apr.–May, Aug.-Sept. 1994; June–Aug. 1995) *Sweet Justice* (NBC, Sept. 1994–Apr. 1995)

Table 1. (cont.)

Multiple Seasons	One Season or Less
1995–2005	
Xena: Warrior Princess (Syn., 1995–2001)	
The Profiler (NBC, 1996–2000)	
La Femme Nikita (USA, 1997–2001)	
Buffy the Vampire Slayer (WB, Mar. 1997–2001; UPN 2001–3)	
Ally McBeal (FOX, 1997–2002)	
Sex and the City (HBO, 1998–2004)	
Any Day Now (Lifetime, 1998–2002)	
Felicity (WB, 1998–2002)*	
Charmed (WB, 1998–)	
Providence (NBC, Jan. 1999–2002)	
Judging Amy (CBS, 1999–2005)	
Once and Again (ABC, 1999–2002)	
Family Law (CBS, 1999–2002)*	
Popular (WB, 1999–2001)*	
Strong Medicine (Lifetime, 2000–2006)	
That's Life (CBS, 2000–2002)	*The Huntress* (USA, 2000–2001)
Dark Angel (FOX, 2000–2002)	
Gilmore Girls (WB, 2000–)	*Kate Brasher* (CBS, 2001)
The Division (Lifetime, 2001–4)	*Philly* (ABC, 2001–2)
Witchblade (TNT, 2001–2)	*The American Embassy* (FOX, 2002)
Alias (ABC, 2001–6)	*The Court* (ABC, 2002)
Crossing Jordan (NBC, 2001–)	*For the People* (Lifetime, 2002)
Wildcard (Lifetime, 2003–5)	*Girls Club* (FOX, 2002)
MISSING (Lifetime, 2003–)	*Presidio Med* (CBS, 2002–3)
Joan of Arcadia (CBS, 2003–5)	*Birds of Prey* (WB, 2002–3)
Tru Calling (FOX, 2003–4)	*Karen Sisco* (ABC, 2003–4)
Cold Case (CBS, 2003–)	*Wonderfalls* (FOX, 2004)
The L Word (Showtime, 2004–)	
Veronica Mars (UPN, 2004–)	
Desperate Housewives (ABC, 2004–)	
Medium (NBC, 2005–)	
Grey's Anatomy (ABC, 2005–)	

* These series debut as female-centered but undergo changes that reconfigure them into ensemble series.

scription to the pay-cable network HBO, the service now offers the HBO Signature channel, which is described by a network senior vice president as "the destination for women" and promoted as "entertainment for a woman's heart, mind, and spirit." Cinemax offers WMax, a channel with "movies for every woman," and Showtime programs ShoWomen.[6]

The appearance of so many female-centered dramas and the emergence of three "women's" cable networks invites critical analysis of the institutional environment that made possible the production of diversified female characters and the subsequent production of similarly diversified female audiences—as well as analysis of these forms. This book starts from the empirical fact that a profound increase in programming explicitly targeting women occurred on U.S. television at the end of the twentieth century. Specifically, a particular television form—dramatic series centered on one or more female characters—multiplied to an unprecedented degree in the number of series and the variety of forms taken by these series. The number and range of these series reached a high point in 2000 and began waning in the early years of the twenty-first century, but they remain more pronounced than in previous years. A second relevant phenomenon has occurred simultaneously. Female-targeted cable networks expanded from one (Lifetime) to three (Lifetime, Oxygen, Women's Entertainment) during the late 1990s and early 2000s, while other networks targeting women—although less explicitly—were also launched during this period.

In terms of dramatic structure and setting, the shows airing in the late 1990s are unprecedented in their plurality and diversity. The most similar moment in U.S. television history might be the mid to late 1970s, during which four dramatic series about women aired for a number of seasons: *Police Woman, Charlie's Angels, Wonder Woman,* and *The Bionic Woman.* As anyone even vaguely familiar with these shows will recognize, a plurality of shows existed, but they were very similar in form and in the types of stories their action/adventure format allowed. The multiplicity in series types and variation within type among the shows in the late 1990s makes it particularly crucial to consider any one show within the larger context of other shows airing simultaneously. Significantly, the women in these series share a great deal of demographic similarity: most are white, heterosexual, single, employed in highly professionalized careers, and live in upper-middle-class, if not upper-class, worlds.[7] Despite this significant demographic similarity, however, the series explore a new multiplicity of stories about women and their lives.

The expansion in cable networks targeting women mirrors the contribution of the dramas, as they provide additional venues through which stories about women can be told. These networks also expand the range of stories told about women and their lives through a diversity of programming genres and sensibilities. The distinctive brand identities created by these networks indicate significant psychographic variation in their intended audiences despite similarities in audience demographics.

Much of the increase in addressing female viewers has resulted from changes in the competitive environment of the television industry in the United States and adjustments in the strategies networks and advertisers use to pursue this audience. The expansion of sex-specific niche-audience targeting from cable to broadcast networks illustrates the importance of female audiences, a crucial target of industries now defined by media convergence and corporate conglomeration. Broadcast and cable networks enact intricate program selection and marketing strategies to acknowledge the variation among tastes and ideologies of different groups of women. This market segmentation now expands beyond classification by series to the identification of discrete networks as the primary location for specific subgroups of women. Such labeling may not be as explicit as "Television for Women," but a review of programming schedules and an analysis of series reveals exactly which type of female audience member networks and their advertisers desire.

A variety of institutional changes have altered the conditions under which networks and production studios create programming about and for women. The establishment of a new institutional context and evidence of narrative changes illustrate the need for examining the intertwined questions of what these series suggest about the status of female audiences, under what conditions stories about women are constructed and shared, and what these series indicate about female audiences' narrative preferences. My analysis of female-targeted cable networks and female-centered dramas indicates a new plurality and multiplicity in the stories being told about women's lives on U.S. television, particularly in dramatic genres. This circulation of a multiplicity of stories about women does not categorically suggest a more feminist environment. Rather, my analysis identifies and explores the types of stories about women these series and networks proffer in order to establish the variation among the series, as well as to differentiate these narratives from previous norms. This narrative environment reflects changes in the status of media targeted to women and variation in the dominant stories told about their lives. It also indicates the need for reassessing critical feminist media frameworks and building theories that are able to analyze a robust range of textual context.

This introductory chapter pursues the related work of contextualizing and explaining the expansion of female-centered dramas and female-targeted networks, identifying the causes of this alteration of textual norms, and exploring the consequences for critical media scholarship about gender and television. The evolving institutional structure of U.S. media has enabled many of the textual developments examined here, as industrial reorganization privileges the targeting of niche tastes and narrowcasting. Such changes demand that we interrogate inherited scripts for evaluating media, engage with broader conversations about gender and media, and reevaluate the dominant language of critical discussion.

Targeting the New Woman: "Women's Programs," 1970–95

The widespread emergence of the "working woman" or "new woman" character in the 1970s provides an important precedent in which norms of gender representation can be clearly linked to cultural and institutional changes.[8] The growth of the women's movement and the gradual increase of career options for women contributed to the changing cultural milieu, while industrial factors also supported new attitudes toward women as media consumers. Feminist television scholars, including Eileen Meehan, Jackie Byars, Lauren Rabinovitz, and Julie d'Acci, identified a number of factors occurring in the 1970s that contributed to making white, middle-class women an even more desirable demographic than advertisers had previously considered them to be, the foremost being advertisers' discovery of "working women."[9] Women had always been a primary target of television advertisers because of their perceived influence on most household buying, but their importance increased when many upper-middle-class women entered the workforce. Advertisers believed that career women controlled much of their disposable income and had more of it to spend than housewives.[10]

Rabinovitz argues that programming with a specifically feminist valence emerged in the 1970s because "it was good business," as a result of the organization of new marketing data into a greater number of demographic categories and what she considers a simultaneous coming of age of "a more independently minded female generation."[11] The cultural examination of women's liberation in the 1970s suggested to advertisers that programming targeting the most desirable audience—upscale, career women—could be inscribed with more liberal discourses and representations than previously had been associated with women on television.[12] Rabinovitz contends that "[a] generic address of 'feminism' became an important strategy because it served the needs of American television executives who could cultivate programming that could be identified with target audiences whom they wanted to measure and deliver to advertising agencies."[13] The arrival of feminist discourses in sitcoms such as *The Mary Tyler Moore Show* (1970–77), *Maude* (1972–78), and *Rhoda* (1974–78) marked networks' attempts to reach women who were experiencing changes in their economic and familial status with stories infused with "lifestyle politics."[14]

Byars and Meehan identify a range of economic, technological, and industrial changes that combined to alter the competitive television environment throughout the 1980s, which further adjusted the status of female viewers and led to the creation of a cable network targeting women.[15] They too emphasize the increase of women in the workforce but explain this as a broad and complex phenomenon.[16] The employment gains feminists secured through consciousness raising and activism led some women into the workforce in the 1970s, but by the 1980s, economic recession forced many middle-class families to send women into the public sphere because of the need for dual incomes. Many women became employed outside of the home out of necessity rather than by choice, a significant enough shift that A. C. Nielsen added the category of "working women" to its demographic measurements as early as 1976.[17] d'Acci notes that specific targeting of the "professional woman" arose from advertisers' recognition of women as a market that was "essentially a conglomeration of fragmented and continually shifting elements," of which professional women were the most conspicuous consumers.[18] Advertisers may have recognized the diverse composition of the women's market at this time, but it was twenty years before programmers and networks would hail women in distinct subgroups.

The economic restructuring after the 1980s recession and destabilization of labor led advertisers and networks to compete for a narrowed "consumerist caste," the "proportion of the population with disposable income for unnecessary goods."[19] This led advertisers to target upscale viewers who had the greatest buying power, a move Byars and Meehan and Jane Arthurs argue led to the creation of hybrid prime-time series such as *Cagney and Lacey* and *St. Elsewhere,* which were designed to attract upscale male and female audiences by combining narrative strategies and generic features for broader appeal.[20] Advertisers considered another option for reaching consumers at this time, as cable reached 50 percent penetration in 1988—the reach forecast to be necessary for financial viability. As cable delivery continued to expand, advertisers realized that although cable channels draw smaller audiences, they also draw large numbers of the consumerist caste and often provide narrowly targeted audiences (specific demographic groups such as children or women), which made advertising buys on cable increasingly valuable for those selling demographically specific goods. The events chronicled by Byars and Meehan suggest an increase in women's status as valuable prime-time audience members, and the events explored in this book suggest that advertisers now ascribe even greater importance to female audiences.

These realizations were not limited to cable programmers. Broadcast networks also began courting female audiences more aggressively in prime time, and throughout the 1980s and 1990s, much of the attention paid to "significant" or "noteworthy" representations of women focused on the increasingly professional roles female characters occupied. Narratives decreasingly emphasized women in the public sphere as exceptional, a shift that corresponds to second-wave feminism's investment in expanding professional opportunities for women. A revolution of some sort transpired almost every other season throughout the 1980s, as *Cagney and Lacey* offered a series centered on two female cops in 1982, Jessica Fletcher commanded a mystery narrative in *Murder, She Wrote* in 1984, four women dominated comedies with *Golden Girls* in 1985 and *Designing Women* in 1986, and opinionated women took center stage across the socioeconomic spectrum with *Murphy Brown* and *Roseanne* in 1988. This regular trickle of series centering upon female protagonists (many of which were lauded for including at least moments of feminist politics) offered important predecessors to the comparative tidal wave of series and depictions emerging in the late 1990s, but it was not until the 1997 success of *Ally McBeal* that female-centered dramas moved into the mainstream in multiple and diverse forms.

Various forces shape the way advertisers and networks view female audiences. The current situation could be very different if not for the liberal feminist project of seeking legal equality in the 1970s, the economic shifts of the early 1980s, and technological changes such as the emergence of cable as a viable distribution system and the creation of affordable video-recording systems.[21] All of these developments altered traditional approaches that were established during the early years of radio for seeking female audiences and designing women's programming.

The institutional context critical to understanding the textual phenomena studied in this book results from the transition toward a "post-network era" of industrial organization in the U.S. television industry. This industrial reconfiguration begins with the "multichannel transition," a dynamic period that coincides with the rise of female-centered dramas and female-targeted cable networks. These institutional adjustments enabled a change in competitive strategy from broadcasting to narrowcasting. The fragmentation of audiences resulting from the new array of programming options has made it possible for networks to profitably target niche-specific audience groups, which is extremely important for "women," a specific yet sizable audience group.

Gender and Media at a Crossroads

The National Organization for Women (NOW) began producing an annual study in 2000 that rates the gender portrayals on prime-time television.[22] NOW's methodology draws from mass communication content analysis approaches to develop rankings of prime-time television shows on broadcast networks. Slight methodological variation exists among the three studies between 2000 and 2002, but the survey results generally are based on one or two viewings of each prime-time broadcast network series. The study assigns "field respondents" from around the country to particular nights and networks, although it is unclear whether multiple respondents provide data on a given show. The report assigns a score (1–100) to each series in the categories of violence, gender composition, sexual exploitation, and social responsibility. The scores are then averaged to provide an overall score for the show, which the report uses to rank the show and determine network rankings.[23]

The NOW study continues the legacy of some of the earliest U.S. feminist media scholarship that developed alongside the second-wave women's movement and drew attention to the manifold ways mainstream media perpetuate sexist ideologies. In communication, this research primarily took the form of content analysis—studies that counted the number of women relative to men or sorted and counted different character types. These studies documented the limited range of women's representations, either in terms of their underrepresentation in televisual worlds or their overwhelming confinement to roles in which they are primarily defined as wives, mothers, love interests, or potential sexual conquests. Such studies argued that this limited indication of the range of women's experiences reinforced beliefs that these were the roles appropriate for women.[24] Scholars described this type of early quantitative research as looking at "sex roles" and eventually "gender roles" (throughout the book I denote this theoretical and methodological approach as the "role model" framework), and such studies were based on a transmission model of communication that postulates direct relationships between mediated images and their social effects.[25]

Such quantitative measures are valuable for surveying expansive amounts of media content but are ill-suited for determining what meaning audiences make or what such character categorizations might mean to viewers. Content analysis provides limited tools for exploring the stories and ideas expressed in television series because they are based upon a framework that understands the process of meaning-making in simplistic terms. Criticism of this method's assumption of a passive audience and skepticism about the correlation between "distorted" media images and social effects appeared as early at the late 1970s.[26] However, role-model research has persisted in framing discussions about women and media and has been dominant in influencing U.S. public policy so that character categorizations such as positive or negative representations, working women, or sex objects have become the dominant language for discussing gender and media.[27] The push for "positive" representations of women came to be the primary terms through which gender issues in media were discussed outside of academic studies, in some ways making the legacy of this approach more significant than the research.[28]

Feminists who came to television from film studies emphasized entirely different analytic frameworks.[29] Some of the earliest studies of film also looked at stereotypes in explaining the limited roles available to women, but these perspectives were quickly discounted.[30] By the late 1970s, feminist film scholarship moved away from questions of whether depictions were "realistic" and instead emphasized psychoanalytic approaches that theorized the gendered dynamics of viewing pleasures. Film studies' relationship with literary studies also resulted in its emphasis on textual analysis, both in terms of the visual construction of the film image and ideological analysis of narrative. Film studies also has emphasized genre in exploring and understanding gender and film. Feminist scholars trained in literary theory and film studies brought these distinctive theories and emphases to examinations of television throughout the 1980s as coterminous but mutually exclusive bodies of research about gender and television developed in mass communication and film.[31]

Feminist television scholarship emerging from British cultural studies offers alternative frameworks of theory and method. The territorial tensions among communication, film, and television study in Britain mirror and diverge from those of the United States, but British feminist television scholars were particularly central in shaping television studies.[32] Definitions of culture that emphasized the "everyday" rather than "high culture," which had been common in studies of literature, film, and art, gave this work a particular focus. The cultural studies project of valorizing the popular led to extensive research on denigrated cultural forms, which resulted in the sophisticated and thorough examinations of the soap opera that are now central to television studies.[33] As part of the popular project of cultural studies, scholars turned from texts to audiences to develop more comprehensive understandings of meaning-making than the effects tradition that dominated mass communication's examinations of audiences.[34]

Cultural studies theorized a contrasting approach to the mass communication tradition of combating negative representations or stereotypes. Rather than calling for "positive" representations, cultural studies theorists advocate the creation of a multiplicity of images of whatever group has been stereotyped in order to make the stereotypes "uninhabitable."[35] Cultural studies offers a more complex theorization of the meaning-making process, insisting that media do not affect all people the same way. As Stuart Hall argues, meaning cannot be fixed, although dominant ideology structures the range of possible meanings in an "attempt to fix the one true meaning" of images and language. So-called positive representations are ineffective in combating stereotypes because they too cannot "fix" meaning. To intervene in a dominant meaning system one must engage the stereotype—"use" it to prevent a fixed meaning from becoming established and to reveal "representation" as a practice.[36]

All three approaches to studying gender and media have developed distinctive bodies of scholarship and possess clear intellectual histories, although film and cultural studies have been more conversant in developing feminist analyses of television. All three areas continue to produce vital contributions to their own disciplinary conversations; however, examples such as the NOW report and its relationship to variant approaches to studying gender and media illustrate the continued influence and problematic legacy of the role-model framework beyond the academic realm. Additionally, the adjusted cultural, technological, generational, and representational context explored here further suggests limitations in this traditional approach and language for discussing gender and media.

NOW established its media activism campaign in 1999 "with the mission of promoting positive and diverse portrayals of women and girls in the media."[37] As one of the most visible and powerful feminist activist groups, NOW apparently identified quantitative measures as the best strategy for influencing policy. Despite this, subtle evidence in NOW's reports indicates that the authors sensed the inadequacy of their method, although they do not call attention to this point. In the 2000 report, NOW triangulated their quantitative measures with a separate diary-based study in which feminist viewers recorded all of the prime-time programs they watched over two weeks. Notable discrepancies exist between the shows most watched by feminists and those scoring highest on the quantitative assessment. Five of the top ten shows in the quantitative assessment did not rank in the top twenty-one shows viewed by feminists, while only two of the top ten shows viewed by feminists rated in the top fifteen shows of the quantitative ranking (see table 2). This diary method was not replicated in subsequent reports, perhaps because it suggested that the quantitative tool did not adequately determine "feminist" shows.

In its 2001 study, NOW included a list of ten shows it recommends within the text of the report that summarizes findings; however, only four of these series ranked among the top ten list created by the quantitative matrix. The report does not explain why it recommends these shows over those that performed best in their quantitative analysis—a discrepancy that popular press coverage of the report acknowledged.[38] In 2002, the report used only a single viewing of each show, a unit of analysis unlikely to result in reliable data.

Table 2. Results from 2000–2002 NOW Prime-Time Report

2000

Quantitative Ranking	Diary Viewing
1. *Family Law*	1. *ER*
2. *Chicago Hope*	2. *NYPD Blue*
3. *Once & Again*	3. *The West Wing*
4. *ER*	4. *Who Wants to Be a Millionaire*
5. *Sabrina the Teenage Witch*	5. *Judging Amy*
6. *20/20*	6. *Family Law*
7. *Providence*	t. *Frasier*
8. *Becker*	8. *Ally McBeal*
9. *Touched by an Angel*	t. *Dateline*
10. *Friends*	t. *Law & Order*
11. *The Hughleys*	11. *Will & Grace*
12. *Kids Say the Darndest Things*	12. *Friends*
13. *City of Angels*	13. *Providence*
14. *The Practice*	t. *Star Trek: Voyager*
15. *Jungle 2 Jungle*	15. *That '70s Show*
16. *Judging Amy*	16. *Once & Again*
17. *Malcolm in the Middle*	17. *The Practice*
18. *The Grammy Awards*	t. *The Simpsons*
19. *The West Wing*	t. *Sports Night*
20. *Ally McBeal*	t. *The X-Files*
21. *Winning Lines*	21. *Biography*
22. *Party of Five*	22. *Dharma & Greg*
23. *Greed*	t. *7th Heaven*
24. *Law & Order*	
25. *Dateline*	
26. *Little Richard*	
27. *That '70s Show*	
28. *Who Wants to Be a Millionaire*	
29. *Frasier*	
30. *Phenomenon*	

2001

Quantitative Ranking	"NOW Recommends"
1. *Gilmore Girls*	*Gilmore Girls*
2. *Sabrina the Teenage Witch*	*Girlfriends*
3. *Felicity*	*What about Joan*
4. *What about Joan*	*My Wife and Kids*
5. *Popstars*	*That's Life*
6. *Kate Brasher*	*Buffy the Vampire Slayer*
7. *Girlfriends*	*Felicity*
8. *Star Trek: Voyager*	*Boston Public*
9. *7th Heaven*	*Ed*
10. *Bette*	*C.S.I.*
11. *That's Life*	
12. *Moesha*	
13. *My Wife and Kids*	
14. *Weakest Link*	
15. *The Weber Show*	
16. *The Hughleys*	
17. *Boston Public*	
18. *Steve Harvey Show*	

Table 2. (cont.)

2001 (cont.)

Quantitative Ranking

19. *Jack & Jill*
20. *The Parkers*
21. *Dawson's Creek*
22. *Buffy the Vampire Slayer*
23. *Popular*
24. *Ed*
25. *Boot Camp*
26. *All Souls*
27. *Charmed*
28. *The Geena Davis Show*
29. *DAG*
   t. *Yes, Dear*

2002

Quantitative Ranking

A+ *The Ellen Show*
A+ *ER*
A+ *Girlfriends*
A+ *Judging Amy*
A+ *Providence*
A *60 Minutes II*
A *Family Law*
A *George Lopez Show*
A *Gilmore Girls*
A *My Wife and Kids*
A *Primetime Live*
A- *Amazing Race*
A- *Bernie Mac Show*
A- *Felicity*
A- *The Guardian*
A- *Once & Again*
A- *Reba*
A- *Touched by an Angel*
A- *The West Wing*
B+ *Boston Public*
B+ *For Your Love*
B+ *Law & Order*
B+ *Maybe It's Me*
B+ *Under One Roof*
B+ *Will & Grace*
B *20/20*
B *Becker*
B *One on One*
B *The Practice*
B *Sabrina the Teenage Witch*

In 2000, the survey only looked at ABC, CBS, FOX, and NBC, and also in-cluded movies airing on television. In 2001, the study only looked at new shows added that season and shows on The WB and UPN and discontinued assessing films. In 2002, the survey transferred numerical rankings to a letter-grade system and included ABC, CBS, FOX, NBC, The WB, and UPN. All data available at www.NOW.org.

This report included some analysis, but it remains clear that narrative devices such as satire and parody cannot be incorporated into the quantitative survey. The curious equal weighting of all four categories of analysis (violence, gender composition, sexual exploitation, and social responsibility) also continued to produce haphazard assessments.

The NOW study provides meaningful evidence about the effect of various approaches to studying media on broader popular discussions and policy deliberations about media. My analysis of the study is highly critical, but I affirm NOW's endeavor. As a feminist television scholar, I would like NOW to contribute to the discussion of how ideas about gender and feminism circulated by media affect cultural understandings of gender roles and issues. Aspects of the studies' methodology and assumptions about media, however, make the NOW reports problematic and even harmful to feminist media endeavors. The more flimsy findings of the study undermine its valid discoveries, such as the limited demographic range of female characters on television and the general tendency for narratives to provide individualized solutions when they raise structural problems. There is ample evidence that even the NOW constituency is uncertain about the shows the quantitative method advocates, but its insistence upon continuing with this framework prevents the organization from exploring nonquantifiable narrative and aesthetic aspects.

Additionally, the theorization of an inactive audience that is central to the role-model framework might negatively affect the feminist project by yielding findings that alienate potential feminists. Many of the young women who come through my classrooms express hesitancy about a "feminist party line" they believe they must follow if they are to identify themselves as feminists. The NOW survey's simplistic quantitative matrix offers no way to understand how factors other than violence, gender composition, sexual exploitation, and social responsibility contribute to viewing pleasure and can lead to a disjuncture for feminist audience members who enjoy a show that ranks poorly. *Buffy the Vampire Slayer* clearly resonates with young, even feminist women, evidenced in their exceptional fan activity surrounding the show.[39] Yet the series merits only a C- by the 2002 NOW survey, which clearly dismisses what viewers find important about the show because it lacks a sophisticated way to assess stories relative to the violence and predominantly white cast. Finally, it is ironic that "experience" remains absent from the survey's measures, given that it has had such a central role in feminist praxis. Feminist methodology has been highly critical of the lack of reflexiveness common to scientific ways of knowing; yet this feminist research endeavor completely lacks alternative measures of knowledge.

Perhaps because of its primacy as an approach for studying media, or perhaps because of U.S. society's proclivity for quantifiable measures, the assumptions and assertions of the role-model framework transcend the isolated circles of academic media study.[40] The role-model framework became the standard bearer of policy and activism initiatives and the vernacular of journalistic criticism, and evidence of its dichotomous assessments can be found in U.S. academic scholarship beyond mass communication.[41] Many of the books about feminism or women and television produced in the United States in recent years have been written by scholars outside of critical media studies, and while these works provide carefully detailed criticism, most do not address institutional structures or the complexity of textual production in a system in which art and commerce are inextricably connected.[42] The lack of comprehensive studies about television, gender issues, and feminism from a media studies perspective has prevented the development of a complex and multifaceted understanding of the U.S. media environment, as has emerged in other contexts.

I note this as additional evidence of the role-model legacy because these studies tend to make dichotomous assessments of programs or representations as feminist or antifeminist, progressive or regressive, as is characteristic of identifying role models or positive and negative representations. Such work has more in common with feminist research that seeks out role models than that which calls for a multiplicity of images to make stereotypes uninhabitable.[43] Charlotte Brunsdon critiques feminist media criticism that remains stuck in binary assessments in her analysis of what she labels the "Ur feminist article," while she and others have also noted the significance of the changing cultural and televisual environment on the frameworks of feminist media criticism.[44]

A chance constellation of forces combined in the 1970s to allow the feminist study of gender and television to remain distinct from the study of gender in film or mass communication. These three areas share common objects of study yet are marked by clear distinctions and have varied histories in different national contexts. My own training brought me first to the study of gender and media through communication, which I then merged with theories and methods of British cultural studies to find a home in what might be uncertainly termed "media studies" within the United States. Defined primarily in opposition to other areas or fields, media studies is not mass communication in the U.S. tradition, with its emphasis on quantitative methods and examinations of media effects, nor is it as emphatically text-based and theoretical as film studies—although these categorizations are necessarily partial and generalized. Media studies has drawn methods and assumptions from these related fields to develop its own canon of work, yet in most cases it remains without a distinctive institutional home. Its practitioners are scattered throughout a wide range of departments and exist on the margins of professional organizations and journal audiences.[45]

This book centrally speaks to the areas of critical television or media studies that were only beginning to develop a few decades ago. With its focus on narratives about women, the book more specifically might be placed within the subcategory of "feminist television criticism," as specifically applied by Charlotte Brunsdon, Julie d'Acci, and Lynn Spigel in their anthology bearing the same title.[46] Feminist television criticism fuses feminist theory with British cultural studies theories of media content and industries while drawing from many of the central assumptions, methods, and theories of the feminist study of mass communication and film.[47] Feminist television criticism takes a variety of forms, including studies of female audiences; traditionally "female" genres such as soap operas; representational strategies used in depicting women, femininity, and feminism; production histories of women in the television industry; and political-economy studies of women as television consumers.[48]

The particular topic under consideration is less important than the methodology and theoretical framework for distinguishing among various feminist approaches to the study of media. The central methodological feature of feminist television criticism is a synthetic approach to studying media, which is drawn from British cultural studies.[49] This synthesis of methods and theories for studying gender and television emerges after the blending of various contributions of feminism, cultural studies, film studies, and some mass communication perspectives. Feminist television criticism primarily focuses on texts within a critical historical, cultural, and industrial context and includes an awareness of multiple sites of investigation (institutions, texts, and audiences), even if these areas are not specifically incorporated within an individual work. Feminist television critics explore representations of women's lives, discourse about their abilities, and stories that dominate cultural narratives based upon the presumption that these series contribute to the audience's perceptions of gender roles and understanding of the world.

I enter these conversations a generation after their inauguration, which accounts for a different training and perspective on the organization, central issues, and debates of the "field" and the permeability of disciplinary boundaries. This vantage point perhaps affords me the opportunity to attempt a more cross-disciplinary conversation. Theoretical and methodological roots are crucial to differentiating variant approaches to the study of gender and media, and I seek to critically engage with, rather than disregard, perspectives that are not central to my approach in the pursuit of theory building and shared conversations. I foreground the legacy of mass communication research on stereotypes and its language of role models and positive and negative representations, even though these categories and the findings of this approach are not commonly recognized by feminist media and film scholars. The mass communication approach frames popular conversations about the relationship between media in society and institutionally supported media-policy objectives to afford it substantial cultural power; I interrogate it as part of a commitment to enabling activist practice and engaging with the cultures of media consumption.

The complexity of cultural studies' theorization of representation offers an important intervention into how feminist cultural critics approach the texts they study. Throughout most of television history, the mass communication approach derived value from the paucity of character types occupied by women and the limited variation among them—a situation that affirmed the dominance of identifying "role models." The multiplicity of dramas centered upon female characters and the proliferation of networks targeting women suggest that a new logic organizes the U.S. commercial television industry. The range of female characters—thirty-four, across the sixteen series I specifically consider here—indicates a diversified narrative sphere in which seeking out role models is of little utility.[50] The role-model approach lacks tools for exploring the narratives that characters inhabit or other artistic components of a storytelling form, and the storytelling capabilities of such a multiplicity of shows would be inhibited if their female characters must all fit some ideal type. Given the expanded privileges some women now enjoy as a result of second-wave feminism, it is impossible to determine what might constitute this ideal due to the diversity and sophistication of contemporary feminist thought. Feminist sites of activism have become exceptionally varied and can even be contradictory.[51]

The multiplicity of and variation among female-centered dramas and networks of the late 1990s consequently requires a reconfiguration of how feminist media critics consider these textual spaces. The specific televisual context alters the significance of each series because each show must be considered relative to a range of other series. Popular and academic critics must be wary of making the same claims or holding the same expectations of every series as they did in eras in which stories about women were more narrowly circumscribed. The changed cultural, institutional, and representational context allows characterizations and discourses of individual texts to *mean differently* than if they were the only series, or one of very few, in a given period.

But Is Ally a Feminist?

Whenever I teach courses such as Women in American Media Culture, our conversations begin by establishing foundational concepts, of which feminism is obviously central. In those first hours of our time together I ask students what feminism is (before assigning reading that would make the answer clear), and I routinely receive responses indicating that most students' perceptions are primarily formed from the vast stew of popular culture. Perhaps feminism is *The Vagina Monologues,* the Spice Girls, and Courtney Love, as the most recent "serious" mainstream journalistic treatment of feminism in *Time* magazine suggests,[52] but as activists and academics know, these popular culture iterations do not even begin to hint at the depth and diversity of feminist thinking. As I write, I am at the end of one of these semesters, and while I graded a response-paper assignment I was reminded of how powerful the popular culture definition of feminists as man-hating, hairy-legged ballbusters remains. Students were generally willing to accept the fight for equality as the determining feature of feminism, but despite our weeks together some still sought to separate this understanding from what those "super-radical feminists" and "female supremacists" advocate, a straw-man (or straw-woman, if I were a "super-radical feminist") version of feminism they set up to embrace its ideals but not the name.

It is difficult to reconcile popular perceptions of feminism communicated through popular culture with the theoretical depth of the arguments dominating many areas of academic and activist feminism.[53] A variety of previous scholars have looked at or for feminism in television texts and provided thoughtful and well-supported textual analyses.[54] My intention is not to rank, label, or analyze television series based on their feminist discourses or representations; the critical feminist contribution of this work develops through my examination of the broader industrial reevaluation of female audiences in narrowcast media environments and how this affects the social perceptions and lived realities of women.

It is unclear whether the development of multiple female-centered dramas is a progressive feminist gain. The existence of a variety of dramatic stories is not itself indicative of more progressive politics, and it certainly is possible for a multiplicity of series and a diversity of stories to remain overwhelmingly retrograde in their gender politics. I do not find the series to be unequivocally conservative (antifeminist) or exceedingly progressive (feminist). My primary argument evolves from the cultural studies framework to explore whether the unprecedented level of multiplicity contributes to making some stereotypes uninhabitable to a degree not previously evidenced, or how the range of stories might allow certain depictions (such as motherhood) to take on new meaning.

My analysis consequently addresses narrative trends and motifs that are recognizable as characteristic of different types of dramas and does not provide an episodic analysis of individual shows as would be common in other types of ideological criticism. I address the feminist politics of some of these discursive and representational trends, although this assessment is far more ambivalent than most similar feminist criticism. Issues of gender politics and discursive constructions of feminism are at the heart of this project, but this preliminary assessment emphasizes narrative rather than feminist criticism. Subsequent research might utilize this book as an intellectual starting point that contributes to the work of explaining and analyzing a particular industrial context from which to develop more detailed assessments of these series and those to come.

Another aspect that complicates my students' understanding of feminism is its diverse and varied nature, which is not at all what they expect after years of media constructions of feminism as a monolithic entity. Although feminist criticism is not the central mode of analysis, the wide-ranging applications of feminism and the more problematic diversity of definitions of postfeminism necessitate that I delineate my use of these terms. Fundamentally, I follow bell hooks's definition of feminism: "To me feminism is not simply a struggle to end male chauvinism or a movement to ensure that women will have equal rights with men; it is a commitment to eradicating the ideology of domination that permeates Western culture on various levels—sex, race, and class, to name a few—and a commitment to reorganizing U.S. society so that the self-development of people can take precedence over imperialism, economic expansion, and material desires."[55]

In the course of a lesson in which I map the different ways feminism has been organized and the utility of each—by theoretical emphasis, by historical period, or by "wave"—I would characterize hooks's definition as emblematic of postfeminism (although she does not characterize it this way). Deviating from the norm among U.S. feminist media scholars, I follow the use of "postfeminism" suggested by Ann Brooks and other scholars writing from locations such as Australia, New Zealand, and Britain. In Brooks's terms:

> Postfeminism as understood from this perspective is about the conceptual shift within feminism from debates around equality to a focus on debates around difference. It is fundamentally about, not a depoliticization of feminism, but a political shift in feminism's conceptual and theoretical agenda. Postfeminism is about a critical engagement with earlier feminist political and theoretical concepts and strategies as a result of its engagement with other social movements for change. Postfeminism expresses the intersection of feminism with postmodernism, poststructuralism and post-colonialism, and as such represents a dynamic movement capable of challenging modernist, patriarchal and imperialist frameworks. In the process postfeminism facilitates a broad-based,

pluralistic conception of the application of feminism, and addresses the demands of marginalized, diasporic and colonized cultures for a non-hegemonic
feminism capable of giving voice to local, indigenous and post-colonial feminisms.[56]

Brooks's definition rehabilitates "postfeminism" and defies its use as suggestive of something that is antifeminist or as a time after feminism. She instead constructs it as a theoretical terrain that results from a breakdown in
consensus during second-wave feminism in the areas of the political effect
of critiques by women of color, the contemplation of sexual difference, and
the intersection of feminist thinking with postmodernism, poststructural-
ism, and postcolonialism.[57]

Although this book is not primarily about different types of feminist
media discourse, my understanding of feminism is crucial to my analyses.
My use of "postfeminism" does diverge significantly from other U.S. scholars such as Bonnie Dow, Andrea Press, Tania Modleski, Mary Vavrus, and
Sarah Projansky, whose work in some ways I continue.[58] I attend to postfeminism less here than in previous publications because the phenomenon
at the core of this book is distinct from postfeminism's intervention into issues of gender and popular culture.[59] Certainly, the multiplicity of narratives explored here and the discourses they produce relate to the changed
context "postfeminism" sometimes distinguishes, but its uncertain status as
a voguish but ill-defined critical term leads me to incorporate it sparingly in
explaining the expansion of female-centered dramas and female-targeted
cable networks.

I earlier characterized my textual analyses as a somewhat ambivalent form
of feminist criticism. Throughout the book I acknowledge the different arguments that might be made of the texts from various feminist perspectives,
perhaps because I cannot quite free myself of the ghost of earlier training in
the mass communication role-model framework. In examining these shows
(I consider myself a fan of some, while others I find tedious for narrative and
ideological reasons), I could see the evidence another scholar might use to
argue that the texts are regressive or antifeminist. As a committed and regular viewer of the multiplicity of series airing in the late 1990s, the old standards of evidence led me to indefinite conclusions. The popularity of these
shows with sophisticated female audiences spurred on the nagging suspi-
cion that the contribution of these texts defied previous analytic frames. As
a result, I offer some less-than-declarative assessments of the feminist potential of many of these shows. This ambivalence results from my understanding of the complex and contradictory ways that casting, character pres-

entation, and narrative intricacies confound simplistic identifications of these shows as categorically feminist or antifeminist.

Instead, I explore questions such as: Does this institutional environment provide a context in which audiences see a range of female characters in such a way as to make their stereotypes uninhabitable? What do these dramas/ networks tell us about the valuation of female audiences? How do the conditions of the multichannel transition contribute to the options facing female audiences? How do these dramas/networks circumscribe the range of stories told and the range of female audience members that are valuable? Do these dramas/networks allow for the telling of nontraditional stories about women? If so, how and why? And how does this expanded address of specifically female audiences relate to feminist goals?

Industrial Context: After the Network Era

Significant adjustments in programming norms do not happen arbitrarily, yet it is also difficult to isolate a singular cause of wide-reaching change. The ascendance of the female-centered drama and the multiplication of women's cable networks must be understood as resulting from an intertwined confluence of industrial and sociocultural factors. The readjustment of the U.S. television industry from the industrial logic of the network era into a period of multichannel transition has radically altered the targeting of female audiences. Exploring the effects of industry-wide changes on the status of female audiences is essential to understanding how and why the popular culture terrain might shift as it did in the closing years of the twentieth century. Cultural studies approaches to media do not presuppose that industrial factors determine content absolutely, and although I emphasize the adjustments from the network era, the simple element of chance—of an unconventional show that succeeds—also plays a significant role in the unscientific process of creating commercially viable art.[60]

Previous changes in the representation of women on television, such as the emergence of the working-woman character in the 1970s, could be explained as much by examining cultural trends as by industrial adjustments: for example, the increasing profile of the women's movement and the career pursuits of female audience members led networks to adjust their address of women. As many feminists have lamented, the late 1990s were hardly characterized by a resurgence in feminist activism. Instead of the reemergence of a women's movement comparable to that of the 1970s, a series of institutional shifts and reconfigurations enabled the appearance of a surplus of female-centered narratives across broadcast, basic, and premium cable networks.

Many of these shifts were not particularly designed or intended to directly advance women; rather, women have been the primary beneficiaries of the shift to niche audiences because of the degree to which they are an identifiable audience subset of substantial size. Limiting a network's appeal to half of the population was an imprudent strategy in the era of three broadcast competitors; however, targeting women and even subgroups of women becomes a viable strategy in the present competitive environment.

A number of institutional adjustments initiated the multichannel transition that began in the mid 1980s and continues through the era this book examines. As "transition" suggests, formal practices and new norms did not solidify during this period; rather, the industry steadily adopted a range of new technologies, services, and ways to use television. Perhaps the most substantial adjustment in business practice resulted from changes in ownership and the steady consolidation of media holdings into a handful of global media conglomerates during the two decades from 1985 to 2005 in which the transition occurred. The purchase of the broadcast networks ABC, CBS, and NBC first altered the ownership structure, as these independent companies become small cogs in larger media portfolios.[61] These media conglomerates often accumulate assets that span production, distribution, and exhibition and own television and film studios, multiple cable stations, Internet holdings, music labels, retail stores, entertainment parks, book and magazine publishing, and cable systems.

Competition in the television industry expanded as new broadcast networks were launched successfully and the technological capabilities of cable slowly reached the broad populace.[62] In 1988, the U.S. cable industry reached 50 percent penetration, the subscription base analysts believed necessary for cable operators to provide a large enough audience to achieve profitability.[63] This subscription level increased from only 19.9 percent in 1980, to 56.4 percent by 1990, and reached 68 percent in 2000. By 2000, nearly ten million additional households received programming via Direct Broadcast Satellite, so by 2004 over 85 percent of U.S. households received television signals through a nonbroadcast provider.[64]

As new broadcast and cable networks expanded viewers' choices, a range of technologies offered them more control. Videocassette recorders provided one of the earliest technological developments to revolutionize viewers' relationship with and control over television entertainment in this era; they were present in nearly 50 percent of U.S. homes by 1987,[65] 68.6 percent by 1990,[66] and leveled off at 85 percent at the end of the century.[67] Recording devices allow viewers to negate programmers' strategies through time-shifting and introduced a new competitor with the home-video purchase and rental market. The VCR established a modest beginning for the consumer electronics industry that has since yielded digital technologies that integrate Internet and television, while digital video recorders (DVRs) such as TiVo and Replay TV further expand consumer control.

All of these changes took place during a period of decreased regulatory control. It is difficult to identify a clear causal relationship, but the deregulatory environment certainly contributed to enabling many of these changes, particularly ownership conglomeration. These developments, along with others such as the rise in multi-set homes and the attendant decrease in family viewing, affect industry operations and how networks value female audiences. These adjustments have helped move the industry through the multichannel transition toward a post-network era, which is likely to be categorized by even more pronounced viewer choice and control after a more thorough reorganization of institutional practices and norms. These changing practices contribute to the proliferation of female-centered dramatic series and female-targeted networks because the adjusted competitive environment revises programming strategies to increase the value of female audiences.

The Significance of Narrowcasting

The changes characteristic of the multichannel transition have affected the economics of traditional broadcast networks enormously. An increase in competitors resulted in smaller profit margins and a reconfiguration of strategies, as broadcasters now compete with cable networks that are able to maintain profits while narrowcasting to a small audience segment. The leaner financial times and constant need for development and innovation also disrupted relations between networks and their affiliates, as each saw the others' profits as gained at their expense.

As a survey of any newspaper's television guide reveals, competition arose mainly from cable networks, which eroded the combined broadcast share, the percentage of those watching television who watched broadcast networks, from ninety to sixty-four during the 1980s.[68] Network share continued to decline during the 1990s, although not at such a sharp rate, with broadcast networks (ABC, CBS, FOX, NBC, The WB, and UPN) reaching an average of only 58 percent of those watching television at the conclusion of the 1999–2000 season and the aggregate cable audience overtaking the aggregate broadcast audience in the 2003–4 season.[69] The audience erosion was particularly acute for ABC, NBC, and CBS, who lost audience share to the three emergent broadcasters and cable networks, both of which tended to draw younger viewers preferred by advertisers.

As other scholars have argued, the rise of female-centered, if not somewhat feminist, sitcoms in the 1970s can be explained by the value afforded to working women as consumers and advertisers' perceptions of their narrative preferences. Attempts to reach the working women of the 1970s and 1980s were complex endeavors, as programmers had to create series that would address the "new woman" but also housewives, husbands, and most people between the advertiser-coveted ages of eighteen and forty-nine. In the era of the three dominant U.S. networks, the top thirty programs earned ratings of thirty to twenty, a number that indicates the percentage of households with televisions who were watching that program. By the 1998–99 season, a point by which network-era norms were clearly disrupted, the highest rated series (*E.R.*) earned a 17.8 rating, while a program could rank in the top thirty with a rating of nine.

This transition offers many important lessons. First, each tenth of a rating point translates into thousands of advertising dollars. Therefore, the significant drop in audience size forced a partial reconfiguration of television economics. Programming is more expensive to produce than it was in the network era, yet smaller audience sizes reduced broadcasters' ability to claim the vast reach previously common. Ultimately, the rise of niche cable networks did not overthrow all conventions because broadcast networks remained the outlet with the broadest reach, and many advertisers still prefer to pay a premium for a widely cast net.[70]

Secondly, the changed competitive environment, in which nine million households (as opposed twenty million) can earn a top-thirty rating, gives smaller segments of the overall audience more significance. Bruce Owen and Steven Wildman describe a primary challenge for mass-media industries such as U.S. television as "a trade-off between the savings from shared consumption of a common commodity and the loss of consumer satisfaction that occurs when messages are not tailored to individual or local tastes."[71] The competition arising during the transition to a post-network era has made it more profitable for programmers to cater to niche audience tastes, which was less advisable when networks sought universal appeal.

The transition to narrowcasting, targeting a niche segment of the overall audience, foremost explains the changes the multichannel transition delivered for female audiences. In an environment characterized by narrowcast competition, smaller, specific audiences gain value, which makes demographic groups such as women—and even more specific groups, such as eighteen-to-forty-nine-year-old working women, African Americans, and other subgroups of the overall heterogeneous audience—increasingly important. The value of niche audiences results from two factors. As noted, some advertisers have little need for a mass audience and instead seek particular audience segments. Therefore, programs delivering specific groups (such as fourteen-to-forty-five-year-old women for Tampax, or wealthy, retired couples for Cadillac) offer exceptional value.

Additionally, creating programming for a specific audience allows for distinct narratives that resonate with that group, a strategy that Michael Curtin and Thomas Streeter describe as sharply defining the "edges" of the intended consumer, which networks do through aesthetic and demographic means.[72] For example, Curtin argues that *Absolutely Fabulous* succeeded because of its willingness to address a subset of the female audience in an affront to other audience segments. Its comedy is built on in-group humor that "beg[s] viewers, who are not on the inside, to stay away," a strategy that "makes the programs even more attractive to those who appreciate the jokes."[73] Curtin maintains that the contemporary competitive environment rewards those who hail a specific audience, even if this means repelling others, instead of appealing to the largest possible audience through "least objectionable" programming strategies.

Developing programming with "edge" contrasts with the network-era strategy of devising programs to appeal to a diverse range of audience segments. In an effort to reach the largest audience, a series such as *E.R.* utilizes an ensemble cast designed to offer different segments of the audience an identification point. The series features African American and female doctors and nurses, in addition to the staple variety of white males. The cast includes young single characters as well as more senior professionals, many of whom have complicated personal relationships. The series incorporates aspects of the action genre in its rapid pace and examination of life-threatening injuries, and it borrows from the soap opera with its melodramatic storylines about suffering and loss, many of which extend over weeks of narrative. Combining multiple elements to draw a broad audience is difficult, though; and for all of *E.R.*'s success in attracting a large and diverse audience, many more series have failed while enacting similar strategies.

Many of the successful series, formats, and networks arising in the past two decades have utilized a narrowcasting strategy. New broadcast networks—FOX in 1986, then The WB and UPN a decade later—broke into a zero-sum industry by targeting a small segment of the audience that was not specifically hailed by the more general programming of the Big Three networks. FOX grew quickly with its irreverent family comedies (*Married . . . with Children; The Simpsons*), teen-focused drama and melodrama (*21 Jump Street; Beverly Hills, 90210*), and series dominated by black actors and inner-city settings (*In Living Color; Martin; New York Undercover*). Narrowcasting has been especially important in the formation of cable networks such as Lifetime Television and Black Entertainment Television (BET) that define their brand by targeting gender- and ethnic-specific groups.[74] It is also a central strategy of networks such as ESPN or A&E that brand their identity with distinct programming formats.

Many of the female-centered dramatic series appeared on cable networks, and only a quarter of the series I focus on aired on ABC, CBS, or NBC. *Any Day Now,* a series rejected by the broadcast networks, appeared on Lifetime, along with *Strong Medicine, The Division, MISSING,* and *Wildcard.* USA Network pioneered the form by offering *La Femme Nikita* as one of the earliest successful original cable series, while Turner Network Television (TNT) aired the action series *Witchblade.*[75] The executive producers of *Sex and the City* deliberately chose a cable network for their series, despite an offer from ABC. This series defies traditional program formats in exploring the lives of four single women in their thirties and airs on Home Box Office (HBO), a premium cable channel that requires a monthly fee but is free from commercials and the content restrictions of broadcasting. Upstart broadcaster The WB has aired many of the female-centered dramatic series, particularly those targeting a teen or young-adult female demographic. *Buffy the Vampire Slayer* debuted as an early entry in the now expansive range of female-centered dramatic series;[76] and The WB also airs *Charmed* and *Gilmore Girls.* The more established upstart, FOX, programmed *Ally McBeal, Dark Angel,* and *Tru Calling* (see table 3). In terms of the institutional structure of television, the appearance of diversified female-centered dramas is at least partially made possible by the increased status of the female audience after the network era. If only as a function of the increased number of programming outlets, efforts to reach and represent female demographics and their concerns have expanded beyond those found in the network era.

Female audiences are among the first niche groups to clearly benefit from a narrowcast environment because of the extent to which they are and are not a niche. At over 50 percent of the U.S. population, women have long been considered a "minority" group because of the history of male domination that forced secondary economic, social, and political status upon them. But power is computed differently when considering television audiences, and female audiences have commanded advertisers' attention because of their control of family spending (advertisers believe that women control 85 percent of personal and household-goods spending), although this status historically has not translated into empowered and diversified depictions of women.[77] This is not to say that the U.S. commercial media system provides empowerment for women, but it does affect their perceived status. In the current media envi-

Table 3. Late 1990s Series by Network (1995–2004)

CBS	UPN
Judging Amy (1999–2005)	*Buffy the Vampire Slayer* (2001–3)
That's Life (2000–2002)	Veronica Mars (2004–)
Kate Brasher (2001)	**Lifetime**
Presidio Med (2002–3)	*Any Day Now* (1998–2002)
Joan of Arcadia (2003–5)	*Strong Medicine* (2000–2006)
Cold Case (2003–)	*The Division* (2001–4)
FOX	For the People (2002)
Ally McBeal (1997–2002)	MISSING (2003–)
Dark Angel (2000–2002)	Wildcard (2003–5)
The American Embassy (2002)	**USA**
Girls Club (2002)	*La Femme Nikita* (1997–2001)
Tru Calling (2003–4)	The Huntress (2000–2001)
Wonderfalls (2004)	**TNT**
The WB	*Witchblade* (2001–2)
Buffy the Vampire Slayer (1997–2001)	**HBO**
Charmed (1998–)	*Sex and the City* (1998–2004)
Gilmore Girls (2000–)	**Showtime**
Birds of Prey (2002–3)	The L Word (2004–)
NBC	**Syndication**
The Profiler (1996–2000)	*Xena: Warrior Princess* (1995–2001)
Providence (1999–2002)	
Crossing Jordan (2001–)	
Medium (2005–)	
ABC	
Once and Again (1999–2002)	
Alias (2001–6)	
Philly (2001–2)	
The Court (2002)	
Karen Sisco (2003–4)	
Desperate Housewives (2004–)	
Grey's Anatomy (2005–)	

*Shows highlighted in this book.

ronment, specifically hailing women in promotional and programming content is an insignificant gamble because 50 percent of the viewing audience is significantly greater than any show regularly amasses. The competitive environment enabled by the end of the network era allows for networks to target variant tastes within the female audience through a diversification of series, genres, and networks. Perhaps now more than ever, complex and contradictory industrial practices characterize U.S. television. Various institutional forces contribute to the type of programming created for and targeted to female audiences, and these forces constantly shift in relation to the composition of the television industry and the strategies different technologies make available.

Defining "Female-Centered Dramas"

What I term "female-centered dramas" belong within a category more generally described as "women's programs" throughout the seventy years of narrative broadcast programming that began with radio. Television's history of women's programs correlates with artistic forms such as film and literature that have developed similar distinctions and categorizations for narratives and forms more commonly preferred by female audiences, although the components required for such classification vary considerably.[78] Those series classified as women's programs are not uniform in genre, structure, or ideology but represent an amalgamation of narrative strategies. "Female-centered" is a textual rather than audience-based distinction.[79] These series construct their narratives around one or more female protagonists, regardless of whether the audience—intended or hailed—is predominately female.[80] This categorization excludes dramatic series pairing a male/female dyad in the buddy tradition, as well as those emphasizing an ensemble.[81] Many of these series are formally similar to the series I consider; their exclusion primarily results from a need to delimit a manageable breadth and to emphasize those series that contribute a significant variation in narratives about women.

Writing about film genres, Andrew Tudor observes that "[g]enre is what we collectively believe it to be," and as the types of series I list in the next section indicate, the generic categories that "we" have traditionally relied upon may have lost some of their explanatory power.[82] As Jason Mittell identifies and seeks to remedy, television scholarship has lamentably undertheorized television genres, applying inadequate theory from literature or film.[83] Rather than engage Mittell's compelling argument for a cultural approach to genre that accounts for how industries, audiences, texts, and contexts converge to delimit generic distinctions, I use "drama" as a much less sophisticated textual classification.

Depending on where one looks, different groups of Tudor's unified "we" (the Academy of Television Arts and Sciences, the Hollywood Foreign Press, various television critics, programming marketers) organize television series in discrepant categories, although drama and comedy dominate. Even these distinctions are undefined, and as Mittell argues, they result from many different factors (features as arbitrary as program length lead to unreflective categorization of hour-long series as dramas and half-hour shows as comedies). In the late 1990s and early 2000s, even distinct categories of drama and comedy are uncertain and seem to have gone the way of other grand narratives, leaving behind an infinite recombination of various styles.

Perhaps my object of study is most clearly distinguished by acknowledging the textual forms I exclude. In addition to ensemble dramas, I do not consider either traditional situation comedies or made-for-television films. These forms offer interesting and important characterizations and narratives but have narrative features distinct from the form that appears in this era in such an unprecedented multiplicity. Additionally, previous scholarship analyzing female characters and the stories American television has told about women's lives has attended to these forms in considerable depth, while the relatively unexplored nature of dramatic series in concert with the exceptional success of the female-centered form in the late 1990s invites critical analysis.

The centrality of the sitcom in feminist television criticism is evident in Patricia Mellencamp's work on *I Love Lucy* and *The George Burns and Gracie Allen Show*, Kathleen Rowe's examination of unruly women in comedies, and Rabinovitz's focus on the sitcom as the "preferred fictional site for a 'feminist' subject position."[84] Dramas are able to construct characters differently and explore different types of stories than sitcoms. Similarly, made-for-television films and serial ensemble dramas have been primary sites of feminist criticism and considerations of female audiences.[85] These forms decreased in importance in the late 1990s, while the contained narrative structure of made-for-television films requires a distinctive theoretical framework. The book does include a broad array of broadcast, cable, premium-cable, and first-run syndicated programming, a range mandated by the contemporary institutional environment but more expansive than considered by most previous scholarship.

Types of Contemporary Female-Centered Dramas

After years of relegating female characters to the limited dimensions of situation-comedy characters, networks have begun to employ a variety of approaches to telling stories about women and finding female audiences. These series can be categorized by distinct narrative features, types of stories emphasized, and demographic features of the audience drawn. This variety must be analyzed for how it works as a marketing strategy to hail certain sections of the female commodity audience and for what the narratives indicate about the status of women and the issues affecting them in contemporary society. An examination of each dramatic type listed below organizes chapters 2 through 5.

ACTION DRAMA   The action drama is one of the most clearly distinguishable dramatic styles and possesses the longest history of exceptional female characters. Contemporary examples include *Buffy the Vampire Slayer* and *Xena: Warrior Princess,* both of which follow predecessors such as *Wonder Woman, The Bionic Woman, Charlie's Angels, Get Christie Love,* and *Honey West.* Obviously, these series are not identical in their narrative composition, and significant variation exists among the contemporary series included in this category. Such series as *The Profiler, Charmed, La Femme Nikita, The Huntress, Dark Angel,* and *Witchblade* utilize narrative elements that primarily categorize them as action dramas, although each deviates substantially from the others.

Many of the current and historical versions of the female action drama distinguish themselves by offering female characters an atypical physically empowered status. Such series feature protagonists that can be characterized as action heroines in the most extreme cases, but at least as females possessing extraordinary physical, intellectual, or mystical power. Media critics writing in the popular press often describe these series as having feminist attributes by virtue of presenting female characters in arenas traditionally inaccessible to fictional and actual women.[86] Such assessments often do not account for the various ways a series can undermine empowerment at a narrative or visual level, such as through structured subordination to Charlie or Bosley on *Charlie's Angels,* or the emphasis on traditionally feminine costuming for characters such as Wonder Woman.

Because they share narrative time with the spectacle of chases and fight scenes, these series sometimes lack the textual complexity of other dramatic narrative forms. Many action dramas structure their narratives episodically, inhibiting long-term character and plot development.[87] An episodic structure also defies the serial form most commonly used to address female audiences, not only allowing for but requiring closure by episode's end. Female action dramas tend to center on one extraordinary protagonist, unlike most serial narratives targeted toward women that feature a multiplicity of characters. Series such as *Xena: Warrior Princess, Buffy the Vampire Slayer, Charmed, Witchblade,* and *Dark Angel* all incorporate fantastic elements that clearly position their narratives and characters outside of familiar reality. This strategy is significant to assessments of what these characters might indicate about the status of women beyond the narrative.

COMEDIC DRAMA   The term "comedic drama" may appear an oxymoron in relation to traditional narrative categories, but it functions as an appropriate distinction as a result of contemporary narrative structures and theories about television genres. Comedic drama replaces the increasingly common industrial term "dramedy," which has been used more frequently in response to a shift from traditional situation-comedy forms throughout the late 1990s, but lacks theoretical delimitation or precise use. Comedic dramas bear more similarity to dramatic series than sitcoms, but they incorporate elements of comedy into their narratives to such an extent that they eliminate or make secondary many of the melodramatic elements more commonly found in dramas. "Getting a laugh" remains a primary narrative goal for these series, even though they refuse many sitcom conventions. They eschew laugh tracks and the "joke per page" rhythm common among television comedies. Contemporary series that center upon female protagonists and are exemplary of this form include *Ally McBeal, Sex and the City,* and *Popular. The Days and Nights of Molly Dodd* precedes these series in experimenting with this form.

As they emerged in the late 1990s, comedic dramas continued the tradition of the new-woman character type, updating the form to account for the post–Baby Boom, post-second-wave generation of characters. Like new-woman series before them, *Sex and the City* and *Ally McBeal* focus on characters' work and dating experiences, although new dilemmas develop as a result of the changes in previous gender norms. These series explore gender-based legal and social issues through the eyes of a multiplicity of female characters who possess distinct viewpoints, emphasize issues that are more personal than explicitly political, and display ambivalence toward feminist gains, which distinguishes their narratives from previous new-woman series.

PROTAGONIST-CENTERED FAMILY DRAMA   The complicated identification of the third type of series as protagonist-centered family drama denotes the narrative multiplicity, yet structural similarity, of the dramas in this category. These series offer some of the most substantial innovations to dramatic storytelling about women's lives, as well as the most successful ratings performance. Unlike *Sisters* (1991–96), the most successful previous series of this type, contemporary shows tend to center upon one female character and explore her struggles with professional and family responsibilities. *The Trials of Rosie O'Neill* (1990–92) and *Sweet Justice* (1994–95) attempted this organization earlier in the 1990s but did not attract audiences large enough to succeed. Series such as *Any Day Now, Providence, Judging Amy, Once and Again, That's Life,* and *Gilmore Girls* exhibit characteristics common among protagonist-centered family dramas.

Many similarities appear across the shows and primarily take the form of three motifs that do not manifest uniformly but appear in variation in each series. Despite the homogeneity repeated motifs may suggest, the series tell remarkably different stories, with discrepancies often resulting from the se-

ries' emphases of family or the protagonist. Series highlighting family continue the narrative features evident in the few female-centered dramas airing in the 1980s and early 1990s, such as *Sisters* and *Dr. Quinn, Medicine
Woman*. Those focusing more on the protagonist's experiences in the public sphere draw from a legacy that includes *Cagney and Lacey, China Beach,*
and *The Trials of Rosie O'Neill,* as well as various characters in ensemble series or male/female buddy series that were not designed or marketed as
"women's programs."

The protagonist-centered family dramas draw the largest audiences of the
series considered in the book, and most air on generally branded broadcast
networks. These series consequently indicate how "women's stories" can
move into the mainstream and introduce complexity and diversity to depictions of women as family members.

WORKPLACE DRAMA   No dramatic form possesses a more substantial television history than the cop, doc, or law show. A fourth type of female-
centered drama has developed as a result of significant innovations in mixed-
sex ensemble series and attempts to recast these traditional workplace
franchises as female-centered universes. Lifetime Television currently presents the most expansive exploration of reconfigured narrative environments,
with the medical drama *Strong Medicine* and the cop drama *The Division*. Located in a Philadelphia women's clinic, *Strong Medicine* depicts two female
doctors from different backgrounds who must learn to work together. *The
Division* features a primarily female homicide squad. The core of four female
detectives and their female captain dominate the squad room, creating a very
different dynamic than that of *Cagney and Lacey*. These series indicate an advance from women's issues receiving occasional focus in cop or medical dramas to their weekly emphasis in series focused on the struggles encountered
by a diverse range of female protagonists in locations highlighting female experiences.

The institutional settings of workplace dramas optimally position these series to explore stories chronicling medical and criminal situations most likely
to affect women. *Strong Medicine* and *The Division* use different strategies to
accomplish this and are joined by series such as *Family Law, Third Watch,* and
Law and Order: Special Victims Unit in emphasizing stories about female
workers and those they encounter.[88] The turn to female-centered workplaces
demarcates the next step in this evolution, one arguably impossible and
unimaginable in the network era. Their isolation on Lifetime indicates the
niche status of these stories, although broadcast networks have begun testing
their viability. A brief examination of broadcast networks' ensemble series il-

lustrates how these networks incorporate elements of the reconfigured workplace drama to expand the narratives available for women in their series.

* * *

The constant appearance of exceptions frustrates any attempt to distinguish narrative types, and this set of four is not immune from hybrid and boundary-crossing forms. Although exceptions exist and some classifications initially may seem tenuous, chapters 2 through 5 indicate that the general concepts hold. The possibility of demarcating distinct types of dramatic series understandable as women's programs or female-centered programming underscores the significance of the contemporary programming environment. Throughout most of the fifty-odd years of U.S. television, a rare season featured one or even two dramas centering upon a female protagonist or hailing a specifically female audience. The female-centered dramas airing in the late 1990s and early twenty-first century must be considered for how they tell specific types of stories and address particular female audiences.

On its face, the new preponderance of outlets in which female audiences can see their struggles and concerns dramatized may seem an obvious gain. The new series expand the options for female viewers, but at the same time, these new images and narratives have not appeared out of the goodwill of network programmers seeking to right the historical lack of dramatic female representation. Rather, they emerge in abundance because programmers came to perceive the female-centered drama to be a valuable strategy for drawing the audiences advertisers seek. The intersection of art and commerce enacted by U.S. television makes understanding the ideological implications of any narrative far more intricate than superficial assessments indicate. Female audiences may see their lives reflected in more complex and sophisticated ways as a result of their new inclusion in dramatic narratives, but pursuing these pleasures transforms them into commodity audiences for advertisers who seek them through their tastes and preferences.[89] This conundrum is characteristic of a commercial media system that often gives with one hand while taking with the other. Positive and negative assertions can be made about the changes chronicled in this book, and I attempt to consider their implications as holistically as possible.

In her study of constructions of femininity in the British magazine industry, Anna Gough-Yates underscores the importance of studying media industries by noting that media spaces are the "place where the cultural meanings and representations of modern femininity are forged, fought over, and understood," while reminding readers that this "place" is simultaneously an "*industry*, with its own particular relations of production and consumption."[90] Likewise, audiences of U.S. television saw substantial adjustments in the number of programs, types of programs, and the number of networks explicitly targeting women during the late 1990s; to understand the cultural discourses contained within these forms we must also consider the economic imperatives enabling them.[91] Arguments about the significance or characteristics of the resulting programming that do not acknowledge the shifting terrain of these culture-producing businesses are necessarily inadequate.

The first chapter continues the broader discussion of the multichannel transition and provides a comprehensive examination of the expansion in the women's cable-network market. I consider the institutional histories and brand positions of the Lifetime, Oxygen, and WE networks by drawing from textual analysis of the networks' programs and promotion as well as interviews with network executives. Similar to the diversified construction of women performed by the multiplicity of female-centered dramas, the multiple cable networks branded as "women's" construct their programming to hail particular segments of the female audience and allow women's interests to be more broadly defined and addressed. The remaining chapters apply the narrative and institutional foundations established here to examine the four types of female-centered dramas for the stories they tell, the narrative strategies they use, and the audiences who view them.

1. Women's Brands and Brands of Women: Segmenting Audiences and Network Identities

Lifetime saw an underserved audience and served it. Now everyone
wants a piece of the pie.
—Kathy Haesele, Advanswers

The development of more than sixteen female-centered dramatic series and at least three cable networks specifically targeting segments of the female audience did not transpire in the dark hours of the morning some time in the late 1990s. There was no revolution or "aha!" moment after which television programs and programming strategies were forever changed. As the introduction indicates, complex interconnections among a variety of institutional factors and adjustments developed over a period of ten to twenty years, and modifications continue with no indication of how a new merger or deregulatory decision may expand competition or signal the establishment of a new era, or what the consequences of these developments might be.

When I began this work in the late 1990s, the multiplicity of female-centered dramas appeared to be the most significant phenomenon relating to television and gender. However, the more long-lasting development may result from the growth in niche cable outlets targeting women. It is not coincidental that female-centered dramas and cable networks targeting women multiplied at the same time; both can be traced to fundamental institutional adjustments that make programming hailing specific audience niches particularly valuable. The phenomena are also connected, as Lifetime's first original dramatic series success with *Any Day Now* was undoubtedly noted by the broader television executive and creative communities, who then sought ways to adjust this form for the audience reach required for broadcast success.

Women were hailed by only one network for most of the cable era, but in the final years of the twentieth century some entrepreneurial voices scrambled to compete for their attention, and multiple brands of "women's networks" developed. A network brand, as in the brand of any good or service, refers to the identity associated with the network, often related to the type of person likely to "consume" it (or the type of person the network's advertisers would like to consume their product).[1] Cable networks, and increasingly broadcast networks as well, establish brands to attract certain audiences to their programming; advertisers then inundate these audiences with appeals for goods and services. This system works most efficiently when programming attracts audiences with specific characteristics that networks can sell to advertisers.

For many years, the slogan "Television for Women" provided enough distinction for Lifetime, since no other network explicitly sought the female audience in this manner. Network slogans and advertising campaigns collectively addressing "women's" lives and needs suggest a generalized construction of women as a coherent and monolithic group. The programming strategies among the "women's" cable networks indicate a much more heterogeneous construction of female audiences. Additionally, the market acceptance and initial success of these networks, as well as the high profile afforded to marketing consultants such as Faith Popcorn, Mary Lou Quinlan, and their firms specializing in marketing to women, indicate that marketers' and advertisers' perceptions of the female buyer have evolved significantly.[2]

This chapter first describes the institutional history of Lifetime, Oxygen, and WE, as their variant histories, ownership, and competitive positions inform their programming options. The expansion of cable networks explicitly targeting women parallels the increase in dramatic stories exploring women's lives, and the variation among multiple female-targeted networks contributes to making stereotypes and dominant stories about women's lives uninhabitable. Proceeding from the assumption that a corresponding relationship exists among representations, stories, and networks, this chapter examines whether these three networks indeed provide a diversity of genres, images, stories, and constructions of "women" and "femininity." The introduction of multiple women's networks and the identities these networks establish through self-promotion and programming content indicate the primary axes by which commercial media divide women as consumer markets and what stories programmers believe resonate with women's varied experiences. Tracing the development and brand establishment of women's cable networks exposes the increased address of the female audience as diverse and fragmented, as well as the strategies networks use to find them.

Creating Women's Cable Networks

Lifetime: Television for Women

The success Lifetime attained by early 2001 stands as one of the clearest indicators of the commercial value of the female niche. Lifetime is considered an industry success not only for its ability to reach female audiences but also because it regularly ranks among top cable networks in audience size. Lifetime's success offers a twofold lesson. Most obviously, it plays a crucial role in understanding changes in institutional perceptions about female audiences and how and why dramatic programs with central female characters began expanding at such a tremendous rate in the late 1990s. Lifetime also illustrates the viability of narrowcasting and similar programming strategies during the multichannel transition.

Lifetime grew out of the merger of two cable networks: Daytime, a joint venture of Hearst and ABC, and the Viacom-owned Cable Health Network. Both were originally launched in 1982. The networks combined as a result of Daytime's difficulty gaining carriage on cable services and the sense that the networks were competing for the same narrow and specialized audience.[3] Lifetime retained much programming from the original networks, with a heavy reliance on advertiser-created series and specials, many of which featured pharmaceuticals and other health-industry products such as hormone supplements and diet aids.[4] In seeking to establish a Lifetime brand, CEO Thomas Burchill initiated a threefold programming strategy that included acquiring female-identified broadcast-network shows (such as *Cagney and Lacey* and *The Days and Nights of Molly Dodd*), creating original series, and producing made-for-Lifetime movies, the last of which proved the most successful (see table 4).[5]

Under Burchill's management, the network initiated programming apparently designed to appeal to upscale heterosexual couples, although it did not openly market its intention to attract both women and men.[6] The network began its signature "Television for Women" branding campaign in 1995, the year it readjusted its focus to begin what Eileen Meehan and Jackie Byars term the network's "established" period.[7] The explicit brand identification and Lifetime's status as the only channel serving women helped it weather complex takeovers and competitive struggles that reorganized the media industry in 1996.

Lifetime's next significant development resulted from its launch of three original narrative series in the fall of 1998.[8] The steady audience gains throughout the cable industry during the 1990s led several of the stronger cable networks to compete more directly with broadcasters by creating orig-

Table 4. Significant Events in Lifetime Television Network's Development

March 1982: Hearst and ABC launch Daytime.
June 1982: Viacom launches the Cable Health Channel.
February 1984: Daytime and Cable Health Channel merge to form Lifetime.
April 1984: Thomas Burchill named network president and CEO.
1988: Lifetime secures second-run license for *Cagney and Lacey.*
January 1989: Lifetime begins airing new, made-for-Lifetime episodes of *The Days and Nights of Molly Dodd.*
July 1990: Lifetime debuts its first original film.
February 1993: Douglas McCormick promoted from executive vice president of sales to network president.
April 1994: Viacom sells its share of Lifetime to Hearst and Cap Cities/ABC (now the Walt Disney Company), its other partners in the joint venture that owns the network.
February 1995: Lifetime announces itself as Television for Women. Lifetime executives describe the network as focusing on "strong stories, strong emotions, and solid entertainment."
1995: Lifetime film *Almost Golden: The Jessica Savitch Story* earns a 7.9 rating.
April 1996: Lifetime Television launches Lifetime Online.
July 1998: Lifetime launches its first sister channel, the Lifetime Movie Network, a twenty-four-hour movie service.
February 1999: Carole Black named president and CEO, Lifetime Entertainment Services.
August 2001: Lifetime launches Lifetime Real Women.
January 2001–March 2003: Lifetime ranks as the most watched cable network in primetime.

inal series similar to those on broadcast television.[9] Although cable series tend to adhere to the narrative structures common to broadcast programming, they often expand status-quo perceptions of what audiences will watch, allowing their programming a distinctive "edge." Cable's less stringent content regulations and the smaller audience size required to be considered successful enabled many of their programming risks.

Producing original series is usually substantially more costly for cable networks than purchasing the license for off-network syndicated series that fill most cable schedules. A quality one-hour dramatic series typically cost a minimum of one million dollars per episode in the late 1990s, while cable networks spent $100,000 to $250,000 per episode for independently produced, low-budget prime-time shows, and often even less for off-network series bought in syndication.[10] Yet despite the costs, cable networks identify the production of original series as an important step toward competing with broadcasters, as well as an essential practice in establishing their network brand. Lifetime spent nearly eight million dollars developing four pilots, three of which aired during the 1998–99 season.[11] The investment paid off when the two-hour time slot in which the network scheduled the three series increased the number of eighteen-to-forty-nine-year-old women viewers by nearly two hundred thousand per week (46 percent).[12]

Despite positive critical reception and some audience gains by the original series, made-for-Lifetime movies remain the network's strongest ratings performer. As other scholars have argued, many of these films feature women as victims or provide them with an extraordinary challenge in the first act that they struggle to overcome.[13] The success and brand identification of these films led the network to create a second network, the Lifetime Movie Network (LMN), in September 1998. Programming for LMN consists of movies, miniseries, and theatrical films from the Lifetime library, as well as some purchased from second-run distributors. Although early market surveys reported a ready audience for the network, with 93 percent of women who watched Lifetime aware of its films, the network had a slow start.[14] Stymied mainly by lack of distribution, a year after its launch LMN reached only five million households.[15] LMN increased its reach to twenty-two million by 2002, an increase largely due to "retransmission leverage exercised by parent partner Hearst."[16] By April 2004, the network reached forty-seven million homes.[17]

The creation of LMN indicates Lifetime's first attempt to leverage its brand and suggests the network's awareness of the need to address the heterogeneity of the female audience. As Lifetime reached its "established" period, it became evident that one network could never serve all women, particularly as competitors emerged to challenge its uncontested status as the network for women. Lifetime's films consistently achieved its highest ratings but were unappealing to some female audiences. The creation of LMN allowed Lifetime to devote less of its daily schedule to replaying older films, while not forfeiting the value of what had developed into an expansive film archive. The main network could then counter-program itself, making space on the Lifetime schedule for content more likely to appeal to women uninterested in the network's films.

At the beginning of the twenty-first century Lifetime entered another transitional phase. Despite six relatively successful years, it did not renew the contract of CEO Douglas McCormick, who had held the position since 1993, and named Carole Black the new Lifetime CEO in March 1999.[18] Lifetime thus employed its first female CEO, recruiting Black from KNBC in Los Angeles, where as general manager she was credited with bringing more women viewers to its newscasts.[19] Upon her arrival, she noted that the lack of a strong competitor had made the network complacent.[20] Although Lifetime had nearly universal cable penetration, research in 1999 indicated that "41 percent of female cable subscribers don't know anything about it."[21] Black consequently increased the marketing budget from eight million to forty million dollars, allowing the network to expand its advertising campaign that had been focused on the twenty markets with the highest female cable viewership to a national level.[22] In addition to the extensive network promotional campaign, Black expanded the programming budget to $236 million, a 20 percent increase over 1998.[23] Less than two years later, Lifetime moved from the number-six to number-one cable network in prime-time viewership.

Black inherited a solid network and expanded its gains. Lifetime earned the sixteenth highest revenue among all U.S. television networks in 2003, with $820 million (eighth among ad-supported cable networks).[24] Lifetime also possesses a large potential audience base, reaching 87.5 million cable and satellite homes, making the network nearly universally available to cable or satellite subscribers.[25] In 2002, Nielsen Media Research ranked Lifetime the second-most-watched cable network, with an average of 992,000 viewers per day (behind Nickelodeon), and more significantly, Lifetime drew an average of 1.58 million viewers in prime time, which earned it the distinction of the most-watched cable network in 2001 and 2002. Despite its viability, Black faced pressure to continue its growth and to prevent new competitors from eroding its grip on the female cable audience. The hype and potential of Oxygen Media led many to wonder whether the upscale female audience Lifetime targets could be split profitably and what assets would prove the most beneficial in the competition. Rebranding by the generally targeted cable networks TNT, TBS, and USA to a more specific identity aided them in reestablishing their top cable ranking in 2003 through 2005. Black stepped down in March 2005 and was replaced by Betty Cohen, who had worked for Cartoon Network.

Oxygen: Like a Breath of Fresh Air

With its history of success and increasing profitability, Lifetime's status as the only network explicitly targeting female audiences made it due for a challenger. In March 1999, Time Warner/Turner Broadcasting Systems announced plans for a women's cable channel.[26] Despite its solid distribution and programming base, Time Warner canceled plans for the Women's Network in August 1999.[27] Sources at Time Warner mainly blamed the demise on the absence of a unified vision for the network, although the competitive environment and startup costs likely contributed to the decision as well.[28] Time Warner's public consideration of a women's network further underscores the attention to the women's market at this time.

Lifetime dodged one competitor, but Oxygen proceeded with its launch plans. Under normal conditions a newcomer to the cable spectrum is not especially threatening to an existing network with solid brand identification.

Typically, a new channel must surpass many hurdles, the largest of which is commanding the financial capital and reputation necessary to achieve significant enough distribution to draw advertisers. Because of this challenge, many new competitors originate from companies connected to a multiple systems operator such as Time Warner, which makes broad distribution possible from the start. Oxygen Media, however, was not a typical newcomer.

Oxygen appeared on the media radar in October 1998, when the joint owners Geraldine Laybourne and Carsey-Werner-Mandabach announced a deal with TCI to launch Oxygen to three million subscribers by January 2000, increasing penetration to at least seven million subscribers within three years.[29] Laybourne was well respected in the cable industry, particularly because of her success as president of Nickelodeon, and was credited with Oxygen's success in finding distributors.[30] Her partners, Marcy Carsey, Tom Werner, and Caryn Mandabach, possessed a library of series, including female-centered comedies such as *Roseanne* (1988–97), *Grace under Fire* (1993–98), and *Cybill* (1995–98). The trio's production company is one of the most successful of its era and one of few remaining independent companies until closing down in 2005. Oprah Winfrey signed on with Oxygen a month later and provided a powerful media reputation and originally contributed the licensing rights to *The Oprah Winfrey Show* library.[31] Additional major investors in the network included America Online, Disney's ABC, Inc., and Vulcan Ventures, an investment company of Microsoft cofounder Paul Allen. Oxygen launched on the clever date of February 2, 2000 ($0_2/0_2/2000$), to an audience of ten million cable subscribers.[32]

In this battle among female-targeted cable networks, Oxygen Media's established Internet presence appeared to provide a key asset, allowing it to promote itself as an integrated media brand that combined cable television and Internet content.[33] Laybourne defined Oxygen Media's mission as "[creating] a media revolution led by women and kids" and argued that the "convergence of content and technology from TV and computers will allow us to bond with our audience like never before."[34] The innovation of developing an integrated cable and Web media brand made Oxygen particularly vulnerable to the retrenchment in the U.S. economy that began shutting down startup ventures in the technology sector in mid 2000. Many industry pundits were quick to forecast its demise, as the changing economics of producing Web content challenged the network before it achieved substantive cable distribution or found its programming voice. Lack of distribution on the analog cable tier in New York City stymied Oxygen during much of its first year, as a prime target market for the network's service-oriented, thinking-women's fare remained unreachable. Eighteen months after its launch, the network reached 12.3 million subscribers and had weathered significant cuts and reorganization in its Web divisions. By April 2002, forty million households received Oxygen, but early Nielsen measurement indicated that only fifty-two thousand households watched it each day.[35] By March 2004, fifty-one million homes received Oxygen, and the network averaged a viewership of 106,000 women.[36]

Although it is only five years old, it is already impossible to speak of Oxygen's programming as a singular coherent entity. Just as Meehan and Byars delimit four periods of development at Lifetime, Oxygen's programming first took the form of "Experimental, Integrated, Non-narrative Launch" (February 2000–September 2001) and later "Edgy Comedy, Talk, and Off-Net Narrative" (September 2001–the present). Such an adjustment is not surprising, but the degree to which the Oxygen brand continues to shift contributes to perceptions of its uncertain future.

The network's first period featured an intensive effort to merge Web and cable content, with two-hour daily blocks of *Pure Oxygen* (a talk show with a format similar to the *Today Show*) and *Trackers*, a similarly formatted show targeting teens. Other nonnarrative programming included half-hour daily and weekly shows such as *Oprah Goes Online* (Oprah and her friend Gayle teaching viewers how to use the Internet), *SheCommerce* (stories about shopping and woman-owned companies), and a remake of the game show *I've Got a Secret*. The network's schedule initially included daily classic films (*The Girl in the Picture*) and documentaries (*As She Sees It*) and countered Lifetime's morning aerobics program with *Inhale*, a yoga show.

Many feminist media critics were intrigued by Oxygen's potential and responded positively to its programming, but this initial phase proved to be unsuccessful commercially for a variety of reasons.[37] The network's initial schedule was unbearably expensive and uncommon at the launch, a time during which making it available on cable systems and increasing audience awareness provided formidable challenges. Network executives also acknowledge misinterpreting what viewers wanted. According to Laybourne, "When we started, we thought women really needed our help. Focus groups showed us that women are not that pathetic. They want to be entertained."[38] Featuring all nonnarrative programming provided the network with a distinctive characteristic to promote, but the necessary magnitude of viewers did not tune in.

Oxygen adjusted its programming in its second period, which is marked by a steady decrease of the Web and cable integration emphasized at its creation. The network shifted from its almost completely nonnarrative origin to include off-net runs of *Xena: Warrior Princess, Kate and Allie, Cybill, La Femme Nikita, Absolutely Fabulous,* and *A Different World*. It added original talk and interview shows such as *Oprah after the Show, The Isaac Mizrahi Show,* and *Conversations from the Edge with Carrie Fisher* and canceled most of the programs from the first period. Oxygen also produces the series *Women and the Badge,* a *COPS*-like show about female police officers and detectives that revises the genre in a less exploitative manner.

Part of the network's branding adjustment features a prominent emphasis on comedy. Its take on the *Candid Camera* version of reality programming, *Girls Behaving Badly,* has clearly demarcated the irreverence and humor characteristic of the brand the network seeks to establish. Oxygen further demonstrated this attitude in its first original narrative series, a comedy titled *Good Girls Don't* (originally announced as *My Best Friend Is a Great Big Slut*) that is reminiscent of a Generation X, Americanized, *Absolutely Fabulous.*[39] Despite the programming shifts, Oxygen has differentiated its brand from the other competitors in the women's cable market. Continued expansion in distribution and exposure to new audiences remain its most formidable obstacles.

Women Have Changed, So Have WE: The Women's Entertainment Network

The Women's Entertainment Network debuted in January 1997 as Romance Classics, a spinoff of, or sister network to, American Movie Classics (AMC). The network first received press coverage in late 1992, when its owner, Rainbow Media Holdings, announced plans for a Valentine's Day 1994 launch. Rainbow sought a way to "maximize the value" of the AMC film library, so Romance Classics developed out of the company's attempt toward "leveraging the AMC brand name."[40] Rainbow tested various "genre channels" in the development of a suitable new network, and romance emerged as the clear winner. When Romance Classics appeared, its programming primarily consisted of movies from the 1930s through the 1980s. In its first year, 5 percent of its schedule provided original programming, and the network reached ten million homes by December 1997.[41] Romance Classics aired its programming uninterrupted by commercials, with appeals from the network's sponsors between programs—a structure enabled by the low cost of programming from an existing library.

By fall 1999, rumors of a name change began circulating, and executives announced a relaunch of the network as Oasis in March 2000.[42] Difficulty negotiating an agreement with the existing cable network Oasis TV prevented this rebranding and instead led to the Women's Entertainment moniker. The appeal of Oasis resulted from the network's perception of its niche. Research the network commissioned in 1997 revealed that female viewers "were interested in escapist fare" and "lifestyle pieces that are reality-based and that can be applied to their lives."[43] Rebranding the network as Women's Entertainment at the end of 2000 did not result in a change in programming content so much as an attempt to more accurately name its programming. Following the relaunch, WE continued to primarily program films with themes of romance and escape and further increased original programming by adding nonnarrative series about famous romances, fashion and style, and biographical shows about extraordinary women. WE reached forty-four million households by mid 2002 and completed an eighteen-month sponsorship deal with Johnson and Johnson as the sole advertiser, after which it shifted to a regular slate of advertisers and began including commercials during its programs.[44] WE adjusted its slogan to "The Space We Share" in October 2001 and simultaneously announced that it would not program any overtly violent or issue-oriented content, which solidified its difference from Lifetime and Oxygen.[45] By January 2003, the network was available in fifty-two million homes and emphasized the slogan "Live, Love, Laugh" as characteristic of its brand.[46]

The institutional history of Lifetime, the emergence of Oxygen, and the rebranding of Women's Entertainment are directly connected to the rupture in traditional practices characteristic of the end of the network era. The existence of cable networks specifically targeting female demographics—especially upscale women and girls—altered historic network strategies for defining female audiences and addressing them as consumers. Understanding the institutional contexts of these networks is necessary to frame their competitive strategies and programming options. In comparison with Lifetime's nearly two-decade existence, networks such as Oxygen, WE, LMN, SoapNet, HBO Signature, WMax, and ShoWomen appear as novices. They have the advantage of launching during a more developed moment of cable history and can take many lessons from Lifetime's successes and failures; however, they will never be the first women's cable network, a status that affords Lifetime a heightened level of brand recognition—for better and worse—that will be difficult for emerging networks to achieve. Lifetime is the standard bearer to which all others are first compared, and its history enables it to stay ahead of those who seek its status as Television for Women.

Fragmentation in the women's cable market continued with the launch of Lifetime Real Women in 2001, and Radio One and Comcast launched TV One in 2004, a network targeting black audiences, but particularly the "demographic sweet spot" of thirty-four-year-old women.[47] The diversity of networks for women on cable matches the strategy pursued by the magazine industry, which also has attempted to specialize "programming" fare.

The economics of cable networks remain very different from the magazine industry, and despite this new proliferation of women's brands, one may ask whether they indeed serve variant brands of women.

Brands of Women: Segmenting Female Audiences

For many years, industry analysts considered Lifetime's pursuit of female audiences to be a highly specialized endeavor. Targeting a demographic that limited audiences to half of potential viewers was unprecedented and daring in the early years of cable. As the competitive practices of the multichannel transition diminished network-era norms, strategic practices began to change. In the first years of the twenty-first century, general-interest cable networks experienced slowed growth and audience loss, while more specifically targeted networks such as Lifetime continued their gains.[48] Oxygen and WE began competing for audiences in these later years that were more clearly characterized by audience and programming specificity.

The female audience can be segmented by a variety of traditional demographic factors: age, ethnicity, marital status, sexuality, household income, geographic location, and educational attainment, as well more particular categorizations based on employment, motherhood, and how women blend work and family responsibilities. Ultimately, income as related to purchasing power and buying practices outweighs all other basic demographic attributes in defining an audience's value—except to the degree that other aspects tend to correlate with income and expenditures. Programmers also segment female audiences by their concerns and interests, what one network vice president of marketing terms "zones of influence," which in some cases are likely to correspond with demographic factors.[49] In surveying programming targeted to women, fashion, design, child care, housekeeping, entertaining, romance, fitness, and careers all emerge as topics of interest to women in general, although different women are likely to rank these and other interests with variant priorities. In constructing their brands, Lifetime, Oxygen, and WE seek to differentiate their programming from their competitors' while targeting the subset of women who order their interests in a specific way. Each network gambles that their brand will attract enough of the most "valuable" audience members to appease advertisers, while seeking a broader audience that can compensate for the limited number of premium eyeballs it delivers.

The ironic aspect of the apparent diversification in women's programming made available by the emergence of multiple niche cable networks results from the relative uniformity of the young, upscale, educated audience members these networks pursue. Admittedly, the niche appeal to a specifically female rather than female and male composite audience clearly enables programs and programming forms that were previously less feasible. However, Lifetime, Oxygen, and WE, as well as SoapNet, LMN, TLC, HGTV, Food Network, E!, Style, and other networks seeking to sell female audiences to advertisers, all pursue the same type of female audience member, although they employ divergent programming strategies to do so. The brand identifications of Lifetime, Oxygen, and WE are not nearly as distinctive as those of *Good Housekeeping, Ms.,* and *Glamour,* nor could they be as a result of current television economics. The model of the magazine industry is helpful for envisioning how a range of differentiated network voices might compete in a way that produces commercial profits while also better serving the diverse needs and priorities of women.[50]

Throughout the network era, the economic imperative of garnering the largest possible audience pushed programming toward middle-of-the-road themes and stories that were as inoffensive as possible. Media conglomerations after the network era—as addressed in Michael Curtin's work—utilize a variety of strategies, including the development of programming with a clearly defined edge that openly hails particular groups while unabashedly repelling others.[51] The moment of competition chronicled in this chapter, which began in the late 1990s and features examples from 2003, must be understood as a time during which executives in the television industry faced diverse challenges. Some struggled to determine how edgy programming could become while remaining commercially viable (Oxygen). And some were forced to focus a broad brand because of the viability of smaller niche markets (Lifetime), while others labored to create an alternative, distinctive identity relative to differentiated competitors (WE, SoapNet). So while the constraints of competing in a commercial media system would normally create an institutional drive toward similar program content, it was also possible to move beyond conventional norms to create distinctive brands.

The institutional push toward similarity results from the fact that all of these networks pursue specific female audiences, who are valued by advertisers and the conventional wisdom of the advertising industry. The networks compete for the funds of the same advertisers, and each seeks the coveted eighteen-to-thirty-four-year-old, college-educated women with a yearly household income above fifty thousand dollars (if not the "upscale" households earning at least seventy-five thousand dollars) for which advertisers pay premium rates. The variation among the networks results from whoever else the networks may catch in casting their nets broadly, but the ideal audience is narrow and specific.

It is difficult to develop a clear picture of the different audiences the networks reach because of the lack of publicly available demographic data, and comparisons are awkward because of the substantial differences in total audience size. Occasionally articles in the trade press include data such as a network's average audience age or income level, but they rarely provide comprehensive information, including all the networks measured during the same period. The networks also commission studies and release information targeted to media buyers in trade-press advertisements and yearly upfront sales kits. This information often highlights the networks' strongest points, and the small print at the bottom of the advertisements indicates that these studies often have small sample sizes and do not address what group of women the sample reliably represents. Such data must be used cautiously, as they are designed to sell the network to advertisers.

Ultimately, demographic variation among the networks' audiences appears to be slight, with the exception of overall size. It is difficult to draw meaningful conclusions about what type of programming resonates with different demographic groups at this preliminary point of competition because of the discrepant network histories and distribution levels. Also, the effect of a gross surplus of channels on viewers' habits remains an unstudied factor of the multichannel transition. Network executives acknowledge that despite the hundreds of channels viewers have access to, they begin their viewing by monitoring what is on eight to ten networks, which might be called default channels. In this competitive environment, executives explained that their goal was for their channel to be among viewers' default surveillance—to have such brand identity that viewers would regularly check their network when seeking a program. Network brand and specific program offerings both contribute to viewing selection. Within this model of default tiers, viewers establish a channel hierarchy based on their perception of what a network is likely to feature. After observing what each channel offers at a specific moment, network identity becomes unimportant, and the viewing decision is predicated on the particular programs.[52]

According to a Magna Global study based on Nielsen data, Oxygen has the youngest audience, with a prime-time median age of 43.7, while Lifetime's is 50.3.[53] WE's audience age has dropped to 53.2 since the rebranding, a significant drop from the upper-fifties-to-lower-sixties average common when the network was Romance Classics.[54] Household income provides another differentiation important to advertisers. Oxygen executives reported that their viewers have an average income around fifty-five thousand dollars, while Lifetime's promotional materials register an average household income of $48,518. WE's 2003 upfront sales kit lists their median household income as $46,500.[55] Women make up 75 percent of WE's audience, 71 percent of Lifetime's audience, and 65 percent of Oxygen's audience when audiences in all dayparts are averaged.[56] Executives at each of the networks asserted that they are concerned with bringing more women to their networks and do not focus on creating programs likely to also draw males, which was not the case when Meehan and Byars did their initial research on Lifetime in the mid 1990s.[57] Lee Heffernan, the senior vice president of marketing at WE, provided evidence that this is the case by noting that she can get a higher advertising rate "selling women" than "selling adults."[58] Table 5 compares other demographic features of the networks based on information they provided. Importantly, these are network-provided figures, and the audience base and periods of measurement are similar but not identical. This demographic comparison is instructive for the similarities that appear despite the differences in the programs the networks offer but lacks the validity necessary to draw meaningful conclusions. The similar-

Table 5. Comparison of Women's Cable Network Audience Demographics

A substantial caveat: The various programming and research executives I spoke with at each of the networks provided the following data for their respective networks (except for median prime-time viewer age). Most is based on MRI Data or Nielsen surveys. I requested information that represents the population of women 18 and over for the 2002–3 year. The audience base I received from the networks varies some, so this comparison can only offer a general snapshot of reasonably comparable categories at a particular moment in time (Summer 2003).

	Lifetime	Oxygen	WE
Audience that is female	71.3%	65%	75.5%
Median viewer age (all dayparts averaged)	47.4	41.7	46.3
Median viewer age (primetime)	50.3	43.7	53.2
Median household income	$48,500	mid $50,000	$48,900
Working women	59%	56%	42.6%
Attended some college	49%	62%	52%
Have children	45%	41%	30%
Median number of people in household	3.2	3.2	3.0
Live in "A/B" counties	69%	73%	71%
African American	17%	6%	16.6%
"Other"	3%	2%	1.43%
Single	23%	19%	18.9%
Married	53%	61%	58.2%
Have computers	67%	73%	72%
Use the Internet	61%	73%	65%

"A" counties belong to the twenty-one largest metro areas and account for 40 percent of the U.S. population. "B" counties are those not included in A that are in metro areas with more than eighty-five thousand households, and total 30 percent of total U.S. households. County designations are based on the 1990 census.

ities among the audiences indicate the need for more refined measurement tools and matrices—a need served by psychographic measures.

Another Segmentation Tool: Psychographics

These sorts of demographic audience distinctions continue to provide crucial information that advertisers consider in buying advertising time, but the industry increasingly uses psychographic features to differentiate between demographically similar audiences and to connect viewers with products in more complicated ways. Psychographic measures—features of lifestyle, lifestage, and attitude—have existed as marketing research tools since the late 1970s but have gained currency as a result of the intensification of niche-audience segmentation. The marketing community continues to debate its validity and usefulness, but networks who sell advertising time increasingly augment their demographic profiles with psychographic information to better specify their audience.[59] Psychographic information is most valuable when research merges information about attitudes, preferences, and opinions with demographic attributes to provide advertisers and networks with sophisticated tools for understanding who their consumers are, where to find them, and what appeal will most likely convince them to buy a product.

Psychographic profiles typically involve segmentation. The VALS (Values and Lifestyles) and VALS2 matrices were among the earliest and most widely used profiles.[60] VALS organizes consumers into eight groups based on an attitudinal survey that identifies motivations. Advertisers can then target their message to resonate with the specific values and priorities of particular groups. Demographic features can be correlated with different attitude segments to provide even more information about target consumers and how to reach them. Other syndicated segmentation surveys correlate factors of attitude from demographic features.[61] ZIP codes and geographic location are central for some surveys, such as ClusterPLUS 2000, which uses street blocs and ZIP+4s to organize neighborhoods.[62] This type of sorting system assumes that similar people live in close proximity and therefore type of neighborhood provides a descriptor of one's personality, beliefs, or priorities, which advertisers use to interpret and predict purchasing behavior.

Psychographic data are particularly useful in helping advertisers target consumers who may be predisposed to buy specific products. For example, Carol Morgan and Doran Levy constructed nine separate psychographic segmentation strategies for the Baby Boomer generation, one of which segments Boomers by their attitudes toward food. Food manufacturers then use these segmentations in designing marketing campaigns. In the case of a new soy-based burger, for example, two particular segments—Nutrition Concerned, those "dedicated to healthful, low-fat meals," and Fast and Healthy, those "focused on convenient foods offering some health benefits,"—compose the primary market for the product.[63] The schema for understanding people's different relationships with food, fused with demographic and geographic information, helps advertisers target their message to reach a higher index of those most likely to purchase a specific product. Rather than broadly targeting consumers of a certain age or gender, the advertiser can promote the product in contexts likely to be seen by those whose preferences correlate with the likely purchaser profile.

The differences between the cable networks targeting women are characteristic of psychographic rather than demographic differentiation—a variation identifiable in each network brand. Interviews with programming and marketing executives at Lifetime, Oxygen, and WE, triangulated with analyses of the networks' programming and marketing materials—both marketing the networks to viewers (on-air spots and billboard advertisements) and to advertisers (advertisements in trade press and upfront sales kit material)—informs the following comparison. The multiple data points illustrate discrepancies in the various networks' voices and their construction of "women" and "women's needs," despite the use of similar descriptors by executives at different networks. For example, each of the networks identifies similar values, such as "empowerment," as a core attribute of their brand. Analysis, however, reveals that the networks manifest their efforts to empower women differently.

The Lifetime Woman: The Everywoman

As it prepared to launch the original series *Any Day Now, Maggie,* and *Oh Baby* in 1998, the director of programming at Lifetime, Dawn Tarnofsky, described the network's typical viewer as "'female, college-educated, around forty-seven-years old.'"[64] The series were targeted to women aged twenty-four to forty-nine, and the network hoped that *Any Day Now* would also draw families. Tarnofsky described Lifetime's goal as offering programs that make women say, "'Wow, that's me up there.'"[65] Little had changed by 2003, when the vice president of marketing, Tricia Melton, described the typical Lifetime viewer as "a woman in her early forties, she is probably a working mom. Psychographically, she is a busy, multitasking woman, very interested in a lot of different things: information about health, parenting, social issues, violence against women and how to break the cycles, so she's a multifaceted person."[66] Although this viewer is only a construction, such explicit articulations are helpful for understanding the viewer executives likely have in mind when making programming decisions. The imagined typical viewer is closely linked to the network's development of its brand identity, which Melton describes as "about inspiration, information, empowerment; it's about emotion, emotional connection, honesty, and relevance." In describing the brand, Tim Brooks, senior vice president of research, stressed the network's emphasis on characters viewers can relate to: "These are supposed to be women that you could be, or that you could know, or that you could relate to on some level." This emphasis leads Lifetime to primarily program series set in contemporary times and prevents it from developing or acquiring fantasy and action-adventure programs. In its selection of made-for-Lifetime films, the network connects the importance it places on characters viewers can relate to by emphasizing true or reality-based stories.

"Issues" are also central to Lifetime's identity—an attribute identifiable in the made-for-Lifetime films and the incorporation of political causes into its original-series programming. Featured as "Our Lifetime Commitment," Lifetime is visible in public outreach initiatives such as Stop Violence against Women, Stop Breast Cancer for Life, Be Your Own Hero, and Caring for Kids.[67] The network emphasizes these initiatives in on-air promotional slots and in themes explored in programming. During a focus on the violence initiative, each of the three original dramas (*Any Day Now, Strong Medicine,* and *The Division*) incorporated plots about violence against women into one night of programming. *Strong Medicine* has provided storylines related to many of the Lifetime initiatives, including ongoing plots related to breast cancer; a story about one of its doctors being raped by a colleague, which included an extended storyline chronicling the collection of the rape kit and her gradual recovery; and a story depicting the other doctor as the victim of domestic abuse. Brooks noted that many of the programs conclude with a tag at the end with phone numbers for viewers to learn more about the issue or to obtain information about service providers if they need help.

Promotional material Lifetime produced for advertisers in 2003 included results from an audience survey that asked respondents to complete the sentence "Lifetime is . . .". The four sets of adjectives listed in response are: entertaining, heartfelt, honest and true, and trustworthy (one must assume these were the most frequent answers, although it is not clearly indicated). The promotional materials also included survey data in which respondents most often classified Lifetime as their favorite basic cable network (33 percent); 38 percent responded that it was the most trusted network for women (as opposed to NBC, ABC, and Oxygen with 4 percent each and CBS, FOX, HGTV, TLC, and WE with 2 percent each).

Because Lifetime is the established women's brand, the newer competitors clearly have defined their brand relative to Lifetime's. The specific features of the Lifetime brand are somewhat difficult to describe because the emphasis on audience breadth makes the parameters comparatively less distinct. Lifetime positions itself as the cable network for all women, while the others are designed to appeal to particular types of women. Lifetime does not serve all women or various groups of women equivalently, but there is a clear inclusiveness in its attempt to construct women as a singular group and invite them all to the network. Lifetime might be understood as the CBS of the women's cable networks (for those familiar with the different brand variations among broadcast networks). It uses a network-era strategy of seeking a broad and heterogeneous female audience, comparable to that utilized by the broadcast networks from the 1950s through the 1980s.

Because of its history as the only female-targeted network, Lifetime has not segmented the female audience, nor has it needed to. With new competitors such as Oxygen and WE initiating such segmentation, Lifetime will have to respond (or face the fate of CBS through the 1990s, drawing a large but older-skewing audience unattractive to advertisers). The extension of the Lifetime brand with Lifetime Movie Network and Lifetime Real Women can be seen as the first step in this response, and Brooks noted that he would not be surprised if the network developed other spinoff networks. The programming of Lifetime Real Women differs from Lifetime in its emphasis on the reality genre, but it is also designed to have a different sensibility.[68] Brooks noted the series *The Things We Do for Love,* which performed poorly on Lifetime because it had a different disposition than the shows scheduled around it. The show has performed much better on Lifetime Real Women, indicating the importance of programming environment and how network identity informs what viewers expect from a show's content.

Lifetime has adjusted its brand focus many times over its long history. Most recently, the ability to spinoff programming to its sister networks LMN and Lifetime Real Women has allowed the "mother" network to focus increasingly on narrative programming, both original and acquired off-net series. Until 2004, Lifetime was the only women's network to offer original, live-action narrative programming, an expensive form that indicates its status as a top cable network. As the discussion of these series in chapters 4 and 5 illustrates, *Any Day Now, The Division,* and *Strong Medicine* exhibit exceptional similarity to broadcast networks' stories about women. Lifetime's focus on narrative series may be evidence of a competitive strategy designed to make the network more similar to broadcast networks, while it also strategically differentiates it from the programming foci and capabilities of Oxygen and WE (see table 6 and figure 1).

Lifetime's primary strength is its broad association with programming for women. Other associations, such as its predilection for stories that construct women as victims in the initial act (while overcoming their victimization in the third and fourth acts), may prevent some women from identifying it as a network for them. Or they may not initially explore Lifetime, but turn there

Table 6. Programming Airing June 2–9, 2003

	Lifetime	Oxygen	WE
Broadcast Day	7 AM–2:30 AM	6 AM–2 AM	11 AM–5 AM
Unscripted			
Original	*I Do Diaries*	*Girls Behaving Badly*	*Full Frontal Fashion*
	Intimate Portraits	*The Isaac Mizrahi Show*	*Single in the Hamptons*
	Speaking of Women's Health	*I've Got a Secret*	*Style World*
	Unsolved Mysteries	*The Knot*	*Winning Women*
	What Should You Do?	*Oprah After the Show*	
		Talk Sex with Sue Johanson	
		WNBA Basketball	
		Women & the Badge	
Syndication	*Denise Austin Daily Workout*	*Birth Stories*	*Great Romances*
	Unsolved Mysteries	*Debbie Travis' Painted House*	*Guest of Honor*
		Skin Deep	*House Calls*
		Sunday Night Sex Show	*Movie Matrimony*
Co-Production		*eLove*	
		Face Lift	
Scripted			
Original	*Any Day Now*	*Hey Monie*	
	The Division		
	Strong Medicine		
Syndication	*Caroline in the City*	*Bliss*	*Felicity*
	Designing Women	*Cybill*	*Two Guys and a Girl*
	Golden Girls	*A Different World*	
	Mad About You	*Kate and Allie*	
	The Nanny	*La Femme Nikita*	
	Once & Again	*Xena: Warrior Princess*	
Films			
	4–5 movies/day	2 movies/day	5 movies, plus 1 repeat/day

before turning to many other general-interest networks. Lifetime leveraged its brand into a magazine title in the summer of 2003 (although it folded in October 2004) and announced plans for a national radio program in 2004, further expanding venues for brand recognition. This broad identification may enable the network to segment in a manner similar to Discovery (once one channel, now at least five—Discovery Wings, Discovery Kids, Discovery Health, Discovery Times, and Discovery Home and Leisure). Whether this segmentation happens by genre (Lifetime Comedy, Lifetime Style) or by addressing different demographic groups (Lifetime Teen, Lifetime Single, Lifetime Working Mom), this segmentation will be commercially successful only if the programming is sufficiently distinct and varied. This should result in diverse representations, constructions, and stories about women. The commercial logic of the cable market rewards networks that offer niche appeal and clear brands, an economic imperative that promotes the continuation and expansion of diverse networks for women.

The Oxygen Woman: Irreverent, Edgy, and Sharp

The founding mythos of Oxygen describes the network's origin as resulting from the founders Laybourne and Carsey finding that there was nothing they could watch on Lifetime that wasn't depressing or overly emotional, that nothing featured as "television for women" represented their taste or sensibility. Oxygen, consequently, must be understood as a reaction to Lifetime, although their competitive relationship is more complex than this suggests. Deborah Beece, president of programming, described the typical Oxygen viewer as "mid-to-late thirties; works outside the home; has children; at least some level of college education; married; very interested in herself—moving herself forward; the kind of person who is not willing to waste her time; [she has a] good moral compass; good sense of values; feels that 'I'm not getting older, I'm getting better; these are the goals I have for myself, this is what I want to accomplish'; not a listless personality; someone who wants to be more aggressive."[69] This profile is not particularly different from the one described at Lifetime, yet there are key differences in how the networks go about addressing this viewer.

Beece explained that Laybourne and Carsey sought to "create a new brand for me and women like me; [a brand] that's optimistic, funny, bold, irreverent, questioning, curious, which doesn't push the pain buttons—which is what a lot of women's media do, whether it's magazines, or Lifetime." Messages such as "you're too thin, you're too fat, your husband is going to leave you" push "the pain buttons" and are often tied implicitly to directives to women about all the things they *need* to do or have. She contrasted the world

Oxygen constructs from the "fearful place" developed in Lifetime's programming. Many examples might attest to this as an apt characterization of Lifetime, however, the strong viewership of the network indicates that its audiences may be reading the material in other ways or deriving some value that may not be apparent in textual analysis.[70] This perception of Lifetime is helpful in distinguishing how the brands are different despite their similar audiences, actual and targeted.

When Oxygen first launched it was—as the network's creators intended—exceptionally bold, curious, irreverent, and questioning, at least by the standards of the U.S. commercial media system. Oxygen initially emphasized a service orientation by exclusively featuring nonnarrative programs designed to inform women about handling money, to provide tools for balancing work and family, and similarly productive and informative programming. These programs clearly addressed an educated consumer, and early shows were unlike anything to air on U.S. television. Women's programs have emphasized a service-orientation since the days of radio (which makes the turn to dramatic narratives in the late 1990s so striking); however, Oxygen differentiated its service voice (from those such as Martha Stewart and magazine self-help columnists) by being much more feminist than traditionally feminine. Oxygen's programming voice emphasizes its audience's happiness and satisfaction rather than topics designed to help women fulfill the needs of husbands and children. In this first programming phase, Oxygen's brand-describing adjectives were connected to news, documentary, and other nonnarrative programming: The teen show *Trackers* included a news package following a sixteen-year-old girl on her first trip to the gynecologist; Oxygen hosted a town-hall meeting with Al Gore as part of the 2000 campaign; and the documentary series *As She Sees It* featured independent and feminist documentaries otherwise unavailable on commercial television.

During its first period, the network also emphasized its effort to integrate Web and cable media content. This convergence remained constantly apparent when viewing the network and contributed to delineating the Oxygen brand. Additional information about program topics and Web addresses scrolled across an ever-present graphics bar along the bottom of the screen (even during commercials). Talk and news shows regularly invited viewer participation in online venues, and narrative programs such as *Xena: Warrior Princess* featured real-time chats that were streamed onto the screen. Oxygen's integrated strategy helped establish who it sought among the vast female audience. Although audience members could experience Oxygen without going online, the emphasis on computer technology characterized it as the women's network of a younger, computer-savvy generation. The inclusion of *Trackers* in its initial programming schedule also reflected Oxygen's pursuit of a younger and more socially relevant audience.

In its second period, the Oxygen brand remains bold, curious, irreverent, and questioning, but less so, and the adjectives describing it are manifest in the network's off-net acquisitions and original comedy development. Clearly, Xena and Nikita are not the "relatable" characters offered by Lifetime, while the female characters in *Cybill* and *Absolutely Fabulous* follow the "unruly women" type and irreverently defy traditional depictions of femininity.[71] Oxygen clearly differentiates itself from Lifetime in its emphasis on comedy rather than melodrama. Lifetime has had little success producing original comedy series and has consequently constructed a heavily dramatic brand through its original series and films (although Lifetime announced new original comedies to debut in 2005). Oxygen's original narrative ventures have been only in comedy, with animated series such as *Hey Monie* and *X-Chromosome,* the hidden-camera series *Girls Behaving Badly,* and the scripted *Good Girls Don't.* Many of these shows utilize sophisticated forms of parody and satire that make for a somewhat ambivalent commentary about gender and women. Oxygen's theatrical selections include many more independent films than the other networks—films such as *Chasing Amy* and *Little Voice* would be unlikely to air on any other network. The network's talk shows frequently defy the bounds of traditional social norms, whether through Carrie Fisher's stream of consciousness interviews with celebrities, Tracey Ullman's insolent look at fashion, or day-in-the-life journeys with Isaac Mizrahi through the streets of New York. Finally, the shows most noticed by audiences, the *Sunday Night Sex Show* and *Talk Sex with Sue Johanson,* offer an explicit and frank discussion of sexuality and sexual pleasure. The emphasis on Web/cable integration has been less pronounced in the second period. The black bar remained at the bottom of the screen into 2003, but the move to narrative diminished the opportunities to utilize it, and having a sophisticated Web presence became the norm rather than the exception among all television networks. In this second period, Oxygen has demarcated itself from other networks much more through comedy than through its Web integration.

In contrast to the Lifetime brand and the stories Lifetime tells, Oxygen now features programming characterized as outrageous (rather than relatable), which results in a very different version of female identity than what is reinforced by nearly all mainstream media. Educational or "edutaining" programming is greatly diminished in the network's second period, while a pro–sexual health/sexual pleasure message remains the primary service-oriented offering of the network. If Lifetime teaches women what to do if they are being battered, Oxygen offers techniques likely to help them achieve orgasm. My point is not to rank these lessons, as both are important, and different women likely prioritize them differently (orgasm is of little importance if you're being beaten). This example demonstrates the value to be gained from the diversification of networks and stories targeting women and supports the assertion that such a variety indeed exists. To continue my analogy to broadcast networks, Oxygen is best viewed as the FOX of the women's cable networks. It entered the market late and has sought to compete by doing things differently and distinctly. Where Lifetime attempts a broad appeal to women, Oxygen has demarcated a clear "edge" to its programming. Oxygen likely makes this gamble because this address may hail the most highly prized eyeballs, although it may also yield a smaller audience overall.

Of the three women's cable networks, Lifetime and Oxygen are the most dissimilar. If charting them on a continuum from most traditional construction of femininity and generalized address of women (Lifetime) to the most atypical construction of femininity and specified address of a particular segment of women (Oxygen), WE establishes its niche somewhere in the middle. This middle-of-the-road status may make WE the most vulnerable of the networks in the competitive environment of the multichannel transition, which rewards networks with clear brand identification. WE's brand remains distinctive from the others, however, and women are certainly interested in more than the dichotomy offered by Lifetime and Oxygen.

WE: Traditional Femininity for a Younger Woman

Promotional materials describe WE as an "entertainment service for women twenty-five to forty-nine, the core target being a thirty-three-year-old working mother," and assert that the WE viewer is "active, fun-loving, a risk-taker and optimistic. When she watches WE our programming engages her because it reflects her lifestyle and interests."[72] WE describes its brand by noting, "Women are ready to lighten up. They want to laugh more, indulge their passions, live in the moment. WE is the only television network for women that provides a positive, inclusive, relaxing viewing experience. Our movies and series reflect our brand positioning—live love laugh."[73] In another brand statement, WE "promises" to "present people you can relate to—people like you. We like you the way you are—no matter who you are. We will connect with you on a positive emotional level. We understand and appreciate those things you value."[74] Perhaps because it remains a new competitor and its middle-of-the-women's-networks status makes its brand unclear, WE explicitly distinguishes itself from the other networks as follows: "While other women's networks seem to be escape-driven or agenda-driven, WE is a place of self-contentment and just enjoying the moment. It's optimistic, friendly and bright."[75]

Lisa deMoraes dubbed WE "the Unthinking Women's Network" in an article reviewing its transition from Romance Classics and its mandate of offering viewers "sanctuary."[76] Clearly, the WE brand was also developed as a reaction to the Lifetime brand and, to a degree, Oxygen as well.[77] With the market for heavy melodrama and moderate feminism occupied by Lifetime and Oxygen, WE emphasizes acquired theatricals such as *When Harry Met Sally, Mystic Pizza,* and *Waiting to Exhale* (generally films it would have aired as Romance Classics), as well as original nonnarrative series on fashion and style and programs showcasing single lifestyles. According to Lee Heffernan, senior vice president of marketing, the theatricals are particularly beneficial in drawing viewers to the network because the films have known attributes and stars and consequently require little promotion. Viewers will see promotions for the network's original series during commercials, which she hopes will lead them to sample more of the network's fare. The films the network purchases contribute to the establishment of its brand, but because it does not create the content, film selection offers limited information about the network's brand specificity.

WE's original series can be grouped into three categories: dating and marriage, style and fashion, and profile/interview. WE primarily utilizes unscripted formats in its original series, a distinction likely attributable to its limited programming budget, but the unscripted emphasis also distinguishes it from Lifetime's dramatic and Oxygen's comedic emphases. The network's *Single in* (the Hamptons, New York, Los Angeles, South Beach, and Las Vegas) series follows single women in different cities each season; it is perhaps best described as *Sex and the City* meets *The Real World.* This show defines dating as the primary activity in its "characters'" lives, and when combined with *Bridezilla,* which follows women as they plan their weddings, and *How We Met,* in which couples share the stories of their first meeting and courtship, the story of heterosexual dating and coupling appears as a central zone of influence for the network brand and consequently for the type of women it targets. *Full Frontal Fashion* primarily explores the upscale fashion industry, *Style World* offers a style-focused travelogue of the fashion, art, and architecture of different cites around the globe, and *Mix It Up* blends the coupling and style areas by chronicling conflicts between roommates and couples when their decorating tastes do not match. Like the features of women's fashion magazines, these series provide a glimpse of the fashion and style options available to upper-income women who have or make time to emphasize design or appearance. WE's interview shows include *When I Was a Girl,* a beautifully shot series in which female celebrities describe childhood memories, and *Winning Women,* which profiles female athletes, many of whom compete in extreme sports. The network also features off-net series such as *Felicity* and the comedy *Two Guys and a Girl.*

Despite the inclusiveness suggested by the claims about "women" in its promotional materials, the network's promise to "understand and appreciate those things you value" and present "people like you" is obviously only true of women for whom dating, fashion, and style are of prime importance. Unlike Lifetime and Oxygen, WE offers a narrow construction of women's axes of identity, with nonwhite women appearing primarily as window dressing, not as women with a distinctive experience. The worlds of fashion and style the network emphasizes are out of reach for all but a few viewers (although the important appeal of escape should not be discounted), and the stress on dating and marriage provides an overdetermined articulation of the heteronormative experience.

It may now be a network by another name, but WE continues to target a traditional construction of femininity that was more obvious in its original appellation as Romance Classics. In many ways it is the opposite of Oxygen, featuring programming with little edge and offering instead a comfortable female inclusiveness—at least for those young women hailed by its traditional construction of femininity. The network delivers on its promise of escapism and serves the tradition of pleasurable female forms once (and still) filled by soap operas and romance novels. DeMoraes is correct in her assessment of the network's content as a place for the "unthinking woman." The closest parallel WE may offer to Lifetime's education about domestic violence and Oxygen's orgasm instruction is information about Vera Wang's new collection or the best way to accessorize a small living space. If it were a broadcast network, WE would be the ABC (in the mid 1990s) of women's cable networks. The brand only slightly varies traditional programming, with its primary differentiation resulting from updating tried and true forms and themes for a younger generation of viewers. Yet, WE expands the programming material available to women. It is not nearly as different as Oxygen, but its avoidance of "issues" and its emphasis on escape significantly diverge from Lifetime's edutainment and awareness-building programs about women overcoming crises.

Perhaps the particular voices with which Lifetime, Oxygen, and WE hail female audiences can be illustrated best by each network's biography series: *Intimate Portraits, Who Does She Think She Is?* and *Cool Women,* respectively.[78] *Intimate Portraits,* promoted as "Her Story, Her Words," features biographies of a wide range of female celebrities and public figures and is Lifetime's longest running original series. Models, actresses, and performers, many of whom appear in the biographies, tell the stories of their lives and their rise to fame. Oxygen's *Who Does She Think She Is?* features women in power and tells stories about how women such as Gloria Steinem and Hillary Clinton gained their professional status and assess their life choices.[79] WE finds its niche in the women's biography market by focusing on *Cool Women,* defined as "ordinary women who do the extraordinary," which explores women in nontraditional occupations such as fire fighting and the clergy.[80]

Each of the networks also airs fashion series and films that address female audiences, but in distinctive ways. Consider what the various hosts of the networks' fashion series indicate about their approach to the topic. WE features fashion series hosted by the supermodels Rachel Hunter and Cindy Crawford; Oxygen's fashion series, titled *Visible Panty Lines,* is hosted by the comedian Tracey Ullman and marketed as an "irreverent look at style"; and Lifetime has featured *Operation Style* with Bradley Bayou and *Next Door with Katie Brown,* both Martha Stewart–esque, jacks-of-all-trades who offer decorating, fashion, makeover, and entertaining solutions. These different approaches toward designing programming on the same topics reveal how these networks establish their identity and announce what type of woman they seek.

The range of foci for women's networks' biography and style series only begins to hint at their variant identities. These networks define their brands through constantly shifting programming, attempting to maintain audiences with successful series while subtly shifting to attract new audiences. While I could not care less about the new trends emerging during fashion week in New York (despite its claims, WE does not show "people like *me*"), I can name many female friends and relatives who have great interest in these events. Likewise, some nights I am in the mood for a highly emotional film or melodramatic tearjerker, while other nights I need to retreat to the outrageous comedic worlds of Patsy, Edina, or Cybill, or view the jaw-dropping boldness of the *Girls Behaving Badly* cast. Not only are women different from one another, but individual women have different needs and interests at different times. These three networks still serve only a segment of women's interests and needs, but Oxygen and WE have significantly expanded the address to, construction of, and options for female viewers.

This chapter offers a generalized analysis of the network brands rather than a close textual analysis of a specific show because no one show adequately captures a network's identity, and individual series come and go very quickly on young networks. No one show has yet captured the Oxygen or WE brand as Lifetime's films have arguably encapsulated that network's identity. Even at Lifetime, the central focus of these films has shifted over time, also making them an unreliable indicator of the network brand. Once some of the institutional uncertainties of new networks and new network identities are resolved, close analysis of the messages about women's lives and the femininities being communicated by individual shows and established network brands will provide a rich site for analysis.

* * *

The brand differentiation among Lifetime, Oxygen, and WE should not be primarily understood as a matter of form but of tone. When I asked Beece and Barasch who they viewed as Oxygen's primary competition, they responded VH1, E!, Comedy Central, and TLC. Similarly, when I asked Brooks at Lifetime the same question, he responded TBS, TNT, and USA. I had expected them to first list the other women's networks, and while they certainly remain part of the competition whether acknowledged or not, this response also points to the variation among the networks. Although the industry and academic researchers tend to aggregate cable networks targeting women as a discrete type of network, the responses of these executives indicate the greater complexity of the competitive situation.

To return to the earlier discussion of different tiers of default channels, it may be that some women include all of the women's cable networks among their default channels, while others only select one or two. I observed this behavior in a female friend who turned first to HBO, then MTV, then Oxygen, and stopped on NBC. All viewers likely develop these patterns that may or may not be influenced by sharing viewing with others. It is unlikely that my friend would have ever switched to Lifetime, or WE for that matter, perhaps deciding to pursue interests online, read, or do something else if none of her default channels provided content of interest. The gross overabundance of channels now available requires that we think differently about viewing. Consequently, the primary competition for the Oxygen viewer may not be Lifetime or WE but networks that do not focus their programming toward women yet speak to their audiences with a similar sensibility.

The differentiated brands of Lifetime, Oxygen, and WE make clear that not only multiplicity but diversity has arrived in the women's cable-network market. Female audience members have benefited from the expansion of networks targeting them in a number of ways. First, the arrival of competition drove Lifetime out of its complacency and forced it to expend more money and effort on its programming. The resulting original dramas elevated the brand, leading to its status as the most watched cable network in prime time. The success of its original dramatic series influenced thinking about stories of female characters throughout the television industry and likely contributed to the expansion of the form on other networks. Secondly, the rise of multiple cable networks targeting women has not resulted in Lifetime clones but expanded the type, tone, and form of programming targeting women. Although the networks program to similar spheres of influence generally identified as important to the female audience, they address these spheres with different emphases and tones. The new networks also have developed forms of programming and topics previously absent or lacking, such as Oxygen's attention to comedy and empowered sexuality.

As in the case of the female-centered drama, the multiplication of women's cable networks has led to more varied depictions of women, their interests, and their priorities. This contributes to a more multifaceted construction of "women" by contemporary U.S. television, further augmenting the contribution made by the diverse array of female-centered dramas. In tandem, these developments have helped broaden dominant norms of femininity, the range of "acceptable" female priorities, and the scope of issues with which women are seen to struggle. Although the range of depictions and diversity of stories about women may not yet match those available to men, these networks and the dramatic series emphasized elsewhere contribute to making this programming environment fundamentally different from those that have come before. Hegemonic constructions of women may not yet be "uninhabitable," but the brand proliferation accomplished by these networks makes them more difficult to sustain.

One of the concerns driving earlier feminist work on Lifetime resulted from the network's power to singularly and visibly define women and their interests in the U.S. television sphere and its decidedly less-than-feminist attitude. This power has been diminished by the addition of other cable networks targeting women and by Lifetime's response in diversifying its own brand. de-Moraes apparently intends her description of WE as the "unthinking women's network" pejoratively, yet WE's strategy for serving the needs of its female audience is no less or more valuable than that of Lifetime or Oxygen. Different women have different entertainment needs and sources of pleasure. The ideological significance of various programs can be addressed individually; however, the existence of variant network identities allows the programs and network strategies to indicate different perceptions of the female audience than if only one of these networks was available. If only WE existed, feminist critics would be right to note the stereotypical and constraining nature of this common deployment of femininity. With Lifetime and Oxygen competing with WE, such criticism becomes less valid, as their different identities correspond to variations among women.

The range of programming offered by Lifetime, Oxygen, and WE creates

an atmosphere in which women can seek fulfillment of discrepant entertainment needs, and the networks' resulting program adjustments illustrate
their response to the cultural negotiation of these different forms. Examination of the various networks' audiences and which programs become dominant on the networks and in cross-network competition will indicate a great
deal about American culture and gender roles, much as historical analysis of
U.S. television has argued about the general audience in previous decades.
The exceptionality of the early twenty-first century exists in the possibility
for multiple female-targeted television networks to enact this process of negotiation in the same manner that books, magazines, and music have provided in previous eras.

Figure 1. Description of Women's Cable Network Shows

The following show descriptions are, in most cases, taken from the networks' Web sites (available as of June 2003). In cases in which the networks did not offer a description I have provided a brief categorization. I have not included descriptions for those shows that had well-known broadcast runs.

Lifetime

I Do Diaries   You won't want to miss all the drama and excitement, as two best friends struggle to pick the perfect wedding gown for each other—without any input from the bride herself! Tune in to see what each pal chose and how the brides looked on their big days!

    http://www.lifetimetv.com/shows/weddings/index.html

Intimate Portrait   Delve into the lives of celebrated women! Get a personal perspective on some of the most impressive women in art, entertainment, politics, business, science, journalism, and sports. Learn about their ups and downs, heartaches and happy endings. Listen as they describe their childhoods, careers, and personal relationships in their own words—and hear from their close friends and family, too.

    http://www.lifetimetv.com/shows/ip/about/

Lifetime's Speaking of Women's Health   Talk show with female doctor discussing women's health, fitness, and beauty issues. Sponsored in part by Proctor and Gamble.

What Should You Do?   The best way to protect yourself in an emergency is to be prepared. Hear from real women who have survived harrowing situations and get insider tips on dealing with dangerous dilemmas.

    http://www.lifetimetv.com/shows/wsyd/index.html

Denise Austin's Daily Fitness   Aerobic workout and instruction.

Any Day Now   This heartfelt original drama looks in on the lives of two very different women who became childhood friends in Alabama during the height of the civil rights movement.

    http://www.lifetimetv.com/shows/anyday/index.html

The Division   It's a cop show with a twist. Lifetime's series explores the personal and professional lives of five very different policewomen in San Francisco. *The Division* features action, suspense, crime, and cat-and-mouse chases. It also looks at the ups and downs of romance, family, motherhood, and female friendships. It's good, old-fashioned drama about working women with real-life problems.

    http://us.imdb.com/Plot?0272376

Strong Medicine   Dr. Luisa Delgado ran the South Philly Women's Clinic so that poor women could get the medical help they needed. Dr. Dana Stowe did medical research on cancer to help women. Together they now run a free women's clinic at Philadelphia's Rittenhouse Hospital to help all women.

    http://us.imdb.com/Plot?0252019

Oxygen

Girls Behaving Badly   A hidden camera show with a different point of view. *Girls Behaving Badly,* Oxygen's bold new comedy show, is *Sex and the City* meets *Candid Camera.*

    http://www.oxygen.com/girls/?slot=nav

The Isaac Mizrahi Show   It's an all-new season of Isaac—holding court in his studio, cooking with celebrity chefs, dancing and playing with Hollywood's elite, and stepping out into the streets of his hometown, New York City.

    http://www.oxygen.com/isaac/?slot=nav

I've Got a Secret   Four witty celebrities take turns asking "yes" or "no" questions in an attempt to guess their secrets.

    http://www.oxygen.com/secret/

The Knot   Follows a couple through their wedding plans and nuptials. Produced in part by The Knot, a wedding Web site.

Oprah after the Show   For Oprah Winfrey, an hour of conversation just isn't enough. In this new prime-time series, Oprah kicks off her shoes and dishes with her audience in the party atmosphere that is *Oprah after the Show*.

    http://www.oxygen.com/oprah/?slot=nav

Talk Sex with Sue Johanson   On *Talk Sex*, Sue fields callers live, in her uniquely candid, no-nonsense style. If you've got a burning, embarrassing, or otherwise "unaskable" question, call 1–888–203–8890. A happier, healthier sex life could be a phone call away.

    http://www.oxygen.com/sexshow/?slot=nav

Women & the Badge   Join Pam Grier for this fascinating series that explores the lives of women in law enforcement. From the local to the national level, these real-life female action heroes put themselves on the line to keep our communities safe.

    http://www.oxygen.com/badge/?slot=nav

Figure 1. (cont.)

Oxygen (cont.)

Birth Stories   *Birth Stories* follows people from widely varying backgrounds and values as they face the realities of bringing a new life into the world.
   http://www.oxygen.com/birthstories/?slot=nav

Debbie Travis' Painted House   Hosted by Debbie Travis, *Painted House* is the next wave of home design shows—it's "how to" with all the real-life humor and drama you'd expect from a decorating show that's part confessional, part soap opera.
   http://www.oxygen.com/paintedhouse/?slot=nav

Skin Deep   *Skin Deep* is a documentary television series that explores the common misconceptions surrounding cosmetic surgery. Through patients' own experiences, it reveals who has it, what they have done . . . and why.
   http://www.oxygen.com/skindeep/?slot=nav

Sunday Night Sex Show   Renowned sex educator Sue Johanson knows all about sex—and she isn't shy about sharing her insights. In this intimate call-in show, Sue tackles callers' questions in a funny, informative, and nonjudgmental manner.
   http://www.oxygen.com/sexshow/?slot=nav

eLove   Encounter real-life couples who've met online and track the evolution of their friendships, romance, and intimacy—then watch them meet face to face.
   http://www.oxygen.com/elove/?slot=nav

Facelift   With the help of one person in each house, Debbie and team redesign one room while the others are away. Will they love it or loathe it? Finding out is part of the fun as Debbie revolutionizes renovation via her unmistakably intimate and upfront approach.
   http://www.oxygen.com/facelift/

Hey Monie   *Hey Monie* is an animated comedy that explores the life and longings of Simone ("Monie"), a single, African American, professional woman in big-city America with her best friend, Yvette, by her side. Accented by improvisation from our Second City cast (and real-life best friends who play Monie and Yvette), there is an authentic feel to the show's language and dialogue.
   http://www.oxygen.com/heymonie/

Bliss   Acclaimed women screenwriters and directors have adapted the best of women's erotic fiction to create diverse, edgy, and provocative drama that honestly explores women's sexuality.
   http://www.oxygen.com/bliss/?slot=nav

WE

Full Frontal Fashion   Our weekly series is guaranteed to deliver your fashion fix, as host Ali Landry takes you front-row and center for the hottest collections coming down the catwalk.
   http://www.we.tv/section/0,,key=3&tzOffset=0,00.html

Single in the Hamptons   Follow along as we take you inside the lives of young, sexy New York singles in search of love, a good time, and the hottest beach on the East Coast.
   http://www.we.tv/section/0,,key=3&tzOffset=0,00.html

Style World   Daisy Fuentes takes viewers around the globe to explore the worlds of fashion, art, and architecture.
   http://sales.we.tv/main/content.asp?ID=4&section=Programming

Winning Women   Actress and triathlete Alexandra Paul investigates changes in world of extreme sports and the female athletes leading the charge. They are ordinary working women who spend their weekends conquering mountains, surviving the surf, and challenging mother nature, as they break records and barriers in the world of sports.
   http://sales.we.tv/main/content.asp?ID=52&section=Programming

Great Romances   Documentary-style series that explores the development and journeys of the romantic relationships among notable historical and contemporary figures.

House Calls   A psychiatrist visits couples in their homes to try to help them solve their relationship problems.

Movie Matrimony   Real-life lovebirds Renee Taylor and Joe Bologna host this WE original featuring memorable movie weddings, from the classics to contemporary.
   http://www.we.tv/section/0,,key=3&tzOffset=0,00.html

2. Fighting for Families and Femininity: The Hybrid Narratives of the Action Drama

> In all the great epics, from the Iliad on, the protagonists have been masculine, their destinies a masculine destiny. Now a real shift is taking place, in which some collective identities—those created for the whole culture regardless of gender—are female.
>
> —James Schamus, writer and producer, *Crouching Tiger, Hidden Dragon*

Of the various dramatic types, action dramas have unquestionably attracted the most popular speculation about the significance of their stories of empowered heroines for contemporary femininity and feminism. The heroines of action dramas are commonly either physically, mentally, or mystically enhanced and extend the legacy of an assortment of previous characters that existed in eras that did not offer such ample variation in female characterizations. Predecessors in *Bewitched, I Dream of Jeanie, Wonder Woman,* and *The Bionic Woman* also possessed "superpowers," while other shows innovated by enabling female characters to do "men's" jobs (*Decoy, Honey West, Get Christie Love, Police Woman, Charlie's Angels,* and *Cagney and Lacey*).[1] The characters in each type of series challenged the roles prescribed for women at the time they aired, although narrative emphasis on their sexuality, fantastic settings or powers, or plots that placed them in need of rescue by male partners often muted the significance of their abilities.[2]

Sherrie A. Inness, writing of 1970s series such as *Charlie's Angels, Wonder Woman,* and *The Bionic Woman,* notes that "these early heroines had a dual purpose: they offered women viewers potentially powerful role models, but the shows simultaneously helped to reaffirm that women, while more capable than generally given credit for, were still less competent than men."[3] Many of the 1990s action dramas allowed their heroines to succeed on their own without the backhanded containment more common in the 1970s series. Despite their limitations, precursors such as *Police Woman, Charlie's Angels, Wonder Woman,* and *The Bionic Woman* were the first commercially successful dramatic series to focus on female characters, and perhaps as a result, action series draw particular attention and function as a bellwether for the status of women's television representation.[4] The literal empowerment displayed by action heroines has drawn extensive attention in discussions of what these stories signify about gender roles. The emphasis on characters' physical abilities in popular journalistic discussions overshadows these series' other contributions to the range of stories told about women and their lives.

Many series have exacerbated the contradiction of the dual purpose Inness notes by constructing heroines who evolve as simplistic revisions of the male superhero. These series attempt to turn the Bionic Man into a Bionic Woman or Superman into Wonder Woman by changing the sex of the hero without more substantive adjustment to the character or her mythology. A truly innovative series must surpass the gender-reversal device to draw complex female characters and tell stories about a distinctly female experience—a trend that emerged with the action dramas of the late 1990s. The creators of many of the characters that precede the 1990s action-drama heroines forced their characters into men's worlds, with the protagonist's gender intended to hail female as well as male audiences. This innovation is fairly superficial, the sort likely to be well regarded by content analysis and measures that seek out attributes such as "dominance patterns." Narrative analysis that considers the stories in addition to their characters' physical abilities reveals that the more significant contribution of the late 1990s cycle of action-heroine series has little to do with their physical abilities.

Despite their emphasis in journalistic outlets, I place no more importance on action dramas than the comedic, protagonist-centered family, or workplace dramas. The development of distinct types of dramatic stories about women that transcend female characters' historical confinement to action narratives diminishes the significance traditionally afforded to this narrative type. In contrast, the action dramas appearing in the late 1990s provide female characters with expanded opportunities from what gender-reversal series allowed. Many limitations continue to contain the innovation of the action drama; however, the existence of other venues for telling stories about women, particularly unprecedented dramatic types such as protagonist-centered family and reconfigured workplace dramas, decreases the centrality of their narratives in telling stories that address female audiences with complex depictions.

The 1990s action dramas are significant primarily because of their rewriting of formal conventions and their increased emphasis on telling women's stories instead of telling stories about superheroes who happen to be women. These series blend textual strategies theorized to appeal to male and female audiences to create a narrative form that features spectacular fight scenes as well as complex characterizations depicting the negotiation of psychological struggles and emotional desires.[5] This chapter considers how the stories told in series such as *Buffy the Vampire Slayer*, *Charmed*, *Dark Angel*, *La Femme Nikita*, *Witchblade*, and *Xena: Warrior Princess* construct narratives about characters with psychological depth, while acknowledging evidence that characters continue to be drawn for the fantasy of male audiences.[6]

Specifying the Action Drama

Action series that construct narratives around a central female character appeared with considerable multiplicity in the latter half of the 1990s, to the extent that clear variations in narrative structures and story function emerge. This chapter focuses primarily on one type of action series, the action drama. Many series feature characters who are supernaturally empowered and contribute to establishing a specific programming context, but distinctions in their narrative forms distinguish them from the action drama. In addition to the shows listed above, an all-encompassing examination of female-centered action series would need to consider *The Profiler* (1996–2000), *The Huntress* (2000–2001), *V.I.P.* (1998–2002), *Cleopatra 2525* (1999–2001), *Relic Hunter* (1999–2002), *Sheena, Queen of the Jungle* (2000), *Queen of Swords* (2000–2001), *She Spies* (2002–4), and perhaps even *Sabrina the Teenage Witch* (1996–2003), *The Secret World of Alex Mack* (1994–98), and *The Mystery Files of Shelby Woo* (1996–2000).[7]

Series that feature female characters with extraordinary human or supernatural abilities can be classified in many ways: according to the type of network on which they air; whether they are a first-run network series or sold in syndication; the series' intended audience composition or size; or the age of the heroine (all other demographic factors are essentially the same). My classification results from the types of stories the series explore. I focus on the action drama partially because of its innovation in traversing the mainstream and cult audience, but primarily because of its relationship to the other series I discuss. Dramatic series with central female characters targeted to female audiences provide the book's unifying object of analysis, and these action dramas contribute the most to this focus. These series resemble others that feature supernaturally empowered female characters, but the action dramas tend to make their empowered women seem more ordinary. The variety of stories that exist simultaneously—including series about tough female law enforcement officers, adventure series, supernatural girl adventure/comedies, science fiction series, as well as action dramas—reiterates the substantive changes in the multiplicity and diversity of dramatic stories about female characters emerging in the late 1990s.

The confluence of the premieres of multiple television series and films featuring female action heroes has led many journalistic critics to assess the phenomenon. The aggregated presence of *Crouching Tiger, Hidden Dragon,* the film version of *Charlie's Angels,* and *Girlfight* in metroplexes in late 2000 with the arrival of *Dark Angel, The Huntress, Queen of Swords,* and *Sheena* on the small screen made the expansion of empowered heroines too significant to ignore. Critics also noted the physical empowerment of characters in ensemble-based series such as *Lexx* and *Farscape* and even acknowledged the Cartoon Network's *Powerpuff Girls* as part of the trend. Initially, many of the articles were careful to note the historical predecessors of these contemporary empowered heroines, such as Sigourney Weaver's character in *Aliens* and TV heroines in the 1960s and 1970s. Yet these articles continued to appear, gradually with less historical contextualization or acknowledgment of the multiple forebears of the type, which is particularly curious in those discussing sequels. (The release of *Charlie's Angels: Full Throttle, Lara Croft Tomb Raider: The Cradle of Life,* and *Terminator 3: Rise of the Machines* in the summer of 2003 returned attention to the story of female physical empowerment, sometimes as though it were a new phenomenon.)[8]

The stories action dramas tell about female heroines are particularly important because audience members and critics quickly identified these empowered female characters as indicative of feminist gains.[9] Critics immediately acclaimed the arrival of female characters who could fight and destroy men as a representational advance, but their analyses rarely attended to the series' overall narrative construction. Many articles employ "role model" terminology, usually suggesting that the action heroines provide positive role models.[10] The more critically rigorous articles acknowledge the feminist conundrum created by the heroines' reliance on sex appeal, accordance with conventional beauty standards, and use of violence to express ambivalence about what the shows indicate about contemporary gender roles. These discussions of women's rights and progress tend to use empowerment literally, suggesting that female characters' ability to vanquish male opponents with physical prowess indicates the achievement of equality.

The late 1990s action dramas deviated from previous action series that featured female characters by developing stories that surpassed simplistic gender reversals. The competitive norms of the multichannel transition afforded new possibilities for creating action heroines with distinct attributes and identities instead of transferring the traits of male heroes onto female bodies. Some of the characters successfully establish their own narrative lineage, even though audience members and critics may be quick to link them to empowered women of decades past. The fact that many of these characters come from other media forms (films: *La Femme Nikita*, *Buffy the Vampire Slayer*; comic books: *Witchblade*; or other television shows: *Xena: Warrior Princess*) complicates their creative histories, but the competitive environment allows for their emergence and success as television series.

These series include much more narrative complexity than is commonly acknowledged in examinations of the heroines' physical abilities. Rather than physical empowerment, these series' greatest innovation results from their narrative hybridity, the stories this hybridity allows, and the breadth of audiences consequently reached. The particular narrative features of the action drama differentiate these stories from other dramatic types. Female-centered action dramas blend elements of the traditionally "masculine" adventure series with the melodramatic depth of quintessentially "feminine" serial narratives about complicated and tested relationships to tell distinctive stories about women. Although my aim is to identify common attributes within the type, regular viewers of these series will also note the variation among them despite their recurrent devices and features.

Narrative Features of Female-Centered Action Dramas

Episodic versus Serial Structure

The six series focused upon in this chapter employ a variety of narrative strategies and techniques, which both differentiates the shows and indicates their comparability. Most of the series function with a dual episodic and serial structure—a specific threat must be vanquished in each episode, but characterization and other narrative elements contribute to the ongoing development of the serial narrative. Many of the action dramas emphasize the episodic story more than any other type of female-centered drama. This narrative device indicates a significant departure from the conventions of serialized narratives commonly associated with women's viewing pleasures.[11]

The episodic organization of these series features distinctive components. The introduction of an evil force at the beginning of an episode structurally requires its elimination by episode's end, yet the outcome is never in question. Viewers' extensive familiarity with the conventions of series television yields a fairly assured knowledge that the threat will be vanquished. The final victory is narratively less important than the process of preparing for battle, re-

searching the opposition, determining strategy, and establishing each character's role.[12] This results in a balance between character-driven drama and spectacular battle sequences that set the action dramas apart from adventure series. The dramas I consider here achieve a balance weighted on the side of
narrative; they include moments of spectacular fight or chase sequences, but
these moments do not dominate the storytelling. The series primarily advance
narratives motivated by characters' psychology and desires rather than using
tenuous narratives to create the opportunity for spectacle. The episodic narrative consequently does more than prepare the payoff of a fight sequence that
leads to closure. Many of the foes exist to expand the characterization of the
heroine, so that while the narrative structure appears similar to standard adventure series, the narrative motivation and results are much more complex.

Action dramas airing in the 1990s developed complex narrative structures
that corresponded to their intended audiences, institutional placement, and
the stories each creative team primarily sought to tell. Although action dramas emphasize episodic stories more than some other narratives targeting
female audiences, these series also utilize serial plotlines. These continuing
stories are often very general and mainly chronicle the protagonists' development: *Buffy the Vampire Slayer* and *Charmed* depict their recognition of
and attempts to balance their supernatural skills with their "regular" lives; in
La Femme Nikita, Dark Angel, and *Witchblade* the characters seek freedom
from organizations and individuals who seek to control them and their powers; and *Xena: Warrior Princess* ultimately explores the relationship of Xena
and Gabrielle in Xena's quest to atone for crimes as a warlord.[13] It is the outcome of these stories that viewers are uncertain of—and unlike the decades-
long narratives of soap operas, these serial stories are resolved so that the run
of the series completes the heroine's finite personal journey. Many of the action dramas increased their seriality from season to season, perhaps because
of the creative freedom afforded by their success rather than the limitations
mandated by their origin as gender-reversal narratives.[14] Even those series
that are more episodic than serial (*La Femme Nikita, Charmed, Xena: Warrior Princess*) maintain some consistency in setting and secondary characters
that allow their narratives greater depth than is possible in *Charlie's Angels* or
Wonder Woman.

Solo versus Team-Based Heroines

Whether a series focuses on a single heroine also differentiates it and illustrates further variance from conventional appeals to female audiences. *Dark
Angel, La Femme Nikita,* and *Witchblade* feature the individual; *Buffy the Vam-*

pire Slayer and *Xena: Warrior Princess* enable a single character with powers but allow her the support of a community; while *Charmed* requires a multiplicity of female characters with superpowers to work together to maximize their power.[15] The dominance of *individual* empowered heroines deviates from the use of a multiplicity of female characters—common in soap operas—as a textual strategy that allows a diverse female audience various points of identification.[16] The centrality of the female heroine serves to attract female audience members, despite the lack of other points of identification in some of the shows. Female audiences may generally seek multiple points of identification, but American storytelling also has a well-established tradition of narratives about extraordinary individuals. Those series with a single protagonist continue the tradition of the sole superhero while not using an expansive cast of female characters once thought to be a key attribute of narratives that women find pleasurable.

Those series empowering a collective deviate from the conventional hero narrative but indicate the value of a cast with a plurality of female characters for telling stories about women's lives.[17] Multiple female protagonists allow these stories to explore the friendships and sisterhood that develop among women. The relationships of Buffy and Willow, Buffy and Dawn, Xena and Gabrielle, and the sisters of *Charmed* are defining features of these series. Such emphasis on the complexity of relationships among women previously had not been as prevalent due to the lack of dramas featuring multiple central female characters.[18] Comedies have provided the primary venue for the exploration of female friendships, while soap operas often highlight contentious relationships among women.

Although these series deviate from the television forms traditionally correlated with high female viewing, they also include narratives that would have been impossible during the norms of the network era. The depiction of female physical empowerment and the consistent vilification of hegemonic constructions of masculinity provide some commonality among the series, while the type of world the heroines inhabit and their heroic function differentiate them. Regardless of how they utilize these characteristics, each of these series tells stories about friendship, family, heroism, and loyalty, although they prioritize them differently and depict the characters struggling with their competing demands in variant ways. The action drama's incorporation of fantastic elements enables it to explore stories distinct from other narrative types while also potentially containing the heroines with the otherworldliness that empowers them. The 1990s versions of these stories indicate expanded narrative opportunities from their 1970s predecessors and must be understood in relation to the other female-centered series airing coterminously.

Recurrent Motifs and Points of Differentiation

Gyneco-centric Legacies

The manner in which each series incorporates a number of defining aspects of the 1990s action drama circumscribes the narratives it can tell and how it tells them. The inclusion of one (or more) primary female characters who possess extraordinary physical abilities provides the most crucial distinction among female-centered action dramas. In the majority of the series, this power is supernatural and part of a legacy only available to women. Buffy is the "one slayer in each generation," part of an all-female lineage given superhuman strength and skill and called upon to fight vampires, demons, and other evil forces lurking everywhere. The three Halliwell sisters, Pru, Phoebe, and Piper (and later Paige), compose the "Charmed Ones"; they received powers including telekinesis, future visions, and the ability to manipulate time upon the death of their grandmother as part of a matrilineal destiny of witchcraft (that was also passed to their already deceased mother).[19] The Witchblade, an ancient weapon worn only by women, chooses Sara Pezzini to be its human conduit. The weapon provides her with full body armor, extraordinary strength, visions of the future and past, and a sword and dagger; it also connects her with an ancestry including Joan of Arc, a Celtic warrior named Cathian, and a fictional U.S. spy, Elizabeth Bronte, who secured the code that led to Germany's defeat in World War II. In a variation, government scientists seeking to create the ultimate soldier genetically engineer Max Guevara of *Dark Angel,* enabling her to see in the dark and run and jump like an animal. Finally, Nikita and Xena possess no superhuman enhancement but are highly trained and astute combatants (on some occasions Xena is empowered with immortality). The heroines with special powers (*Buffy the Vampire Slayer, Charmed, Witchblade,* and *Dark Angel*) may possess extraordinary abilities in comparison to Nikita and Xena, but they do not control their powers absolutely. Overconfidence, selfish motivation, and genetic defects counterbalance their apparent infallibility.

The repeated use of gyneco-centric destiny as the foundational mythology behind these series is crucial to the innovation in the types of stories they tell and the way they hail female audiences. These narratives effectively disempower men through exclusion, disinviting them from identifying with the heroine by making it impossible to share her power.[20] In a culture dominated by tales of patriarchal right and privilege, the decision to empower these female characters through a rite obtained by gender effectively constructs female gender as valuable. For example, in *Witchblade,* Sara repeatedly faces a primary foe named Kenneth Irons. The series constructs him as an exceptionally wealthy businessman, perhaps to be understood as capitalism personified. Despite repeated attempts to buy or influence his way into its possession, Irons cannot wield the Witchblade and bears physical scars from his attempts, indicating a boundary to the effective scope of patriarchy and capitalism in the acquisition of power. In its final season, *Buffy the Vampire Slayer* emphasizes the gender dynamics of the slayer lineage by adding to the established slayer mythology. Time travel reveals to Buffy that male spiritual leaders constructed the slayer power and empowered the first slayer through a process more than slightly suggestive of a rape, which provides a disconcerting narrative development that the usually highly introspective series leaves uninterrogated until the finale. After a season of episodes in which Buffy, her gang, and a group of girls who are "potential" slayers seem increasingly unlikely to succeed in vanquishing the evil entity named "The First," the series concludes its cumulative story by deviating from its founding myth. The only way to destroy The First is to magically defy the slayer legacy as belonging to "one girl in every generation" and to bestow the slayer powers on all the potentials; this is depicted in the episode as symbolically empowering girls everywhere.[21]

The significance of the source of empowerment in these narratives is reinforced by considering other kinds of empowerment myths the creators might have used. The bite of a radioactive spider (Spiderman) or the repair of injuries from a parachuting accident (Bionic Woman) provide a founding mythology that is far less impressive or useful for constructing the allegorical level on which many of these series operate. *Buffy the Vampire Slayer, Charmed,* and *Witchblade* provide an affirmation of female identity as a narrative component that was not a central part of previous empowerment legacies and is important to the types of stories the series explore.

Narrative Worlds

The type of world the characters inhabit also affects the stories the series tell. The characters' empowerment primarily distinguishes a series as the action-drama type, but the narrative world delimits the range of stories available in each show. With the exception of the heroines' abilities and their knowledge of the evils they must battle, most characters exist in realistic, contemporary U.S. cities. *Buffy the Vampire Slayer* is set in Sunnydale, California, a Los Angeles suburb. *Charmed* takes place in San Francisco, and *Witchblade* depicts New York City at the dawn of the second millennium. *La Femme Nikita* never exposes its location; most action takes place in a dark, seemingly underground compound that houses Section One, an antiterrorist organization that dispatches Nikita and the other agents to distinctively European locales. In contrast, *Dark Angel* tells its story in the year 2019 in a postapocalyptic Seattle, an Orwellian nightmare of rogue police, failed technology, and U.S. destitution. *Xena: Warrior Princess* provides even greater variation with its setting of premodern Europe and Asia and revisionist versions of Greco-Roman mythology and pre-Christian history.

These settings are important to the stories the series can tell in a variety of ways. Otherworldly components allow a far greater breadth of material than what is available to the "realistic" narratives of the other drama types. This enables the action dramas to explore a broader range of literal and allegorical themes than the standard law, medicine, and family dramas allow. Yet, the "real world" settings for characters with otherworldly power aids in the construction of fantastic stories rooted in reality so that these dramas produce allegories less veiled than those in the science fiction genre—a form long acknowledged for its ability to contradict and deviate from dominant ideology because of its futuristic settings.[22] The supernatural aspects of these series may suggest that women require otherworldly intervention to achieve empowerment, but it is also notable that empowered female characters are not so fantastic as to require their confinement to exotic locales and galaxies far, far away.

Men and Masculinity

It is crucial to acknowledge the role played by male characters and the type of masculinity they depict because many of these series rely heavily on characterization for much of their narrative complexity and distinction from more spectacle-driven series. Many of the series feature a male guide for the heroine: Giles as "watcher" in *Buffy the Vampire Slayer*, Leo as the Charmed Ones' "white lighter," Nottingham and Danny as Sara's physical and emotional protectors in *Witchblade,* and Logan as "Eyes Only" in *Dark Angel*.[23] These male characters function as counsel for the heroines, aiding them in understanding their supernatural powers and duties. They often have access to information unknown by the heroines, but none use their knowledge to control the female character. (The role of these male characters is consequently very different than Bosley and Charlie in *Charlie's Angels* or Steve Trevor in *Wonder Woman.*) None are able to maintain an objective distance from the heroines placed in their charge (only Logan is not sent specifically to guide Max), with romantic relationships developing between Leo and

Piper and Logan and Max, while a father/daughter dynamic bonds Giles and Buffy.

The deeply felt emotional bonds do not undermine the heroine's ability or independence. These men play a crucial role in their lives, but the heroines do not prioritize these relationships above others or above their duties. Such emotional investments are atypical of action narratives, and these relationships define the dramatic depth of these series. The heroines' attachment to a variety of friends and caregivers compromises many of the missions and battles, but these relational connections indicate the characters' humanity rather than weakness. By regularly forcing them to choose among competing interests, these stories explore the kinds of decisions many women make in an effort to balance familial, personal, and professional demands. Consequently, these relationships should not be understood to contain the characters, regardless of what having a "watcher" might suggest on a superficial level. The heroines have equitable relationships with the men in their lives.

Male characters also function as sidekicks and heterosexual romantic interests who complicate the heroines' ability to prioritize "work" and personal desire. Importantly, the various male companions embody a nonhegemonic masculinity. Consider characters such as Xander and Oz (*Buffy the Vampire Slayer*), Joxer (*Xena: Warrior Princess*), Birkoff (*La Femme Nikita*), and Jake, Danny, and Gabriel (*Witchblade*). Even male romantic interests—Angel, Riley, and the neutered Spike (*Buffy the Vampire Slayer*), Michael (*La Femme Nikita*), Leo (*Charmed*), Logan (*Dark Angel*), and Conchobar (*Witchblade*)— defy hegemonic portrayals of masculinity. Those male characters who do exude a hegemonic masculinity—exhibiting physical power and control, achieving occupational success as valued by capitalism, controlling a family as a patriarch, manifesting characteristics of the frontiersman, and displaying heterosexual power—are most often villains (Ares in *Xena: Warrior Princess,* Operations in *La Femme Nikita,* Lydecker and White in *Dark Angel,* and Kenneth Irons and Captain Dante in *Witchblade*).[24]

The consistency with which these female-centered action dramas affirm a revised masculinity and demonize hegemonic masculinity indicates an important development evident across the series explored in this book. Apparently, the empowerment of these heroines requires male companionship, romantic and familiar, that deviates from patriarchal norms and standards of phallic dominance. This trend expands across the series considered in other chapters and more generally to many series airing in the late 1990s and early twenty-first century, although the inclusion of "sensitive" men has been a noted attribute of television preferred by women for some time.[25] The empowerment of action heroines only seems possible when male companions embody a masculinity that does not threaten women, consequently making hegemonic masculinity "evil."

Among the action dramas, this dichotomous construction of masculinity is most clearly embodied in the *Buffy the Vampire Slayer* character Angel. The series introduces him as a vampire with a soul. Once among the cruelest of vampires, Angel is cursed by a gypsy tribe with the reinstatement of his soul, which causes him immense pain for the suffering he has inflicted. In his soul-intact state as Angel, he is dark, brooding, and quiet, cares greatly for Buffy, and defers to others, clearly exhibiting a nondominant masculinity. When the curse is broken, however, his identity as Angelus returns, and he becomes loud, cruel, and manipulative, embodying the search for control and power characteristic of hegemonic masculinity.

The significance of this clear refutation of hegemonic masculinity must be considered in relation to the other aspects of the series, such as their articulation of a revised femininity as indicated by heroines' physical empowerment, but also their visual containment within hegemonic femininity in their depiction and adherence to dominant beauty standards. Even within individual series, the action dramas defy traditional gender constructions in some ways while reinforcing them in others. The consistent vilification of hegemonic masculinity as a threat to empowered female characters, however, indicates the narrative inability for empowered heroines to have nonadversarial relationships with such men.

Desiring and Empathetic Heroines

The series can also be linked through their depiction of female desire or the heroine's motivation. Female friendships are crucial priorities in all but *La Femme Nikita* and *Witchblade* (which may relate to the explicitness with which these series target male audiences) and become essential to the narrative tensions of conflicting loyalty that the series develop. In her analysis of *Cagney and Lacey,* Julie d'Acci examines homoerotic interpretations of the title characters' friendship as the series' primary depiction of desire.[26] Her textual examples and evidence of audiences reading against the heterosexuality of the characters prepares the text of, and audience response to, *Xena: Warrior Princess*—a narrative more open to interpretations of Xena and Gabrielle's relationship as lesbian.[27] Although it is possible to read the female relationships in *Buffy the Vampire Slayer* and *Dark Angel* as homoerotic, I focus on the use of friendship as a strategy for creating familial relationships and as balanced with heterosexual desire.[28]

The serial narratives of *Buffy the Vampire Slayer* and *Xena: Warrior Princess* ultimately explore the heroines restarting their lives and facing various forms of evil while developing and maintaining non-blood familial relationships that become of primary importance. Threats from demons or warmongers revolve weekly, but the self-discovery required to care for others and balance others' needs with the heroine's own builds from season to season. The serial narrative of *Charmed* also examines interpersonal relations, as the three initially estranged sisters must learn to work together to maximize their power. *Dark Angel* features more complex yet less developed relationships; the series begins with a quest-narrative motif, as Max primarily seeks to find the other Manticore escapees—her similarly genetically modified "brothers and sisters." This goal grows increasingly elusive when the others are captured and killed, which leads to an emphasis on the community of friends that serve as Max's "family" in Seattle. The depiction of Max growing to place others' needs before her own marks her evolution, as she is the most reluctant heroine among this set. The narrative attributes her reticence to the difficulty of postapocalyptic life and the abuse and mind control she suffered at Manticore.

Others have more fully explored the significance of the supernatural to the development and maintenance of female friendships as depicted in these series.[29] I acknowledge the centrality of these relationships because they result in a constant source of tension for characters who must reconcile personal desires, the wishes and needs of their friends, and their duties as heroines. As a result, stories about loyalty become the primary narratives of these series, as heroines attempt to negotiate divided allegiances with a focus uncommon in any of the other action drama types. Even those series that do not develop complex relationships depict struggles over loyalty. Nikita regularly chooses to disobey commands in favor of her more humane sense of justice or in defense of Michael. Because allegiances within Section One shift constantly, viewers are never aware of a character's true motives or which scenarios are tests and which are real. Consequently, the series' priorities, and by proxy, the heroine's, are difficult to discern until the end of the series.[30] Loyalty and trust are central to the *Witchblade* narrative as well, as Sara must negotiate Kenneth Irons's attempts to control her, codes of law enforcement, and knowledge gained through the Witchblade.

The Function of the Heroines

The purpose of the heroines in the cumulative story of each series results from the form of their empowerment and the narrative world they inhabit, and it provides a crucial commonality among the series. Although they articulate their function in different ways, each heroine primarily exists to rid the world of evil and protect innocent lives. The series demarcate good and evil simplistically, following general designations within dominant American ideology. The greatest deviation from dominant standards results from the occasional depiction of science, law enforcement, and capitalism as forces of evil or as easily led astray from altruistic purposes. Most of the characters are reluctant heroines, at least initially, as all but Xena articulate a desire to be "normal" or be freed from the duties that result from their enhancement.[31] Characters located in the "real" world particularly struggle with balancing their empowerment and its effects on those around them; they frequently express a desire for a more ordinary and simple life and companionship free from constant threat.

The heroines' reluctance and the regular narrative construction of saving the world as the "work" they must balance with personal lives filled with friends that function as family contribute to the sophistication of these narratives in comparison with adventure series and previous heroines in *Charlie's Angels* or *Wonder Woman*. The series of the late 1990s feature heroines with complex psychological motivation. Rather than a cartoonish calling to defend the world from evil, the series often depict the characters negotiating interpersonal dynamics, multiple allegiances, and moral ambiguity. The heroines are fallible, another unusual trait for characters possessing superpowers. Despite their extraordinary abilities, they are intensely devoted to friends and willing to prioritize the well-being of those they love over the greater good of society. When faced with the ultimate choice of personal sacrifice, two of the series have concluded with the martyring of the heroine to save the world or the fate of multitudinous souls.[32]

The characters' varying empowerment, the worlds they inhabit, and their understanding of their roles perform important storytelling functions, enabling more sophisticated narratives than previously evident in the action drama or adventure series. The complexity of the stories told beyond the heroines saving the world from evil foes expands the range of narrative pleasures the series can fulfill. Rather than emphasizing the lineage of these series with previous versions, criticism might more usefully explore their innovations.

These action dramas provide a fascinating modification of the dramatic form when examined in relation to Byars and Meehan's suggestion about the strategies programmers used in the early 1980s to make cop and doc franchise series more attractive to female audiences.[33] Programmers at that time perceived women to be more interested in characters' emotional involvement than linear plot development. In many ways, action dramas appear as even more complex attempts to integrate storytelling components traditionally valued by women with those of episodic narratives driven by male protagonists. The shows feature a female action heroine, which can be viewed as an attempt to attract mixed-sex audiences, drawing female audiences by bestowing physical empowerment on a female character and heterosexual male audiences through the appeal of heroines demonstrating dominant beauty ideals and action plots. The female-centered action dramas feature spectacular fight and chase scenes, but in most cases they rely on hand-to-hand combat rather than weapons such as (arguably phallic) knives and guns. This offers explosive physical action in a personal and intimate manner. Indeed, the choreography of these scenes has as much in common with dancing as fighting. The series develop narratives that support the spectacle with intricate stories of divided loyalties and heroines forced to make heartbreaking decisions in prioritizing their desires, the interests of those they love, and their duties in advancing the forces of good. These personal struggles provide the characters with psychological depth that allows viewer identification with their turmoil.

Much has been made of the allegorical level on which these series operate, particularly *Buffy the Vampire Slayer* as a comment on the horrors of adolescence. The balancing of personal interests with those of others can also be interpreted as an allegory for the multiple demands on women, such as the work/family dichotomy and women's pursuit of "having it all," developed more explicitly in comedic and protagonist-centered family dramas. The action dramas tell a similar story to the other dramatic types, but because they work on an allegorical rather than a literal level, the heroines appear sympathetic while depictions of "real" women can draw critique for appearing whiny (as was the case with Ally McBeal). Buffy and Xena are forced to prioritize among their desires and those of their friends and to make difficult decisions, sacrificing some lives to ensure the survival of others. This resonates with research that consistently finds women exhausted by daily demands that require them to choose among the needs of their jobs, children, partners, and themselves.[34] The impossibility of the situations in which the heroines find themselves explains the centrality of reluctance as a component of their characterization. The fact that they cannot escape their destiny as warriors makes the allegory more comparable to the situation of lower- and middle-class women who have worked outside of the home since well before second-wave feminism. Unlike the bourgeois female characters of *thirtysomething* or *Baby Boom,* they cannot choose to stay at home; they work because of economic necessity. Like the action heroines, they are condemned to a frustrating negotiation of duties to ensure the survival of those they love.

The final section of this chapter explores the construction of loyalty in *Buffy the Vampire Slayer* and *Xena: Warrior Princess.*[35] Although the spectacle of their beauty and power earn the women who inhabit these series much fanfare, focusing on their psychological complexity and the series' consistent stories about negotiating divided loyalties indicates a narrative trend as important as the physical empowerment of lithe young blondes able to kill the things that go bump in the night. Many nonviewers likely miss the narrative significance of the female action drama, assuming that the depth of the phenomenon extends only to physical empowerment.

Loyalty, Duty, and Forgiveness in *Xena: Warrior Princess*

In a plot arc that spans and concludes the series' third season, Xena and Gabrielle experience a cleavage that nearly destroys their friendship. Gabrielle's refusal to follow Xena's wishes leads to great emotional pain for Xena and gives her cause to distrust Gabrielle. The story begins when Dahak, an evil god whose entry into the world is constructed as similar to Armageddon, impregnates Gabrielle. She refuses to believe the child she bears is the "Child of Darkness" and opposes Xena, who matter-of-factly orders that she destroy the child. Gabrielle cannot bring herself to do so, but she knows that Xena will, so she leaves the baby, Hope, in a reed basket in a stream and tells Xena that she followed her demand.[36] Gabrielle's sense of loss builds; her disagreement with Xena's assessment of Hope leads her to doubt Xena, which bears significant consequences.

Two episodes later, Xena pursues a foe with the expressed purpose of exacting revenge. Although Xena explains the history of the relationship and why the situation necessitates that she kill the ruler, in an uncharacteristic reversal of personalities, Gabrielle cannot break from her clearcut demarcation of good and evil. As the philosopher counterpart to Xena the warrior, Gabrielle questions Xena's motives and intervenes by informing their foe of her plan. Xena is consequently captured and nearly executed because Gabrielle distrusted and betrayed her.[37]

The two continue, apparently unaffected by these conflicts for a few episodes, but then the story reveals Gabrielle's other betrayal with devastating consequences. Hope returns and kills Xena's son, Solon, who was being raised by a surrogate family for his protection.[38] At this point, Gabrielle "kills" Hope, who disappears for a few episodes, but the supernatural child had grown strong enough to return nine episodes later in the season finale in which Dahak threatens to enter the world. The series breaks from its tenuously constructed reality following the episode in which Hope murders Solon and provides a surreal, dreamlike episode in which Gabrielle and Xena fall into an alternate world (marked by the musical form of the episode) to negotiate Gabrielle's betrayal, express Xena's grief and rage, and attempt reconciliation.[39] Xena exhibits her rage in this alternative world by killing Gabrielle, although her actions have no consequence in the "real world." The two emerge from the emotional struggle exhausted and reconcile.

Although Xena forgives Gabrielle, the violation prevents her from fully trusting her. In the season finale—the final battle with Hope and Dahak— Gabrielle again acts suspiciously. Viewers know that she has learned that Xena will die if she kills Hope. Gabrielle struggles to deter her from killing Hope, without appearing to still seek to save Hope. Xena struggles with a desire to believe the two have reconciled but cannot help being suspicious of Gabrielle's motives. The season concludes when Gabrielle sacrifices her life to kill Hope, with both falling into depths of "hell."[40]

Gabrielle inflicts unimaginable pain on Xena through her repeated betrayal, which is exacerbated by the results of her actions (Gabrielle's refusal to kill Hope leads to Solon's death; Xena is tortured and nearly killed). Despite her grief, Xena forgives Gabrielle, but only after having the space to enact her rage without consequence. In the broader context of the series, this plot arc is central to the lessons the characters teach each other. Although Gabrielle typically sees greater complexity in situations, in this case her rigid understanding of good and evil results in her heroic "failure" at this preliminary point of the series and necessitates that she make the ultimate sacrifice in the finale of season three because of her mistakes. Xena avoids giving her life (until the finale of the series) due to her warrior training, Gabrielle's more typical influence as a peaceful mediator, and by valuing her relationship with Gabrielle above all else.

While thus condensing narrative simplifies and omits many plot nuances, this summary reveals the complexity of the struggle Gabrielle and Xena endure in maintaining their relationship and the importance of these plots for the series. These episodes feature elaborate and spectacular fight scenes, but they also depict a deep melodramatic struggle that results in palpable emotional pain. The series features many stand-alone episodes that do not directly advance these relational issues, while other episodes feature important developments in the relationship plot as well as typical episodic plots. The brief summaries in *TV Guide* likely would not have noted any of these relational plotlines, yet the hybrid nature of the narrative allows it to tell episodic stories about vanquishing a particular foe while also constructing a serial narrative about the complicated development and maintenance of the relationship between the primary characters. Consequently, the series magnifies the struggles and challenges involved in developing a significant relationship and externalizes intimate feelings of trust and love to bear hyperexaggerated consequences.

Love, Trust, and Friendship in *Buffy the Vampire Slayer*

Themes of loyalty, duty, and forgiveness also occupy central narrative importance in *Buffy the Vampire Slayer*. A multitude of plot arcs reflect the centrality of developing and maintaining interpersonal relationships in this series: the episodes leading to The WB series finale, in which Buffy sacrifices her life for her sister's; Willow's abuse of witchcraft and her friends' struggle to return her to the side of good; the conflicts that develop in the final season as Buffy disregards Giles's and the others' opinions and leads the team into battle with disastrous results. Here I focus on an oft-cited set of episodes that conclude the second season and illustrate the multiple levels on which the series tells its stories. The melodramatic plot arc begins with Buffy and Angel's first sexual encounter. This moment of happiness ends the spell that had returned vampire Angel's soul. Angel is gone from the bed when Buffy wakes after their night together, which begins the series' enactment of a banal high school situation in a monstrous way (as is its tendency in early seasons), to elevate the clichéd story of a boyfriend's postcoital rejection to a horrendous level. Not only does Angel reject Buffy, but now restored to his vampire state, he seeks to enact revenge on those who made him most human.[41]

Buffy immediately must make choices that prioritize her relationships. Embarrassed by Angel's rejection, she initially hesitates to tell anyone what has happened, which delays the group from determining that Angel is now evil and how he became that way. Although she is deeply hurt, Buffy cannot fully grieve the loss of Angel as her love before facing the possibility that she must destroy him. The complexity of the choices she faces multiplies rapidly as Angel brutally murders a teacher who had become a mentor to her friend Willow and a developing romantic interest for her watcher Giles. While Buffy comes to understand Angel's "change" as demonic in nature and not a reflection on her, her friends become increasingly vengeful, now grieving a loss of their own and angry with Buffy for not sharing her suspicions sooner. The tension among the group builds over three episodes until Buffy recognizes that she has no choice but to kill Angel.

Willow discovers a spell that will return Angel's soul at the last minute, but anger divides the group of friends so that they cannot agree about using it. Some seek Angel's destruction, while others accept the solution that will "save" him out of deference to Buffy. Typical plot complications disrupt the spell-casting and leave Buffy to believe she has no alternative but to kill Angel. Willow proceeds with the spell and returns Angel's soul in the midst of a fight to the death with Buffy. Buffy does not know that soul reinstatement is possible because Xander allows his jealous hatred of Angel to consume him and does not share the crucial information. Buffy recognizes a change in Angel near the end of their fight, but it is too late. Angel has set events in motion that will lead to the "end of the world" without his death. Bearing the heavy burden of her own love for Angel, her friends' desire for revenge, and her duties as the slayer, Buffy subordinates her own desire and kills Angel.[42]

The melodramatic depth of these events results from the guilt Buffy feels because her desire for Angel placed her friends in harm's way and because her ill-advised decision to pursue a romantic relationship with a vampire (in possession of a soul or not) resulted in a friend's death and near catastrophe for the others. The decisions the characters make here will come to define their relations in future episodes. Buffy runs away immediately following this incident, leaving her mother and friends worried and then angry with her upon her return for needlessly inflicting concern. Their emotions seriously trouble the friends' relationships, although they slowly begin to mend. Their relations are tested soon after when Buffy first hides Angel from the others after he returns in a tortured and destroyed state. She experiences overwhelming guilt for the pain she has caused him and because she now hides his presence from the others. Like *Xena: Warrior Princess,* the series requires regular viewing to understand the intricacies of relationships and the significance that can be found in apparently banal plots because of the characters' history. Scenarios such as this force Buffy to subordinate her own needs and desires for the good of her friends and humankind. The narrative even questions her willingness to have friends and family in her life, with these relationships constructed as a luxury she cannot afford.

Buffy the Vampire Slayer enacts a complicated story about options facing empowered and self-motivated women. As in *Xena: Warrior Princess,* the narrative operates at multiple levels. On the surface, the series tells supernatural stories about fighting demons and vampires, but the true marrow of the series results from the melodramatic stories of intense and complicated interpersonal relations. In this era of abundant female-centered dramas, the action dramas surpass initial expectations that the form's primary offering results from their specially empowered heroines' abilities. Although this is an important aspect, the complicated hybrid narratives these series develop to tell impassioned stories about friendship, particularly among women, represent an underestimated contribution to the stories told about women and their lives.

* * *

The emphasis on stories about balancing loyalties and overcoming betrayals that provide the psychological depth for many of the action dramas is significant, particularly in comparison with comedic and protagonist-centered family dramas. These two narrative types tell stories about the individual character, with much less attention to the complexity of relationships with others and the depth of intimacy involved in friendships.[43] The fantastic nature of heroines endowed with superpowers masks the significance of their narratives, but upon examination, the action dramas reveal themselves to be most like soap operas—the narrative form long associated with female audiences—in their depiction of deep, complex, and often painful relationships.

The action dramas of the late 1990s enact a hybridization comparable to that of the workplace dramas a decade and a half earlier. These series combine narrative strategies to broaden the appeal of their narratives in the same manner as *St. Elsewhere*. Thus, the late 1990s heroine action dramas indicate programmers' strategic efforts to hail heterogeneous audiences. The hybridization suggests an attempt to plane the "edge" of these programs, expanding the possible audience instead of specializing audience appeal. In this sense, the action dramas are quite distinct, as the other female-centered dramatic types indicate a more deliberate construction of edge.

Action dramas and empowered heroines are important for all the reasons that journalistic articles featuring titles such as "Attack of the Sexy-Tough Women" may ascribe, but their greatest advancement can be found at the narrative level.[44] By disguising their hybridity much more elaborately than the reconfigured workplace dramas currently confined to Lifetime, they achieve more mainstream success and broader audience diversification, while not sacrificing their ability to explore the struggles women experience. The innovation of 1990s action dramas in comparison with predecessors such as *Charlie's Angels*, *Wonder Woman*, and *The Bionic Woman*, or as contrasted with adventure series such as *V.I.P.*, *Relic Hunter*, or *Sheena, Queen of the Jungle*, results from their narrative complexity and their ability to depict characters with substantial psychological depth. Although the thin, young, white heroines of 1990s action dramas may be cast and costumed using tools of a traditional femininity developed to be subservient to dominant patriarchy, their stories defy these superficial trappings and indicate some of the new narrative possibilities available to female audiences.

3. Sex, Careers, and Mr. Right in Comedic Dramas: The "New" New Women of *Ally McBeal* and *Sex and the City*

Molly Dodd is who Marlo Thomas might have become had *That Girl* stayed on the air long enough to evolve into *This Woman*.
—Phyllis Theroux

Following the lineage Theroux describes, Ally McBeal and Carrie, Samantha, Charlotte, and Miranda of *Sex and the City* indicate the arrival of the most recent generation of single-woman characters who continue a genealogy that can be traced to Ann Marie of *That Girl* and Mary Richards of *The Mary Tyler Moore Show*. "New woman" characters throughout television history primarily have been "single girls," young women who seek jobs in the city prior to marriage.[1] Marlo Thomas recalls that her character was the result of her declaration to the network, "'I don't want to be the wife of somebody, I don't want to be the daughter of somebody, I don't want to be the secretary of somebody, I WANT TO BE THE SOMEBODY.'"[2] Moya Luckett argues that the television version of this character type in many ways emanates from Helen Gurley Brown's prescriptive book *Sex and the Single Girl* (1962) and with characters in such series as *My Sister Eileen* (1960–61), *My Living Doll* (1964–65), *Peyton Place* (1964–69), *Honey West* (1965–66), *The Girl from UNCLE* (1966–67), *The Avengers* (1966–69), and *Julia* (1969–71).[3]

Despite the differences in institutional placement and competitive environment that distinguish *Ally McBeal* and *Sex and the City,* they have much in common with the single-women series that preceded them and continue the tradition of the new-woman character type. Television's original new woman was the fictionalized doppelganger of women entering the workforce in the 1970s, women who chose careers made possible by second-wave feminist activism. The identifier has been since applied to independent, strong, or feminist female characters, but the pursuit of work outside of the home and stories related to being single traditionally have defined new-woman characters.[4]

In the 1960s and 1970s, being a single woman working in the city served as a key site of differentiation for characters in series such as *That Girl*. However, their participation in the workforce would only continue until they married and assumed the more traditional female roles of homemaker and mother that mirrored society's expectations of the characters' real-world counterparts.[5] Professional opportunities for female characters expanded from short-lived, pink-collar roles during the 1980s, with the emergence of stories about a career journalist in *Murphy Brown* (1988–98) and a business executive in *Baby Boom* (1988–89). Female characters also began appearing in ensemble or buddy series that did not emphasize a traditional home life for married women, although work figured less prominently in many of these series than in other new-woman narratives. These series did not bind characters to traditional domestic roles and became a common mode for comedic stories about women, particularly those exploring friendships among women (*The Facts of Life, Kate and Allie, Designing Women, Golden Girls, Living Single,* and *Cybill*).

In addition to workplace involvement, series with new-woman characters emphasize dating and sexuality. A key component of single-woman stories results from their characters' liberation from the marriages that have limited the available stories about women. Many series consequently reproduce family-like relationships in different ways, such as *The Mary Tyler Moore Show*'s replication of familiar roles within its workplace setting—a common strategy by the late 1980s.[6] A cycle of divorced or widowed characters followed *The Mary Tyler Moore Show* and adjusted the boundaries of the new-woman character type, but in a way that clearly continued its trajectory of representation and discourse. Characters in *Phyllis* (1975–77), *One Day at a Time* (1975–84), *Alice* (1976–85), and *Kate and Allie* (1984–89) enacted narratives similar to those of previous new women, except that they encountered the new woman's independence because of a marital change. Many of these characters had children who functioned as their family (*One Day at a Time, Phyllis, Alice, Kate and Allie*), while others found family in the workplace (*Alice*) or in a female buddy (*Kate and Allie*). The 1990s series continued these possibilities, with the four friends in *Sex and the City* fulfilling each other's companionship needs, while co-workers who are also friends comprise Ally McBeal's primary support community. This community of friends provides an important distinction between comedic dramas and protagonist-centered family dramas. In the latter, families present a primary narrative focus even though most of the characters are single, which underscores how character demographics (such as marital status) alone do not provide a reliable prediction of narrative type.

A Turning Point in Form:
The Days and Nights of Molly Dodd

The narratives and characters of *Ally McBeal* and *Sex and the City* continue the general legacy of new-woman stories about unmarried working women, but one series particularly prepared their arrival. *The Days and Nights of Molly Dodd* was prescient in its 1987 debut and faced institutional challenges as a result. It began airing on NBC but was canceled after a season and resurrected by Lifetime for two years of additional original episodes. Like other new-woman narratives, *Molly Dodd* explores its title character's haphazard search for companionship and vocation but also breaks from many of the characteristics of the single-woman series in its characterization and form.

Much of *Molly Dodd*'s innovation can be attributed to its narrative and style. The series blends comedy and drama, a newly emergent trend at the time (also evident in *Frank's Place, Hooperman, The Slap Maxwell Story,* and *The Wonder Years*) that had become common by the late 1990s. This form enabled the series to defy the pat resolution of the twenty-three-minute situation-comedy formula to expand the types of stories possible and afforded it a narrative sophistication less available in the traditional sitcoms that had most commonly presented single-woman narratives. This form also allowed serialized plots, which provided another adjustment in narrative strategy that introduced ambiguity and expanded potential interpretations. *Molly Dodd* was unusual because producers shot the series on film with a single camera and omitted the laugh track, which aids its blending of humor and melodrama. Characterization motivates humor rather than jokes, and the film format allows for cinematic images and the incorporation of nondiegetic sound, which enhances the visceral reception of the stories.

Like *Molly Dodd, Sex and the City* and *Ally McBeal* blend drama and humor and break from realist traditions by incorporating devices that draw attention to their status as texts. The importance of this form derives from its effect on the narrative rather than inherent features of mixing humor and melodrama. *Molly Dodd, Sex and the City,* and *Ally McBeal* use first-person narration, characters' conversations with themselves and imaginary people, and fantasy sequences to create rich character development that exposes perspectives and information unavailable through conventional narrative structures. These techniques exhibit the inner lives of the characters and effectively strip a layer of surface to reveal their uncertainties and flaws to a degree that is less evident in other dramatic narrative types. The nakedness of the characters' innermost thoughts, fears, and desires creates an intimate relationship between audience and character. The bald honesty of exposing the complicated expectations and desires of the characters has yielded ample critique from journalistic and academic feminist critics, particularly when their inner lives reveal perspectives unbecoming of a role model.[7]

Molly Dodd also marks a point of departure from previous new-woman comedies because the series constructs Molly as a much more ambivalent new woman. Partly because of the introspection made possible by the unconventional narrative form, she airs her uncertainties and insecurities as she psychologically negotiates her own and others' expectations for her professional and personal lives. *Molly Dodd* provides a valuable precursor to series airing in the late 1990s because of its formal and narrative composition, as well as critics' uncertainty about its title character. In her analysis of the industrial and textual negotiations *Molly Dodd* endured, Pamela Wilson recounts that critics were delighted by its "quirky" characters and "hybrid" form.[8] She notes that a dichotomy developed among assessments of Molly, with some critiquing her as an "off-balanced woman whose control over her own life was tenuous at best," while others applauded her imperfection as realistic and representative of her generation's values and life experiences.[9] Television critics recycled nearly identical assessments writing about *Ally McBeal*'s debut ten years later.

Ally McBeal and *Sex and the City* clearly continue the tradition of the new-woman character type with some notable adjustments. *Molly Dodd* disrupts the trajectory of new-woman characters confined to situation comedies by illustrating the possibility of more sophisticated narrative forms. In 1987, it was not yet feasible for such an innovative series to air successfully on a broadcast network, which reaffirms the significance of the changed institutional context following the network era for enabling a greater diversity and multiplicity of female-centered stories. *Ally McBeal* and *Sex and the City* are greatly indebted to *Molly Dodd,* as they now indicate the possibilities for complex characterization, story, and style in a way that makes conventional sitcoms seem inadequate storytelling vehicles.[10] The different narratives that organize this book illustrate the fragmentation of the single-woman story into multiple story types. Some readers may query my decision to include *Ally McBeal* and *Sex and the City* in a book about female-centered dramas while excluding shows that more directly continue the narratives and form of previous single-woman sitcoms such as *Caroline in the City, Suddenly Susan,* or *The Nanny.* The multiplicity of dramatic narratives and new stories enabled by hybridized forms decreases the importance of conventional sitcoms in the late 1990s because they retell established stories in an era that allows for greater innovation.

Including *Ally McBeal* and *Sex and the City* in a collection examining female-centered dramas is consistent with the book's focus on exploring types of stories rather than applying generic categorizations. The single women in these series are similar to and distinct from the single-woman characters considered in other chapters. Throughout this book I specifically consider sixteen series that focus on thirty-four female characters. Of these thirty-four, only three are married at the series' start, and an additional nine get married and six divorced or separated during the series' run (of which two remarry) (see table 7). Despite the dominance of single-woman characters, only the series in this chapter continue the tradition of the new-woman story. Being single emerges as a consistent character attribute in late 1990s series, although not all dramatic types emphasize stories about being single—a narrative focus that differentiates the series in this chapter from *Providence, Judging Amy,* and *Gilmore Girls,* whose protagonists are also single but do not make this their narrative focus. *Ally McBeal* and *Sex and the City* tell similar stories about young, unmarried women who have fantastic careers, struggle with the social pressure to marry, and wonder whether a suitable companion even exists. They explore female friendship in contexts devoid of other family members and include, but are not defined by, workplace settings.

Ally McBeal and *Sex and the City* draw from and provide numerous innovations to the new-woman form, which likely results from their historical context and the possibilities afforded by the multichannel competitive environment of niche-audience strategies. The series' use of particular narrative conventions—mixing episodic and serial plots, blending humor and drama, incorporating first-person narration, and utilizing parody—aids their telling of stories distinct from the others addressed in this book. Unlike the single protagonists in many of the action and protagonist-centered family dramas, these shows construct narratives around a multiplicity of female characters. This expands the locations for identification and leads to sophisticated representations of women's lives because of the variant female perspectives that develop (particularly in comparison with single-character series such as *That Girl*).

How stories about single women are told and how contemporary versions deviate from previous forms indicate much about the types of stories that now circulate. As in the other types of narratives, the composition of the series—particularly their settings and characters—greatly predicts the types of stories they tell. Ultimately, the emphasis on characterization allows them to tell compelling stories, even though plot action is usually minimal and

Table 7. Characters' Marital Status (all drama types)

Series	Central Female Characters (Single unless otherwise noted)
Buffy the Vampire Slayer	Buffy
	Willow
Charmed	Pru
	Phoebe
	Piper, married during series, then separated
	Paige
Dark Angel	Max
La Femme Nikita	Nikita
Xena: Warrior Princess	Xena
	Gabrielle
Witchblade	Sara
Ally McBeal	Ally
Sex and the City	Carrie
	Charlotte, married during series, divorced, remarried
	Miranda, married during series
	Samantha
Any Day Now	Mary Elizabeth, married at start of series
	Rene, married during series (finale)
Gilmore Girls	Lorelai
	Rory
Judging Amy	Amy, divorced
	Maxine, widowed
Once and Again	Lily, divorced, remarried
Providence	Sydney, married during series (finale)
That's Life	Lydia
The Division	C. D., married at start of series, then divorced
	Jinny, married during series, divorced, remarried (finale)
	Magda, married during series, then separated
	Katelyn, divorced
	Rana
	Tracy
Strong Medicine	Lu, married in last season
	Dana
	Andy, married at entrance to series, then divorced

conversations about emotions play a central narrative function. Each of the series explores stories about how the characters experience life and manage the prosaic predicaments they encounter. The blending of comedy and drama is crucial to developing these stories, because purer forms of situation comedies and dramas commonly emphasize plot more than character.[11]

A Sociocultural Turning Point:
The Post-Second-Wave Generation

In addition to the distinct narrative form of these series, the generational difference of the characters from previous new-woman characters provides a significant distinction. Admittedly, the characters in nearly all of the female-centered dramas considered throughout this book indicate a transition from telling stories about the Baby Boom/second-wave-feminist cohort. Particular narratives arising from the generational difference are more pronounced in the comedic drama narrative type than any of the others.

The characters in *Ally McBeal* and *Sex and the City* came of age experiencing the gains achieved by second-wave feminism. Consequently, the narratives of these series must be understood to be located in a modified cultural milieu and their characters expected to possess a different worldview from those who preceded them. Cultural events and experiences bind writers to contexts that become imprinted in stories and character construction. *Molly Dodd* bears the markings of upper-middle-class white women's lives in the 1980s; Mary Richards grew from the emerging feminist movement of the 1970s; and *Honey West*—while somewhat sexist and retrograde by contemporary standards—arguably negotiated the possibilities available in the 1960s. The generational discrepancy is more specifically apparent in the particular life experiences that contribute to characterizations. Where Molly's quirky eclecticism results from the psychological and cultural challenge of reconciling her 1960s flower-child identity with the consumerism surrounding her as a 1980s yuppie Baby Boomer, Ally's offbeat neuroticism derives from the complicated expectations faced by post-second-wave women raised with the belief that they can "have it all."

Jane Arthurs and Laurie Ouellette also note generational identity as a vital component in understanding the characterizations in these shows.[12] Drawing on the work of David Brooks, Arthurs uses the categorization of the "bourgeois bohemian," or "bobo," to distinguish the class and taste culture represented particularly by *Sex and the City*.[13] Brooks argues that the bobo replaced the yuppie as a dominant class fraction in the 1990s, in part because bobos reconcile the contradictory impulses of social liberalism and materialism that manifest as yuppie guilt. Arthurs suggests that whereas white upper-middle-class female yuppie characters of the 1980s displayed their guilt through the lost opportunity for marriage and children, the white upper-middle-class bobo characters of the 1990s have been freed from the sexual constraints of bourgeois respectability, resulting in the complicated melding of postfeminist irony and feminist literalism.[14] Decades of feminist activism also likely enabled the more open and empowered sexuality of the 1990s new-woman characters, who date in a world of very different sexual politics than in Mary Richards's days. The significance of this changed generational context requires more substantive exploration than can be provided here, but this adjustment must be understood to have considerable consequences for the characterizations that the series develop and their relationship to previous new-woman characters.

The changed historical and cultural environments substantially affect the two primary components of single-women stories: the status of dating and marriage, and career opportunities. As society has become more accepting of single women, the possibilities for single-woman characters have increased. By the late 1990s, series depicted marriage more as an option than a necessity, although the pursuit of an *ideal* heterosexual partner defines the narratives of both shows. Paradoxically, 1990s characters discuss their search for this partner more openly than those in the late 1970s through the 1980s. The return of discussion about finding or desiring romantic partnership has led those maintaining a role-model framework of analysis to assert that the recent depictions suggest a return to a pre-second-wave consciousness.[15]

The status of careers for characters in the 1990s series also illustrates an adjustment from the positions of assistant, nurse, and girl Friday held by their predecessors. Series in the 1980s began to depict a transition, evident in the appearance of characters who occupied highly professionalized careers, such as in *Murphy Brown*. In contrast, work is unimportant to Molly Dodd despite expanding opportunities. An artist at heart, Molly floats in and out of jobs singing, selling real estate, and working in the publishing industry. Although 1990s characters' careers (particularly in *Sex and the City*) are not especially significant to the series' narratives, the fact that the series allow them careers, depict them as talented, and suggest that they pursue work as more than a pastime until marriage indicates a noteworthy development.[16] Carrie's career as a writer is an organizing narrative device; however, she never experiences "office politics" or worries about her job in the way that a narrative emphasizing characters' careers would likely explore.

Series in the 1990s eased the construction of the working woman as tough and assimilated into male corporate culture. Female characters' pursuit of work outside the home is a defining feature of all the dramatic types considered throughout this book, yet the attention afforded to work and the way the series construct work varies significantly among the dramatic types. For comedic dramas and their new-woman characters, it is crucial that the characters have careers, but the actual depiction of them engaged in work is often minimal. Arthurs describes the distinct space of work for the *Sex and the City* characters as a collapse of work into the private sphere.[17] *Ally McBeal* also constructs unusually permeable boundaries between work and home, particularly through the device of the office bar as the primary nonwork space (yet occupied by the same people who determine Ally's public world). The 1990s comedic dramas depict women finding alternatives to the trappings and behaviors of the previously all-male public work spaces. Such depictions help diminish stereotypical constructs such as the "working woman" as it emerged in the 1980s by indicating a diversity of possible depictions of working women and what stories can be told about their lives.

Assessing Feminism in a "Postfeminist" Environment

Journalistic criticism often loosely connects the physical empowerment of the action drama heroines with female empowerment, but academic and journalistic critics have examined the characters of comedic dramas as though they indicated the second coming of feminism (at least in the television age), and most were displeased. Scholarship about these series and the new-woman character in general has primarily sought to assess the feminist or antifeminist attributes of these series, and such research often ignores their contradictory and sophisticated aspects in efforts to categorize between these binary poles. Some of the critiques bear evidence of the role-model framework and use the characters' unwillingness to inhabit a feminist posture in all occasions as evidence of antifeminist perspectives. The uncertainty about the feminist significance of the central characters in *Ally McBeal* and *Sex and the City* provides a valuable illustration of the utility of cultural studies models of theorizing representations in redefined cultural and institutional contexts. This subsection departs from the primary arguments of the book, but the extratextual debate about the feminist meaning of these shows was so significant as to require some assessment of these discussions relative to the broader phenomenon of female-centered television in the late 1990s.

   Time magazine's use of Ally McBeal as an icon of contemporary feminism, resulting conversations among journalists in the United States, Britain, and Canada about the series, and a reflexive moment in which David E. Kelley used the series to comment on the confining nature of role-model expectations in response to the *Time* discourse capture the complexity of the series' narratives, their extratextual significance, and inadequacy of the role-model framework, even when it is employed through critical analysis. Seven months after the *Time* story, Kelley began an episode with a dream sequence typical of the series.[18] In her dream Ally is waylaid in the courthouse by a representative of a group called Women for Progress. She announces that Ally has been nomi-nated as a professional role model and lists Ally's features that deviate from the role-model ideal, recalling many of the opinions expressed in journalistic outlets the previous summer. Ally grows irritated with the woman's criticism and ends the sequence by biting her nose off and spitting it across the room.

This narrative moment is important for underscoring the limitations of feminist criticism built on the role-model framework and for considering is-sues such as appropriate units of analysis when examining a series with over one hundred hours of narrative. This scene fits within a broader narrative context of the episode and amidst transepisodic plotlines, and it represents Kelley's response to Ginia Bellafante's assertion in *Time* of the series' con-nection to feminism. Yet Mary Vavrus uses this scene as an indicator of Kel-ley's and the series' stance on feminism.[19] The text arguably lends itself to Vavrus's interpretation, but her reading—in a book otherwise about news—divorces this moment from the goals and purposes of a fictional narrative. Vavrus argues, "Ally's pure disdain for feminism—or even being a role model for young girls—is obvious at a glance."[20] Her "disdain" is not obvious, nor should a "glance" be the unit of analysis through which such a determina-tion is made. Kelley included the snipe back at the series' critics in an isolated moment of an episode focused on telling a story unrelated to Ally's dream; this broader episodic narrative—let alone the hundred other episodes un-mentioned by Vavrus—are highly relevant to explaining the character's re-sponse and the series' politics.[21]

Vavrus is offended that Kelley did not seek for his character to be a role model, which illustrates why this framework is inadequate for providing a comprehensive analysis of storytelling. Limiting academic and journalistic discussions to a character's role-model attributes misses the narrative con-tributions made by these series. Further, the infallibility that being a role model suggests precludes the telling of compelling and complicated stories. This analytic framework does not provide a way to understand how or why the stories resonated with a substantial audience and its content achieved the water-cooler-conversation status pursued, but not obtained, by so many series. That characters in this and other series do not openly claim to be fem-inists offers valuable evidence about popular misconceptions of feminism, and the discussions of the series by journalists provide artifacts of cultural discourse that returned feminism to a topic of popular discussion, albeit in a superficial media form. Assessments that search for an idealized example of feminist characters or role models fail to engage the complexity of story-telling in these series and the narrative pleasures audiences derive from them.

Academic scholarship about *Ally McBeal* reveals the inadequacy of criti-

cal models derived from the role-model tradition. The findings of such critics seem preordained by their methods and theoretical frameworks. Rachel
Moseley and Jacinda Read, Jane Arthurs, and Brenda Cooper construct textual analyses that acknowledge the narrative complexity of the series and
look beyond literal interpretation, and they understand each series as one of
many voices contributing to contemporary discourse.[22] They acknowledge
the series' internal contradictions to identify their feminist and antifeminist
attributes and to explore the presence of conflicting ideas as symptomatic
of a particular textual, cultural, and institutional context. Contrarily, Mary
Vavrus, Rachel Dubrofsky, and L. S. Kim deemphasize the narrative functions of storytelling to identify antifeminist components of the series.[23] Their
studies reflect isolated examinations of the series that do not acknowledge
the broader programming context in which they air or the fact that this context is radically altered from previous eras. Their research is neither poorly
developed nor badly constructed; given the framework with which these
scholars approached their studies, their findings are well supported and rea-
soned.[24] The method and units of analysis each scholar utilizes allow each
to produce persuasive arguments and valid, although contradictory, findings. This conundrum suggests the need for feminist media critics to reevaluate our methods and theoretical foundations.

Feminist media criticism and media texts reached a point of complexity
by the late 1990s that enables dichotomous understandings of the feminist
valence of these series.[25] Feminist media scholars may produce varying analyses based on different definitions of feminism, but the range of findings that
result from method and framework indicates some fundamental problems
for contemporary feminist media criticism. Academic scholarship about gender and late 1990s television inordinately attended to the series I classify as
comedic and action dramas and rarely acknowledged the much broader proliferation of female-centered dramatic series. These other series created an
unprecedented context of reception in which the comedic dramas told their
stories, thus affecting the meaning of these stories and their relationship to
broader cultural discourses.

Additionally, the comedic dramas use irony and parody to complicate and
confuse textual analysis and the more literal frameworks common in role-
model analysis. It is impossible to argue persuasively that these series are either feminist or antifeminist because of their contradictory nature and their
sophisticated use of narrative devices, as well as the complexity of their textual form and the programming context in which they circulate.[26] Elsewhere
I have identified postfeminist attributes of these series, but I cannot deny the
possibility of antifeminist interpretations. I take exception to such interpre-

tations when they do not account for parody and satire, multiplicity of female perspectives, or variation and inconsistency over the cumulative narrative. Although one might prefer clear unassailable findings, scholarship must acknowledge the ambivalence that results from textual or contextual complexity rather than willfully disregarding such confounding variables.

* * *

The following pages explore the stories *Ally McBeal* and *Sex and the City* tell and the strategies their creators use to tell them, rather than continuing to link their texts with previous iterations of the new-woman form that have resulted in feminist scholarship to which this work is greatly indebted.[27] The limited scope of the comedic drama form allows for more detailed analysis and attention. Despite the fact that only two series take this form, these dramas contribute greatly to the diversity of stories about women that began to appear in multiple forms and as commercially viable products in the late 1990s. With so few shows of this type, it is impossible to discern whether the similarity among these series results from their uncommon form or whether using an uncommon form enables the particular stories these series tell. *Ally McBeal* and *Sex and the City* predominately explore stories about single women, not only in the demographic categorization of their characters but also by emphasizing stories about being single. Both series feature a multiplicity of single, thirtysomething women in professional careers who live in urban settings, but their characters are differentiated by disparate worldviews and characterizations. Finally, both series blend features of drama and comedy in a manner that makes their narratives distinct from the myriad female-centered situation comedies that previously have drawn attention for their female portrayals, as well as from action, workplace, and family dramas considered elsewhere in this book. The comedic dramas therefore contribute to the diversification of stories told about women by varying the traditional form of the new-woman series, while also differing from the other dramatic types considered in other chapters.

Many Characters, Many Stories

Despite their different narrative bases, *Ally McBeal* and *Sex and the City* both use a variety of distinctly drawn characters to explore the dilemmas single women face. Both present casts that illustrate the multiplicity of perspectives women may have on dating, marriage, and careers; and importantly, the series do not construct one perspective as "correct" but depict an environment in which a plurality of stances are equally viable. This narrative development has important ideological implications, allowing the texts to acknowledge the diversity of women's experiences, the range of possibilities available to each, and the variety of desires among them. Significantly, though, the variant perspectives of the characters are not tied to aspects of identity, as neither series attends to factors such as ethnicity, class, or education as a way to explain their divergent views. Series such as *Golden Girls* (1985–92), *Designing Women* (1986–93), and *Living Single* (1993–98) preceded these series with ensembles of diversified female characters.[28] They located a "voice of reason" distinctly within one character (Dorothy Zbornak, Julia Sugarbaker, and Khadijah James). The relationship among characters in a comedic drama is more fluid, and there is less demarcation among the women in voicing particular outlooks. Narrative devices such as first-person narration aid the shifting and less narrowly circumscribed identities of the characters in comedic dramas.

Carrie and Ally's roles in their respective series require specific analysis. In some ways, the narratives mark these characters as the series' center, yet neither plays the role of the reliable narrator common to such central characters. Carrie provides viewers' initial entry into the series, but despite her voiceovers, *Sex and the City* affords the other characters autonomous storylines and action independent of her. Similarly, although Ally is the title character, and the cumulative narrative tells "her" story, she is a similarly unreliable central character. Audience members cannot use her response to events and situations to assess the valence of the narrative, which contributes to the contradictory ways this series can be understood. Martha Nochimson notes, "looking at Ally as a role model was inappropriate in a show in which the feminism was located not in Ally, but between characters, in new relational paradigms."[29] This assertion may be even more true of *Sex and the City*. Perhaps this distinction is most clear relative to characters in other dramatic types; in comparison with the characters in *Ally McBeal* and *Sex and the City*, Buffy, Xena, Amy of *Judging Amy*, and Sydney of *Providence* serve as more conventional, dependable central characters. The narrative deemphasis of Carrie and Ally allows the other characters an independence crucial to the series' construction of varied female identities.[30]

Sex and the City

Despite the demographic similarity among the characters in *Sex and the City*, their distinct perspectives variously enable and constrain their actions and choices. Each episode focuses on a socially regulated concern or issue (such as motherhood and aging) to which the characters respond. *Ally McBeal* is structured similarly, however, the characters more commonly respond to legal dilemmas—although these stories often relate to aspects of characters' personal lives.[31] Their responses to situations differentiate their priorities, goals, and the possibilities they envision.

Upon superficial examination, the characters seem to exhibit some stereotypical attributes of stock female character types. Closer examination reveals that they shatter such molds in many other respects because of the rich and complex development the series allows. *Sex and the City* loosely positions Charlotte (Kristin Davis) and Samantha (Kim Cattrall) on opposite ends of the virgin/vamp spectrum but considerably modifies this opposition. Charlotte maintains many traditional views eschewed by the others and hopes for the storybook prince who will sweep her away. She unquestionably desires to be a wife and mother, although she does not remain virginal in waiting for the arrival of the perfect mate. Samantha occupies the other extreme by regularly reaffirming that dating is not a means to an end and enjoying her life of serial dating and one-night stands as an end in itself. Despite regular speeches expressing her contentment with dating, the text occasionally suggests that Samantha does not find this life as fully satisfying as she claims.

Miranda (Cynthia Nixon) and Carrie (Sarah Jessica Parker) occupy a less extreme middle ground and appear much more ambivalent about either partnering or remaining single. Miranda often appears the most cynical of the women and the most content with her single status. The series explores her decision to buy an apartment—a choice indicating that she is no longer waiting for someone to establish a domestic space with her—and other situations where societal scripts undermine single professional women's experiences. Miranda faces an unanticipated pregnancy in the fifth season, and her decision to have the baby yields stories and perspectives about motherhood and work that are very different than those offered by Charlotte. Carrie first appears to be a more heavily veiled version of Charlotte—in search of the same mythical partner, but concealing her desire. Her character evolves considerably over the course of the series, and she grows ambivalent about marriage after recognizing that it will require her to sacrifice some aspects of being single that she deeply enjoys.

An episode from the first season indicates how the four characters' diverse perspectives force them to negotiate issues and events. "The Baby Shower" follows them to the Connecticut suburbs where they visit an old friend, Laney, who once rivaled Samantha's lack of sexual inhibition but is now married and pregnant.[32] The four characters each respond distinctively to the realization that Laney's fate could be their own; the concern is particularly acute for Carrie, whose period is over a week late. Laney and her suburban friends offer additional female voices as they interject perspectives on marriage, motherhood, and the suburbs.

The episode begins by alluding to the fable of the city mouse and the country mouse, as none of the city slickers—all dressed in black leather and sucking down coffee—is prepared to drive to the suburbs. Although she barely knows Laney, Charlotte is the most excited about the event and is the only character who remembers to bring a gift. Upon their arrival, Charlotte quickly succumbs to the world of baby clothes and toys and displays obvious envy of the world the suburban mothers share. Laney, however, shatters Charlotte's ideal world near the end of the visit when Charlotte overhears that she intends to name the baby Shayla. This is the baby name Charlotte had planned for her daughter since her own childhood, a name she only disclosed to Laney in strict confidence. Believing the theft of her baby name indicates that all her dreams are lost, upon returning home she destroys the pictures stored in her "hope box," the economy-sized version of a hope chest. Here she has collected pictures of her dream husband (clipped from fashion magazines) and her dream homes (a townhouse in the city and a weekend home in the Hamptons), as well as a pillow with "Shayla" stitched across it. She "mentally scotch-tapes" the pictures back together later in the episode after she meets a man with the potential to revive her dreams of marital and maternal bliss. In contrast, Samantha brings the expectant mother a bottle of scotch and continues a relationship of outrageous one-upmanship. Samantha, ready to show everyone how much better she looks than the eight-months-pregnant Laney, wears skintight pants and a shirt exposing her stomach. The cult of motherhood cannot penetrate Samantha's veneer, and upon returning to the city she throws an "I'm not having a baby" shower as a wild variation of the Connecticut experience.

Miranda has experienced the suburban baby-shower ritual before and serves as an all-knowing guide for the women; she explains upscale suburban phenomena such as electric dog fencing and warns them of the cultlike behavior of mothers. She listens to Carrie's fears that she may be next without revealing her own feelings about motherhood and accompanies Carrie to buy a pregnancy test after returning to the city. Miranda's outlook emerges as she later spends her evening lip-locked at Samantha's party. As Carrie narrates, "Still convinced that marriage and baby equals death, Miranda chose life, also known as Ed."

For Carrie, the whole trip is a vision of what her life could become, as she simultaneously renounces and embraces the displays of motherhood encountered at Laney's home. She purchases a pregnancy test when she returns to the city, but she decides she cannot take it until she is certain of how she feels about the potential results. The day after Samantha's party she scrutinizes mothers and children at play in a city park and realizes that alternative versions of motherhood exist. Consequently, she accepts the potential "positive" outcome of the test, but her period starts before she arrives home.

The diverse perspectives of the four main characters contrast with those of Laney and the other suburban mothers. Although she appears happy with her new life, Laney calls Carrie after the shower and laments that they never see each other. Carrie mentions Samantha's party as an excuse to get off of the phone, but Laney considers it an invitation and tries to resume her former role as life of the party, despite her pregnancy. Carrie spends the evening trying to keep Laney away from the vodka as Laney bemoans that she woke up one day and did not recognize herself. She advocates that someone should warn women about what happens when they choose suburbia and all it symbolizes.

In addition, the suburban mothers directly address the camera to answer Carrie's rhetorical question, "What is still buried deep within the suburban mothers?" The first mother nostalgically recalls her days of sexual promiscuity and discloses, while burping her infant, that she has an Internet lover. The next woman reveals that over two hundred people reported to her when she worked as a senior vice president, but now, as a mother, she only yells at the gardener. A happier mother changes a diaper while saying that she is the same person she was before motherhood and that she loves her life. Nevertheless, every now and then she thinks about "Lisa," suggesting a previous lesbian relationship. The final mother swings a child in the yard as she confesses that she sometimes climbs up in her kids' tree house with her Walkman and smokes a joint while listening to Peter Frampton. All of these insights contrast with the mothers' outward appearance at the shower as happy and fulfilled with their lives as suburban mothers and married women.

In less than twenty-two minutes, this episode provides a complex exploration of various perspectives toward marriage, suburbia, maintaining a career, and motherhood and how these factors affect women's sense of self and career. In many respects, the narrative weighs each of their perspectives equally; it balances caricatures of the suburban mothers with Charlotte's desire to join them and Samantha's overcompensation for her life choices. The only "solution" supported by the text is Carrie's realization that motherhood does not require that she become a suburban mother. This is a somewhat superficial perspective, however, as she arrives at this conclusion after spending a day watching children play and observing a mother who appears to have retained a distinct sense of self. She never talks with this woman or any other mother who affirms that strategies exist for overcoming the negative aspects of motherhood the text constructs. In many ways, Carrie's assumption that motherhood would be different for her is as idyllic as Charlotte's fairy-tale plans for her future.

The conclusion of the episode can be understood as an attempt to provide episodic closure and superficially resolve the source of narrative tension. The ending does not negate the diverse perspectives raised in the episode; although it provides a conservative containment of some of the characters' outlooks, the text judiciously allows for difference. The episode concludes with Carrie's decision, which does not rewrite or invalidate the various other viewpoints and arguments raised during the episode. The array of outlooks and experiences counters essentialist beliefs that all women are nurturing and desire to be mothers and that all other concerns pale or disappear once a woman becomes a mother. By providing so many varied perspectives, the series offers multiple points of identification and refuses to construct a preferred position. The characterization of each woman motivates her stand. No response appears "better," or even more feminist, and the episode denies a monolithic outlook as characteristic of all women.[33]

Ally McBeal

Ally McBeal uses an extensive range of female characters who exhibit complex and contradictory identities. The series includes six regular female characters and one recurring female character.[34] Its character-driven format focuses stories on the exploration of their responses to events (instead of a continuous sequence of events). As in daytime serials, very little "happens" in each episode; instead, characters' reactions to new information or knowledge receive great emphasis. This allows the creation of distinct personalities within the ensemble, which is particularly significant because the series showcases so many female characters.

The eccentric nature of many of *Ally McBeal*'s characters and their constant, substantive redevelopment contributes to the show's ambiguous tone. Much of the cultural debate surrounding the series results from critics' uncertainty about its seriousness, because of its use of narratives that unpredictably shift from realistic melodrama to trifling comedy and fantasy sequences. Such narratives and characterizations allow for varying interpretations of the show's ideology, including the possibility that the dramatic and comedic depictions of characters are parodic—critical of the concepts they explore—rather than making light of them, as others have suggested.[35] Characterizations are thus highly unstable. Additionally, the series reinvents itself considerably in each of its five seasons, which makes generalizations nearly impossible. Analyzing *Ally McBeal* requires specific contextual acknowledgment of the season and even episode.

Ally McBeal focuses on legal issues related to women in addition to exploring its characters' psyches, which provides a narrative component that limits and expands its narrative terrain in comparison with *Sex and the City*. Almost without exception, the firm accepts cases that affect women or are specifically salient to the private sphere. Stories deal with prostitution, sex-based discrimination, sexual harassment, and questions of family or relationships, particularly the legal dimensions of marriage. Consequently, *Ally McBeal* can probe issues that are politically rather than socially enforced; however, these stories also require the series to focus less attention on characters' inner psychological realms, which are so central to *Sex and the City*. The series develops Ally's character with depth comparable to Carrie, Samantha, Charlotte, and Miranda, but it does not draw her castmates as fully.

As in *Sex and the City*, the characters' variance develops through characterization rather than acknowledged demographic difference.[36] Ally (Calista Flockhart) is a whimsical idealist trying to find her way in a world for which she is unsuited. Her active fantasy life and refusal to relinquish the expectation of a Prince Charming figure do not make her the "feminist role model" many critics desire, yet her idealism allows her to express ambivalence toward second-wave-feminist gains in a way that promotes thoughtful introspection into the reconfigured dilemmas women face despite feminism's accomplishments. Georgia (Courtney Thorne-Smith) is most similar to Ally, and her personal life represents everything Ally desires, until her marriage disintegrates in the third season. Georgia's attempts to overcome and utilize her physical beauty also distinguish her, as she seeks to defy others' expectations that she is less competent because of her "Barbie doll" appearance.

In contrast to Ally's and Georgia's uncertain personal confidence, the series characterizes Ling (Lucy Liu), Elaine (Jane Krakowski), and Renee (Lisa Nicole Carson) as experiencing a sense of power derived from their status as attractive women and depicts them strategically using their sexuality to "control" men. The narrative provides variant motivations for their display of sexual empowerment: Renee's brashness developed as a mechanism for coping with adolescent teasing; the text reveals Elaine's hypersexuality to be a performance she uses to draw attention (to compensate for her exclusion as support staff); while Ling's confidence appears simply that of a competent and able woman. These characters often appear far more confident and in control than Ally and Georgia, and consequently they are more emblematic of "strong women." Nelle (Portia de Rossi) remains the least developed female character. When introduced at the beginning of the second season, firm partner Richard Fish (Greg Germann) identifies her as "sub-zero Nelle," a comment on her frosty personality and all-business demeanor. After joining the firm, her personality thaws, but she lacks the eccentricity displayed by the other characters and is often confused by their oddities and attention to emotion. Nelle provides contrast to Ling's "feminist" politics of men as the inferior sex and to Ally's ambivalence toward feminist gains.

When an episode places these female characters in the context of an event or issue, they react distinctively, illustrating the diversity among them. For example, the women each respond differently to a case in which a community organization called MOPE (Mothers Opposed to Pornographic Entertainment) sues Ling because she owns a female mud-wrestling establishment. Richard forces Ally and Georgia to join Nelle in defending her, although their only role is to appear as "women" who support Ling. Nelle, who is also uncomfortable with the case, begins by arguing legal merits such as zoning rather than attacking MOPE's contention that the establishment "degrades" women.[37] When Ling testifies in defense of her club, she replies to the prosecution's query of whether her club exploits women by saying: "Women are exploited by the high-heeled shoe. Women are exploited by the idea that we have to paint our eyelashes every day just to go to work. Pharmaceutical companies spend billions of dollars convincing the world that cellulite is evil. Is that to empower women? If anything, we should be glad to have my club, because we exploit men—in my club women basically control the dumb stick [penis] and take the men's money."[38]

During the speech, Ally marvels at Ling's logic, Georgia laughs over the ridiculous comparisons, and Nelle expresses dismay. Back in her office, Nelle tells Ling that she cannot give the summation because she does not believe in Ling's position, noting, "Progress aside, women are still things to be looked at, objects. These clubs don't help." Before stepping aside, Nelle calls a male lawyer, who also works as a stripper, to testify that he finds women's response to his appearance gratifying, not degrading. Nelle also uses him as an illustration of how the jury does not view him as "objectified" or as a victim. Ally accuses Nelle of using a stunt and critiques her by arguing that the gender reversal is not equivalent because of the power differential between the sexes—a standard feminist response. Richard provides the summation and argues that men need these clubs to understand that their sexual urges are normal. The judge hesitantly rules in favor of Ling, based on his belief that the club reflects community standards.

The variance in characters' perspectives is readily apparent, as the regular characters, as well as the prosecution (representing a female character), all view the issue differently. Ling argues that the club does not exploit women because within its walls women control men and profit from their foolishness. Nelle recognizes that the club does not diminish cultural objectification of women, and the prosecution makes a causal argument of degradation. Neither Georgia nor Ally offers justification for their reluctance to work on the case, which is likely related to their dislike of Ling. The characters' perspectives also result from how the mud-wrestling club affects their lives. Ling benefits financially and finds it empowering to use men's objectification of women against them. Nelle recognizes that the objectification is connected to how men treat her in other spaces because she is a woman and does not find objectification empowering for either sex. The plaintiff from MOPE believes the club diminishes the value of her neighborhood and threatens her home and children. The episode does not offer a clear feminist solution to the diverse perspectives, nor is any position validated because of the grounds on which the judge presents his decision.

The female characters in *Ally McBeal* also enact divergent perspectives on dating, marriage, and the socially regulated gender issues explored in *Sex and the City*. By featuring so many women in primary roles, *Ally McBeal* can depict women as a group composed of varied outlooks in a manner unavailable to series with only one or two female characters whose primary narrative function is as contrast to the perspective of male characters. Like *Sex and the City*, *Ally McBeal* constructs a narrative space in which female characters can debate personal and professional dilemmas that their real-world contemporaries may encounter.

The inclusion of a plurality of female protagonists allows both shows to examine the breadth of female experience and the various perspectives women embody. Their hesitation to assert a dominant viewpoint indicates a shift from previous series such as *Designing Women* and *Golden Girls*, which tended to identify a single character as the consistent embodiment of a feminist perspective (the characters Julia Sugarbaker and Dorothy Zbornak, played by Dixie Carter and Bea Arthur, respectively). By indicating multiple feminist positions, late 1990s comedic dramas express the complex dynamics in which women negotiate their personal politics with the options society affords them, as well as an environment of multifaceted feminist issues and priorities. This opens the narratives to diverse audiences that mirror the complexity and diversity of the characters.

The deliberation among characters in both these series marks a primary variation of the comedic drama from other female-centered dramatic series. Action and protagonist-centered family dramas emphasize a main character. Although other female perspectives commonly surround her, the main character dominates the series and determines an ideological vantage point that is absent from *Sex and the City* and *Ally McBeal*. This likely demarcates the most substantial contribution of the comedic drama to the tradition of

telling stories about female characters. The complexity with which these series construct characters' worldviews and place them in dialogue allows considerable depth to the depiction of female experience.

Single Women and Searching for Mr. Right in the 1990s

Characters' single status plays an important role in their characterization and
in differentiating the stories told about single women in comedic dramas from
those told in other dramatic types. The 1990s versions of the single-woman
story continue the focus on dating and the search for a suitable partner as primary narrative subject matter; this comprises the serial story of both *Ally Mc-
Beal* and *Sex and the City*. Feminist analyses have scrutinized the representation of career women struggling with their expectations of and options for
romantic partnership because of what these stories suggest about social expectations of women. Many previous series have indicated feminist progress
in characters' career options, but feminist critics have illustrated how narratives contain these career gains with fewer personal-life options or depend-
ence on a husband.[39] *Ally McBeal* and *Sex and the City* represent the first generation of television characters who assume the benefits secured by
second-wave feminist activism, and new career possibilities lead many of them
to need to reconcile their independence with their desire for romantic relationships.

The programming context affects how these series tell dating stories in two
ways. First, the generational difference of these characters from their predecessors in *That Girl*, *The Mary Tyler Moore Show*, and *Molly Dodd* afford them
very different worldviews. *Ally McBeal* and *Sex and the City* depict women
who continue the new-woman type, but the characters face different challenges, or at least face them with reconfigured priorities. Although many
gender-based inequities still exist in the U.S. society reflected in and engaged
by these series, the gains that have been made allow the narratives to explore
how these white, educated, upper-middle-class protagonists experience the
choices feminism allows them. The series depict the gains as creating new
dilemmas and challenges for the characters, but they do not present them in
the reactionary manner characteristic of what Dow identifies as "postfeminist" programming of the 1980s, which openly blamed feminism for the new
dilemmas women faced.[40] In fact, nothing seems to be blamed for the problems the characters experience, nor do the narratives suggest that they are
doing or have done something wrong. Rather, their struggles result from the
scale of their expectations. Their desires for close female friendships, perfect
male companionship, particular types of family life at specified times, and

career advancement in jobs they enjoy are grandiose and uncompromising—and, consequently, not easily achieved.

Secondly, the stories these series tell about dating are only one of four types, or indicative of only two of sixteen series. The phenomenon of multiple and diverse series centering upon female characters, particularly in the dramatic series that this book takes as its focus, allows the dating behavior of Ally, Carrie, and their friends to mean something very different than it would have if the shows had aired in the 1970s or 1980s. A multiplicity of stories about dating emerged across the dramatic series, and the different dramatic types offered narratives that varied significantly from the emphasis on dating and marriage in comedic dramas. The multiplicity of female perspectives in the comedic-drama ensembles prevents either show from constructing a monolithic view of female desire in relation to sex and marriage. While Charlotte makes finding a male companion her life's mission, *Sex and the City* balances this portrayal with Samantha, who "doesn't do relationships," and *Ally McBeal* offers a similar range of perspectives.

In the past, new-woman protagonists were often the only single female characters in existence, but stories about young heroines and divorced professionals now provide a much more expansive range of narrative opportunity. Comedic dramas do emphasize stories about romantic relationships with men; however, dating receives much less narrative emphasis in the action and workplace dramas. Examination of the stories told by comedic dramas reveals that the primary challenge for these women is not finding a relationship so much as finding the right one, a subtle variation that is crucial to the available range of interpretations. These women refuse many eligible bachelors as inadequate mates, which makes the pursuit of a partner an active and selective process. To adequately gauge the stories U.S. television tells about women's lives in the transition to the twenty-first century, the stories must be viewed as components of a multifaceted context, not as isolated utterances.

Ally's Search for Mr. Right

In many ways, characters' unsuccessful attempts to find suitable mates structure *Ally McBeal* and *Sex and the City*. Many of the characters in each series express confusion about balancing their professional success with their own and others' expectations of them. Even when they determine what they desire, the characters struggle with their inability to control the timing of meeting a partner or having children. Critics of *Ally McBeal* in particular have interpreted such articulations as indicative of its antifeminist politics and a throwback to 1980s discourses that correlated women's inability to find desirable relationships with their professional careers.[41] The comedic dramas construct this issue with more complexity than this interpretation recognizes, exploring how women negotiate contradictory measures of success and social expectations without posing a return to traditional gender roles as a solution.

Much of the criticism of Ally's character as regressive that circulated in popular magazines and newspapers cited her open dissatisfaction with her personal life as key evidence of the show's antifeminist politics. Journalists and academic critics captured Ally's first-season perspective in quotations such as:

> "I am a strong, working, career girl who feels empty without a man—the National Organization for Women, they have a contract out on my head."[42]

> "All I wanted was to be rich and successful with three great kids and a husband waiting to tickle my feet—[and] I don't even like my hair."[43]

> "If women really wanted to change society they could do it. I plan to change society. I just want to get married first."[44]

Critics used such quotations in support of arguments condemning Ally as antifeminist and as illustrative of the series as a touchstone for contemporary debates about gender. For example, Veronica Chambers notes, "Ally has clearly struck a nerve with twentysomething women who feel both excited and confused by the choices bestowed upon them by the feminist movement. They understand Ally's big questions: 'If I have it all, can I be happy?'"[45] Surveys of audience members found that Ally's confusion, anxieties, and insecurities attracted them to the series.[46] The story told by *Ally McBeal* captures the complexity of negotiating residual and emergent cultural expectations and social scripts as a "mosaic of contradictions," which some viewers acknowledged to resonate with their own experiences.[47] *Ally McBeal* intervenes in cultural debates about the professional and personal dilemmas contemporary single women face by reflecting the difficulty of achieving their chosen life plan in a world where gender roles have been modified but miniscule institutional change has occurred.

Ally's focus on finding the perfect romantic partner often provides her main motivation in plots exploring her personal life. She finds herself in the midst of a life she did not seek and now must make her own. The series' back story reveals that a desire to be with Billy, not a love of the law, led her to pursue her legal degree. She excelled in law school, while Billy opted to leave Harvard for a school where he could obtain a law-review position.[48] Ally consequently finds herself living a successful life by some societal standards, but it is not the life she planned. This explains some of the ambivalence with which she views her professional life, as well as her constant pining for a more sat-isfying personal life. In one early episode she confides to Georgia that her life has fallen short of her expectations. "You know, I had a plan. When I was twenty-eight, I was going to be taking my maternity leave, but I would still be on the partnership track. I would be at home at night with my husband reading *What to Expect When You're Nursing and Trying Cases*—big home life, big professional life—and instead I'm going to bed with an inflatable doll, and I represent clients that suck toes. This was not the plan."[49]

The representation of Ally and her dating discontent varies over the course of the series. In the first two seasons, her ineffectiveness in satisfying her per-sonal desires mainly results from her inability to be with Billy, who moved on from their relationship and married. Once Ally recognizes her relation-ship with Billy is over, her perspective changes and she dates a number of men; however, she finds some fault with each of them. In the third season, her inability to find a long-term romantic partner primarily results from her refusal to deviate from a Prince Charming archetype and the complexity of her identity, which make finding a match for her whimsy and ideal of mas-culinity challenging. She refuses one man after another, men she acknowl-edges are perfect except that they are homeless,[50] laugh oddly,[51] or are bisex-ual.[52] This series of failed prospects may suggest that it is impossible to find a "perfect" man; however, it also functions as a critique of Ally's unwilling-ness to explore a relationship that deviates from her expectations.

Dating becomes less of a concern for Ally following Billy's death near the end of season three. A long-term relationship with Larry Paul (Robert Downey Jr.) dominates season four and allows Ally to explore the complex-ity of negotiating a relationship, rather than the cursory dating of early sea-sons. By season five, the series depicts Ally possessing a new maturity. Her need for romantic partnership becomes subordinated to her responsibilities as a firm partner and the fulfillment she finds as a mother. Significantly, the series concludes with her leaving Boston and the firm to satisfy her daugh-ter's needs. By this point she is more certain that she must simply find her way through the world rather than being anxious about her life's deviation from her plan.[53]

Based on previous new-woman series, one might query whether the deci-sion to connect Ally's newfound maturity and confidence in the final season with her status as a mother simply repeats a common narrative device used to reaffirm that women only mature when they become mothers, or that de-votion to a child becomes a substitute for romance.[54] It is possible to argue that this is the case with *Ally McBeal*, but other narrative developments resist this explanation. The series establishes Ally's mature turn well before her daughter's arrival through her mentoring relationship with Jenny and her decision to buy a house.[55] Further, Ally continues her search for romantic partnership despite Maddie's arrival. She does display hesitance about pursuing a long-term relationship with Victor (Jon Bon Jovi), but this can be explained as a consequence of her slow recovery from the loss of Larry as well as a result of Kelley's decision to end the series with Ally confidently unattached.

The stories of motherhood and coupling in *Ally McBeal* must be considered amidst the broader programming context. While characters in other series alternatively eschew motherhood or acknowledge it as important, but only one component of their lives, Ally finds satisfaction in gaining the family that she has desired. The pervasive nature of stories correlating maternity with maturity contributed to naturalizing this relationship. Previously naturalized constructs regarding women's relationship to maternity become uninhabitable in this textual environment in which motherhood takes various forms and is depicted as cherished by some characters, undesirable to others, and viewed with ambivalence by others yet.[56]

Ally McBeal's main contribution to cultural discussions about negotiating career and family is its ambivalence: it recognizes career gains as an advance, but simultaneously depicts uncertainty about how to evaluate this success compared with other desires. This makes Ally much more a comrade than a role model for female audiences who identify with her struggles. In this ambivalence the series accepts the multiple plans, choices, and goals women may have, consequently allowing for differences among women and discrepancy among equally feminist perspectives. On the whole, the series uses uncertain seriousness, parody, and satire to willfully refuse the coherent and stable characterizations or the plain and discernible narrative required for meaningful content analysis or standard textual analysis.

Sex and the City: *Single and Fabulous! or, Single and Fabulous?*

Similar to Ally's unsuccessful efforts in search of the right partner, Carrie, Samantha, Charlotte, and Miranda experience an ongoing process of dating and reconciling the lives they lead with those they planned. The characters' pursuit of long-term heterosexual mates drives the narrative trajectory of *Sex and the City*, yet the lack of viable candidates forces the women to find fulfillment in their careers, friendships, and short-term boyfriends. By later seasons, the narratives include more psychological introspection and depict the characters weighing the options available in single and married life instead of uncritically pursuing partnership as a dominant social script.

In one of the earliest explicit interrogations of the characters' search for marriage-worthy partners, Carrie poses the question, "Is it better to fake satisfaction with a relationship than be alone?"[57] The episode begins with Carrie arriving late to an early-morning photo shoot for a *New York Magazine* article on being "Single and Fabulous!" Carrie stays out all night the previous evening and falls asleep an hour before she is due at the shoot. She arrives with matted hair and smudged makeup and sucks on a cigarette as the photographer shoots—allegedly testing the lighting. When the article appears, a disheveled image of Carrie provides the cover photo for an article now entitled "Single and Fabulous?" As the four women read the article, a cautionary tale questioning the amount of satisfaction single New York women derive from their lives, insecurities emerge despite their knowledge that a comparable article appears every few years. The characters manifest their lack of certainty about their quality of life in a variety of ways: Miranda rekindles a relationship she gave up on because she has to fake orgasm; Charlotte begins a relationship with the handyman/out-of-work actor living across the hall who deviates significantly from her ideal beau; Samantha becomes atypically lovesick over a man who awakens her desire for companionship by plying her with promises; and Carrie hides in her apartment after seeing pity in the eyes of a street vendor who recognizes her from the magazine cover.

Despite these displays of insecurity, by the end of the episode Miranda realizes that she cannot fake sexual gratification, Charlotte decides that she cannot pretend to be attracted to a man who is not her type, Samantha cannot deny some desire for companionship, and Carrie recognizes that she is not completely secure with being single. Significantly, though the women decide not to feign who they are and what they desire in order to find heterosexual companionship, each acknowledges that she desires companionship—uncritically assumed to be found in marriage—but that marriage is not so important as to pursue it at the expense of other needs.

Other episodes further illustrate how the characters negotiate their search for satisfying personal and professional lives. "The Baby Shower" provides an extensive examination of the characters' desires for family—from Charlotte's jealousy to Samantha's overcompensatory revulsion—while other episodes explore how each character manages the discrepancy between her life and how she desires it to be. For example, when Miranda buys an apartment, real estate agents, brokers, and bankers remind her that she is deviating from social expectations and her hopes for her life as they repeatedly ask if her boyfriend is moving in, if the down payment is coming from her father, or if she is separated. These questions assert traditional expectations, although they do not alter Miranda's decision.[58]

Miranda also displays a complicated ambivalence when faced with a poorly timed pregnancy. She chooses to remain single (an option she can choose because of her economic status as a lawyer) and experiences a loss of some of the aspects of single freedom she enjoyed, while also finding unanticipated joys in motherhood. As in Ally's case, it is erroneous to assume that Miranda's motherhood signifies her maturity or replaces her pursuit of heterosexual coupling simply because the device has often been used this way in the past. Miranda's pregnancy works as a valuable plot device to explore the relationships of the characters and their desires in a new way. Miranda unintentionally becomes pregnant at the same time Charlotte desperately tries to have a baby, learns of problems with her fertility, and faces a rapidly unraveling marriage. The juxtaposition of the two women and the different meanings of pregnancy, work, and motherhood allows the series to explore women's efforts to achieve the extraordinary expectations common among this generation. Again, the stories do not pose feminism, patriarchy, nor any other ideology or entity as particularly to blame for the characters' negotiation of compromised expectations. The narrative constructs these problems as personal rather than systemic—an often-noted criticism of the narratives produced by the U.S. commercial media system.[59] The series gives voice to variant female perspectives but does not affirm any one as better than another despite the personalized solutions.

A later episode revisits the characters' feelings about "singledom" when a scheduling conflict leads Carrie to spend her thirty-fifth birthday alone. In an uncharacteristic (and consequently poignant) speech, Charlotte proposes that the women be each other's soul mates and "let men be just these great, nice, guys to have fun with."[60] By posing and supporting such a proposition in subsequent episodes, Sex and the City tells stories very different from previous and other contemporary iterations of the single-woman series. Female friendship receives unprecedented narrative primacy and is depicted as a viable alternative to heterosexual coupling as the series traces Miranda's experience with single motherhood, Charlotte's infertility, divorce, and remarriage, Samantha's survival of breast cancer, and Carrie's decision to end her engagement after recognizing that she was unwilling to forego aspects of her single life.

When the series concluded in the spring of 2004, Miranda had married Steve and moved to Brooklyn, Charlotte and her second husband Harry were preparing to adopt a child, Samantha had battled breast cancer and found a place in her life for an unlikely partner, and Carrie had returned home from Paris to begin again with Mr. Big. In some ways the series finale reasserted traditional tropes of maternity and coupling, but it also left many doors open, and on closer examination, it did tell stories different from those of previous new women. Cumulatively, the series tells the stories of how the characters determined what among their hopes and desires was most important, and none achieved the contents of her "hope box" without sacrifice and negotiation. The narrative did not punish the women for defiance of some expected behavior in its failure to deliver their ideal lives; rather, it offered stories in which they found parts of the life they were looking for in the lives they were dealt. Importantly, given the types of stories told by this show, one should not assume that "they lived happily ever after." Based on previous episodes, it does not seem likely that Mr. Big and Carrie will last, nor that Smith and Samantha will settle into conventional coupled bliss. For a series that primarily narrated the *process* by which four single friends explore and follow life options, a final episode does not serve as the conclusive end of the journey.

* * *

Ally McBeal and *Sex and the City* began as transparent versions of the series they eventually became. As they drew substantive audiences in initial seasons, their networks and producers allowed experimentation with techniques and stories that increased the characters' depth and complexity. Much of the journalistic criticism of *Ally McBeal* that my analysis challenges was written in the series' first two seasons, which perhaps explains some of the discrepancy of interpretations. Although it is possible to understand the characters' pursuit of male companionship as regressive and comparable to stories told about single women thirty years ago, it is also possible to see these stories as explorations of the challenges this generation of women faces in rewriting social scripts of dating and marriage because of the gains of the past thirty years. When viewing the cumulative narratives over the series' multiseason trajectories, *Ally McBeal* and *Sex and the City* do not tell stories about desperate women whose lives are empty without marriage but instead examine the complicated process of discovering personal identity and how women who lack an inherited social script incorporate careers and companionship into their lives.[61] These women do not all desire the same thing, nor are they flawless, as would be necessitated by a role-model or positive-representation framework. The discrepancy among their hopes and priorities indicates the range of possibilities afforded to women of privileged class, ethnic, educational, beauty, and sexual status.

Creating the same choices afforded to men has been central to liberal feminist activism. The privileged women of these series can choose among more opportunities than most women, as was true of the 1980s characters in *thirtysomething* that Elspeth Probyn describes as the "choiceoisie."[62] Yet the sociocultural context of the late 1990s differs from the mid 1980s, and the series explored here offer reflexive consideration of the rhetoric of choice. For example, within the narrative of *Sex and the City,* Charlotte's decision to marry and then stop working in pursuit of becoming pregnant leads her friends to query the "empowerment" of her decision.[63] Charlotte's decision is depicted as her deliberate choice (in a frustrated conversation with Miranda, she affirms, "I choose my choice, I choose my choice, I choose my choice") and not one of a false consciousness created by cultural expectations. Charlotte pleads with Miranda, "The women's movement is supposed to be about choice," yet it is clear that even women privileged to have the opportunity to make such a choice now face stigmatization if they eschew work, while women who pursue careers continue to be the object of cultural critique. It is certainly important to be suspicious of these articulations as truly indicating the possibility of choice, as many have shown how narratives contain women while using trappings of "progress"; yet it is also important to allow for the possibility of new stories and to acknowledge that changes in context may alter the meaning of signifiers such as characters' decisions to leave work or have children. As Moseley and Read argue, "[*Ally McBeal*] offers us a female subject who admits problems without rejecting feminism as the cause, and it shows us the world through her eyes. It combines an address to traditional feminist concerns in theme and narrative with an address of the new conditions of women's lives in the 1990s, and it does not attempt to impose any idea of appropriate female feminist identities."[64] Ironically, discourses of choosing between home and career in *Sex and the City* and *Ally McBeal* seem to repeat 1980s containment, but the alteration of the historical, generational, and representational contexts allows these discourses substantially different meanings.

These series require critical engagement with questions about why they have resonated with audiences, instead of categorically decrying the characters' feminist potential because their skirts are too short, they are too skinny, or they admit to not finding complete fulfillment in their jobs. Role-model analyses that examine characters in relation to an ideological ideal lack the complexity necessary for understanding the functions and effects of television's storytelling. Moreover, given the complexity of the narratives and the unprecedented programming context, it is crucial that audiences have a voice in criticism. The popularity of these series alone provides an indication of their resonance; precisely what is resonating can only be known by surveying audience members.

As is the case with each of the narrative types this book considers, comedic dramas function distinctly and in concert with the other female-centered dramas that share space on broadcast and cable schedules. To date, comedic dramas have focused on single, urban-dwelling, professional women and explored stories about careers, dating, and friendship in this environment.

These topics recur in other narrative types, but their varied settings, emphases, and strategies yield distinct stories. This chapter only grazes the surface of worthwhile criticism of these texts. Audience research could afford the existing textual criticism greater depth in understanding what meanings different audience segments make of the series and the priority they place on them in comparison with others. The few audience studies completed at the time of this writing suggest that audiences recognize the complexity of these texts and produce nuanced readings.[65] If future comedic dramas represent characters who are not thirtysomething, single professionals, it will help distinguish which aspects of these series result from their narrative structure and which arise from the settings and stories these characters require. *Ally McBeal* and *Sex and the City* unquestionably contribute to the evolution of the new-woman character and indicate the possibilities available in a programming context that supports a multiplicity of series centering upon female characters and a cultural and historical moment characterized by the rise of a new generation of women.

4. Same Story, Different Channel? Returning Home and Starting Over in Protagonist-Centered Family Dramas

> Why don't they make a show about a real woman, a smart woman? I
> mean, she doesn't have to be perfect. In fact, she shouldn't be perfect.
> So maybe she doesn't look like a model, maybe she even has hips. . . .
> A professional woman with an imperfect personal life; a woman who
> is doing her best to figure out where she fits in this crazy world. They'd
> never put a woman like that on TV.
> —Sharon Gless as Rosie O'Neill to her off-screen therapist

In this highly reflexive moment, in which Gless refers to her previous identity as Christine Cagney and her current identity as Rosie O'Neill, executive producer Barney Rosenzweig uses Gless's character as a mouthpiece to express the challenges facing dramatic series centering upon female characters in the early 1990s. Rosie O'Neill was exactly the character Gless—as O'Neill—describes. And she was on television; but her stay was brief, with the show surviving with only thirty-four episodes. Rosenzweig's efforts were not in vain; he was just a little ahead of his time. *The Trials of Rosie O'Neill* (CBS, 1990–92) and *Sweet Justice* (NBC, 1994–95) struggled and ultimately succumbed in their attempts to bring dramatic stories about professional women with complicated personal lives into television viewers' homes in the first part of the 1990s. By the end of the decade, their prescience would be realized, as series built on identical plot devices of characters returning home and simplifying their careers became the most watched shows amidst the rise in female-centered dramatic narratives.

Reconfigured to focus on a central protagonist, revised family dramas proved the commercial viability of female-centered dramas on mainstream broadcast networks. This dramatic type primarily has told its stories in contexts featuring a multiplicity of characters, as in the series *Sisters* (1991–96) or any number of daytime soap operas. *Providence* arrived as a midseason replacement in January 1999 and revived NBC's Friday night by immediately winning its time slot and scoring as the most watched series on any network on Friday nights. The series tells the story of a doctor, Sydney Hansen (Melina Kanakaredes), who returns to her family home from her successful Los Angeles plastic-surgery practice for her sister's wedding but chooses to stay following her mother's sudden death. NBC programmers marveled that *Providence* did not lure audience members from other broadcast series, but that its audience had not been watching Friday television or had defected to cable.[1] Although network programming slates for the next season were already in development by the time *Providence* became the broadcast success story of the year, the achievements of this drama about a professional woman must have weighed heavily on schedulers' minds as they convened to make final selections.

Providence was not the first series to offer a reconfigured version of the family drama in the late 1990s. Six months earlier, Lifetime launched *Any Day Now* with respectable reviews, but much quieter fanfare. Cable original series were still uneven in their quality and regarded with some skepticism. *Any Day Now* explores the lives of two childhood friends who reestablish their relationship as adult women after years of estrangement and traveling different life paths. Mary Elizabeth Sims (Annie Potts), a white, working-class housewife, became pregnant just before high-school graduation and immediately married and began raising a family, while Rene Jackson (Lorraine Toussaint), an African American woman, attended college and law school and pursued a career in Washington, D.C. In the pilot, Rene returns to Birmingham, Alabama, for her father's funeral and decides to stay to continue his civil rights law practice. Set in the South in the present and in the women's 1960s childhood, the series explores the challenges to their friendship, many of which result from their identity-based differences. *Any Day Now* was never the industry front-page story that *Providence* became, but the series plodded along and gained viewers. As *Any Day Now* proved itself by returning for a second season and earning top cable rankings for annual two-hour episodes, the series garnered more attention for the way it related to a developing trend on broadcast networks than for its innovative status.[2]

The protagonist-centered family drama emerged more fully in the fall of 1999, with the debut of the first slate of new series following *Providence*'s success. CBS premiered *Judging Amy* and *Family Law*, while ABC offered *Once and Again*. For the first fourteen weeks of the season, *Once and Again* and *Judging Amy* competed in the 10:00 P.M. Tuesday timeslot, with *Once and Again* winning the first outing, and *Judging Amy* taking and maintaining a solid lead in subsequent weeks.[3] As part of annual schedule adjustments for

ABC following the end of *Monday Night Football,* the network moved *Once and Again,* a series about soon-to-be divorced Lily Manning's (Sela Ward) return to dating and her experience as a single mother, to the 10:00 P.M. Monday slot, where it aired opposite *Family Law.* Programmers may have been surprised by the vitality of these new series, as *Judging Amy,* chronicling the life of Amy Gray (Amy Brenneman) after she divorces and returns to her childhood home to work as a family court judge, regularly drew more viewers than the critical and popular favorite *NYPD Blue. Once and Again* and *Family Law* fought to even ratings in a competitive network hour that also offered the fast pace and deep characterizations of NBC's *Third Watch.*

As the season concluded and networks announced fall 2000 schedules, all three series had survived—a surprising feat. These series placed late thirty- and forty-year-old female characters in central dramatic narrative roles, which provided a marked contrast to the characters in their twenties and early thirties who populated most broadcast series. Although crossover from male and teen audiences might contribute to the success of series such as *Ally McBeal* and *Sex and the City,* these new series offered mothers and grandmothers an unprecedented narrative focus in dramatic contexts and were less likely to draw the younger viewers that are so important to advertisers. Furthermore, the increase from one broadcast success (*Providence*) to four such series likely indicates market saturation; conventional wisdom suggests that audiences may respond to one of these series, but not all of them. Audience response, in this case, clearly deviated from expectations. Not only did *Providence* and *Judging Amy* attract enough viewers to return for a second season, but these two series consistently drew the largest audience of any of the female-centered dramas discussed in this book.

Based on standard industry practice, the seeming absence of new, similar series on fall 2000 schedules was perhaps the most surprising aspect of the success of these protagonist-centered family dramas. Typically, when a successful form materializes, programmers seek series that copy or imitate the form until it fails either by overwhelming viewers with multiplicity or by eliminating any sense of innovation possessed by the original.[4] *That's Life,* an underpromoted series that appeared to have a short life expectancy based on scheduling and promotion, provided the only clear continuation of the protagonist-centered family drama. This series centers on Lydia DeLuca, a character raised in a working-class Italian family, who decides to go to college in her thirties. The WB's *Gilmore Girls* ultimately proved to be a successful variation of the form as well, with its story about a mother who became pregnant as a teen and her relationship with her now teenage daughter.

Understanding the context in which these series arrived and their institutional placement is important because, by a variety of measures, they provide the most significant development of the female-centered drama trend. In terms of the industry, they draw the largest audiences, and most appear on generally branded broadcast networks rather than niche locations particularly addressed to female audiences. Consequently, these series afford an opportunity to examine how dramatic stories driven by a female protagonist move into the mainstream. The textual negotiations of femininity, feminism, and family in these series indicate much about network executives' perceptions of female audiences' narrative desires. Remarkably similar motifs recur across many of them, which could lead to the superficial perception that they are nearly carbon copies. Despite beginning from similar origins in their premises and range of characters, these shows construct distinct narrative identities in a manner that indicates diversity in mainstream women's stories.

Motifs of the Protagonist-Centered Family Drama

Three motifs are common to many of the protagonist-centered family dramas and suggest much about the tensions perceived as central in women's lives. These motifs are also key to setting the boundaries in which these series attempt to negotiate a binary tension between realism and idealism. None of these series sets itself outside of the bounds of accepted reality to the extent evident in an action series such as *Xena: Warrior Princess,* or even the occasional fantasy sequences of *Ally McBeal,* but many of the protagonist-centered family dramas use combinations of three motifs to construct an idyllic narrative world. The lead characters often struggle with issues and dilemmas designed to resonate with audience members in Anytown, USA; however, the use of particular motifs in constructing the context for the story allows the characters options and realities unavailable to most of their viewers. The persistence of these motifs across a multitude of the series suggests their narrative importance to the stories the series tell and the strategies used in their construction.

A Politics of Place: The Setting of a Mythic New England

Contrary to the ubiquitous Los Angeles or New York settings of many U.S. television series, the protagonist-centered family dramas almost uniformly retreat from urban environs and in many cases locate their stories in New England cities and towns such as Hartford, Connecticut (*Judging Amy*), Stars Hollow, Connecticut (*Gilmore Girls*), or Providence, Rhode Island. (The title of the latter highlights the importance of location, as well as the double play on Providence as geographical location and as an explanation of the narrative premise—"it was providence that Sydney would return home.") *Once and Again* offers a subtle variation by basing its story in a Chicago suburb; *Any Day Now* is set in Birmingham; and *That's Life* offers small-town intimacy blended with a more urban environment by locating its story in the New York suburb of Belleview, New Jersey. Although these last three series do not base their narratives in New England, place remains central in nearly all of them, which marks a similarity among protagonist-centered family dramas that deviates from standard television fare.

Among the New England–set series, the sense of place is crucial to their idyllic narratives. In *Judging Amy* and *Providence*, the visual composition ignores the status of Hartford and Providence as large cities. Establishing shots instead emphasize seasonal foliage, often in shots framing the family homes that provide a central narrative location (in fact, it always seems to be autumn in *Providence*). *Providence* makes use of cityscapes to indicate transitions, with Sydney going from home or the church-set, low-income clinic where she works to the big-city hospital. The camera always shoots the "city" from a distance in these establishing shots, and the graceful helicopter pans set to theme music do little to suggest the diversity and grit likely to exist even in this small urban environment. In contrast, when cameras follow Amy to her downtown courthouse workplace, *Judging Amy* makes greater use of gray, snowy days, setting the public space of her work apart from the warm, cluttered space of home. These series mark their settings on a visual as well as narrative level.

Gilmore Girls places even greater narrative importance on setting and place. The fictional small New England town of Stars Hollow is crucial to the narrative in the same way that *Sex and the City* relies upon New York City. The eccentric small town first served as a refuge for Lorelai as a young mother trying to escape her overbearing socialite parents in Hartford. In this series, the city of Hartford symbolizes the antithesis of Stars Hollow's utopian way of life. It is not coincidental that Hartford harbors Lorelai's parents as well as the elitist prep school that Rory eventually attends. *Gilmore Girls* offers an idyllic vision of community life in Stars Hollow, where people not only know their neighbors but care for them; where constant pedestrian traffic makes chance encounters the norm; where small shops and mom-and-pop enterprises have not been destroyed by the suburban sprawl of malls, Wal-Mart, and a Starbucks on every corner (you must travel to Hartford to visit the mall). The rural Stars Hollow and urban Hartford become symbolic of a primary narrative tension in the series, whether Lorelai (and Stars Hollow) has offered Rory a better upbringing than Lorelai's parents (and Hartford) offered Lorelai.

In *Gilmore Girls* particularly, but also in *Providence, Judging Amy,* and *Any*

Day Now, alternative places—locales represented neither as city nor suburb—become a defining aspect of narrative and characterization. The settings in these stories operate as fantasy locations in response to late twentieth-century concerns about the status of suburban life (especially in the wake of the Columbine school massacre), while negative perceptions about the quality of city life for families still abound. The uniform refusal of urban settings that are crucial to the comedic dramas (New York City, Boston), workplace dramas (Philadelphia, San Francisco), and some of the action dramas (such as *Dark Angel*'s apocalyptic milieu) further underscores the importance of alternative spaces for telling stories previously lacking on television. The mythic New England town operates as fantasy for viewers; the space of Stars Hollow belongs to a nostalgic illusion and "Providence" and "Hartford" serve as pseudo-urban constructs extracted from their complicated metropolitan referents and signified by the visual beauty of autumn foliage or blankets of white snow.

The politics of place in *Once and Again* and *Any Day Now,* although different, warrant mention. To some degree, the Chicago suburb of *Once and Again* functions similarly to the New England settings. Despite their proximity, the characters rarely breach the confines of the "city." Coffee shops, family-owned bookstores, and restaurants provide the primary public spaces for interaction, which allows the suburb to seem like an "alternative place." However, location ultimately serves a different narrative function in *Once and Again* when considering the stories told and how they interpellate the viewer. Instead of relying on location to explain the idyllic lives of the characters, *Once and Again* uses the Chicago suburb as a proxy for Anytown, USA, so that viewers recognize the characters' struggles as universal rather than distinct. This series is more melodramatic than the others, and consequently it establishes a different relationship between the protagonist and audience than in *Providence* or *Judging Amy.* The use of a generic setting instead of the differentiated place aids in this identification process.

For *Any Day Now,* location introduces narrative conflict instead of explaining characters' idyllic existence. The series uses the setting of Birmingham in the 1960s and the 1990s to introduce the past and present reality of racism in American society. Like the New England–set series, location provides an essential part of the series' construction and delimits available narratives; however, it also introduces a hazard to the lead characters, their families, and their friendship. Birmingham is constructed as a place where menaces such as the Ku Klux Klan, racist law enforcement, and segregated public spaces threaten the citizenry in both the 1960s and at the dawn of the twenty-first century. The series most often contrasts Birmingham with

Washington, D.C. (where Rene worked prior to the pilot) to denote the different status of race relations and racism in the two environments (as constructed by the series). Birmingham provides both threat and solution. The series does not offer Washington as a place in which racism no longer exists, but as one in which racism is often implicit and hidden. Consequently, despite the threats Birmingham introduces, it also creates a space for dealing with and working to eradicate racism that is not available in places where the threat remains invisible or unspoken in the dominant culture.

Despite the contrasts between *Once and Again* and *Any Day Now*, it is significant that place occupies a central narrative role in many of the protagonist-centered family dramas. The creators deliberately chose to establish their stories in locations unusual for U.S. television, and setting these stories in nontraditional spaces further differentiates them from other female-centered dramatic offerings. This shift in physical location announces that these are different stories than previously available; they depict complicated female characters who exist in unfamiliar spaces.

Rediscovering Lost Connections: Returning to the Childhood Home

Providence, Judging Amy, and *Any Day Now* each returns its protagonist to her parents' home as the point of departure for the series. Viewers' first images of Dr. Sydney Hansen include glamorous open architecture in Los Angeles, as she packs her suitcases in her beachfront home and hurries through professional obligations to make a flight for a weekend in Providence. Likewise, the first images of Rene in *Any Day Now* feature her dashing out of a Washington courtroom, flipping through files, instructing her assistant, and talking on her cell phone. As she departs for another meeting, she receives the call from her mother informing her that her father has died and requesting that she return to Birmingham for the funeral. Neither character anticipates returning home permanently, but when Syd's mother dies during her sister's wedding and Rene reconnects with her mother and childhood friend, both delay their returns.

In slight contrast, viewers never glimpse Amy Gray's life before she returns to Hartford. Much of what happens in the pilot episodes of *Providence* and *Any Day Now* serves as back story in *Judging Amy.* Like the other characters, Amy has lost a parent, her father; however, the parental death does not necessitate or motivate her move home. The pilot begins with Amy, dressed in a wedding gown and veil, expressing uncertainty about the day's events to her mother, who advises her to follow her instincts (David Bowie's "Under Pressure" plays in the background). This scene, which the audience soon learns is a flashback, closes with Amy asking for a quarter, which she then tosses into the air to aid her in discerning the impulse of her "instincts." The scene cuts to Amy waking up alone in bed and a graphic indicating it is "ten years later." She has already returned to her mother's home, and throughout the episode viewers learn that she married, had a child (six-year-old Lauren), and spent the intervening years in Manhattan as a corporate attorney. She returns to Hartford to "start her life over" after "her marriage died" and a college friend nominated her for a family judgeship.[5]

Other series exemplary of the protagonist-centered family drama do not utilize the returning-home event as their narrative beginning, but they do use similar strategies. *Gilmore Girls* offers a more figurative return home, as Rory's acceptance to Chilton in early episodes necessitates that Lorelai reestablish a relationship with her parents as part of requesting a loan to pay for her daughter's tuition. Although Lorelai only physically returns home for weekly dinners as her mother's mandated condition for the tuition money, reestablishing the relationship after years of estrangement is arguably as significant as the complete physical relocations outlined in *Providence, Any Day Now,* and *Judging Amy. That's Life* begins with Lydia's decision to attend college in her mid thirties. The character makes much of her independence, but by the close of the first season she returns to her parents' home (located in the same town) because of the financial challenges of paying tuition and working full-time. *Once and Again* provides the most substantial exception; here the separation of the lead character, Lily Manning, from her husband announces the series' beginning. Instead of emphasizing the negotiation of familial relations between the protagonist and her parent(s) and siblings, Lily endures the struggle of briefly understanding herself as a single mother, then as a woman with children dating a man who is also divorced and has children.

In many series—particularly *Providence, Judging Amy, Any Day Now,* and *Gilmore Girls*—the return home and its implications for family life are closely interrelated with the politics of place. Sydney, Amy, Rene, and Lorelai all relocate from urban environments to locales that are presented as more nurturing and safe. For the first three characters, this move from unforgiving and harsh professional worlds is furthered by their return into the space of the family—into the physical space of their childhood rooms and figuratively into the dynamics and functioning of a family unit. Even in *Gilmore Girls,* Lorelai's childhood room serves important narrative functions. The room remains a veritable shrine to 1980s teen culture as she left it and continues to symbolize the pain of her relationship with her parents during her teen years. The room later becomes a battleground in the passive-aggressive struggle between Lorelai and her mother, Emily, over Rory's best interests. Emily redecorates the room to make it Rory's; although as when it was Lorelai's, Emily filters all decoration and artifacts through her notion of acceptable and appropriate expressions of teen culture.

That returning home functions as a repeated motif in series telling stories about the lives of adult women with successful but complicated professional and personal lives is a surprising turn of events. A defining motif of previous new-woman series involved characters' decisions to leave home, evident in the opening credits of *That Girl* and early seasons of *The Mary Tyler Moore Show*, in which the characters traveled to their new homes in urban environments. None of the series pose this move home as a result of a failure on the part of the protagonist. In *Providence*, Sydney's younger sister and brother both remain in the family confines despite being adults. A sense of family responsibility and a need to assume the role of caretaker left vacant by her mother's death clearly influence Sydney's decision to stay. Amy also shares the house, at least occasionally, with one of her brothers. Initially, Vincent, an underemployed writer, remains in the family home, and their older brother Peter returns home in the fifth season when he separates from his wife. The series articulates the challenge of single motherhood as a primary motivation for Amy's decision to live with her mother, with whom she has a much more antagonistic relationship than that depicted between the other protagonists and their parents. Rene decides to remain in Birmingham for many reasons: concern for her mother's well-being, the duty of continuing her father's law practice, and a reevaluation of corporate life as unfulfilling.

The widespread narratives about female characters who return to their childhood homes unquestionably causes concern in the same way that the maternity narratives in *Ally McBeal* and *Sex and the City* seem reminiscent of previous narrative devices used to contain the options afforded to female characters. Despite the individual narrative constructions of the return home as a result of uncontrollable circumstances and not the characters' failure, the preponderance of this motif may indicate a more implicit evaluation of the ability of professional women (as these characters represent them) to abide on their own. The reinsertion of protagonist characters into their birth-family settings should be approached with recognition of the historical use of such narrative devices to restrict women, but critics must also remain open to the possibility that the device is not used regressively. Dramatic narratives require a site of conflict, and I consider these series together because they take the family as their site of conflict, as opposed to forces of evil, the bittersweet search for a romantic companion, or workplace settings. The uniform denial of the traditional nuclear family as it appears in series such as *thirtysomething* or *7th Heaven* makes these family dramas unusual and likely results from writers' waryness of reproducing environments traditionally dominated by patriarchal gender norms. Given the multiplicity of series about women that circulate alongside the protagonist-centered family dramas and do not emphasize traditional family constructs, it would be shortsighted to categorically denounce stories about women and their families as antifeminist or inherently conservative. These stories could be told as a critique of their inability to succeed, but the series considered here deny that interpretation and allow much greater depth to their protagonists than afforded to the self-sacrificing mothers who have often inhabited dramatic narratives.

It is also important to acknowledge that my analysis aims to note similarities. While each series utilizes a return-home narrative, it would be reductive to assume that each tells the same story and negotiates familial situations in the same way. *Any Day Now,* for example, focuses little attention on the mother/daughter relationship after the first season, instead utilizing Rene's friendship with Mary Elizabeth and the crises of her friend's family for its primary narrative content. Similarly, *Gilmore Girls'* refusal of physical relocation aids its exploration of how a community of non-blood relatives can serve as family and leads it to consider stories very different from those of *Providence* and *Judging Amy.* These stories about women who renegotiate familial roles of daughter and sister as adults provide uncommon narratives instead of rehashing repeatedly told domestic stories in situation comedies. At the same time, however, the repeated use of this strategy obscures other possibilities for family constructions. Could Amy or Sydney find support in a community of friends as seen in *Sex and the City?* Is there a different support structure available to aid Amy in raising her child? Must Sydney adopt a conventional maternal role to help her siblings and father through the loss of her mother? And why must she be the caretaker?

Reinventing Careers: Doing Something That Will Make a Difference

As the protagonists return home to an idyllic New England community, many also reevaluate their careers and discard their original career path for work that provides a sense of contributing to the larger society. This motif appears most distinctly in series with characters that physically return home: *Providence, Judging Amy,* and *Any Day Now.*

In *Providence,* Sydney decides to stray from her specialization as a plastic surgeon to work as a family-practice doctor in a low-income community clinic. The pilot depicts Sydney's Los Angeles practice as overrun with celebrities and others seeking elective surgery to enhance their image. Despite the narcissism that defines some of the patients who try to woo her back to L.A. in early episodes, even preliminary characterizations reveal that she originally entered plastic surgery for altruistic reasons and sought to help disfigured children. A description of the series released by NBC notes that she "entered the field of cosmetic surgery with noble ambitions, but several years of performing collagen lip treatments and nose jobs for celebrities and over-privileged teenagers in Los Angeles began to erode her sense of purpose."[6] Explaining the series' premise, the description continues, "Sydney's disenchantment with her career combined with a relationship breakup and a family crisis prompts her to move back to the *safe haven of Providence* where she *finds fulfillment* working in a low-income medical clinic."[7]

Similarly, Rene in *Any Day Now* chooses to leave corporate law for the grassroots civil rights work that defined her father's firm. The narrative is vague in explaining the type of work she performed in Washington, but her economic status confirms that it was financially well rewarded—especially in contrast to the pro bono work she frequently performs in Birmingham. The series regularly depicts her representing clients who are discriminated against because of ethnicity, gender, sexuality, or religion or pursuing cases in which she defends underdogs who occupy the moral high ground. The series mythologizes her father in 1990s remembrances and 1960s portrayals, depicting him working with Martin Luther King Jr. and playing a vital role in bringing civil rights to Birmingham's African American population.

Amy's move from corporate law takes place prior to the opening of the series; however, the dialogue affirms her career change as a result of seeking work that offers a less materialistic sense of fulfillment. Amy's sense of duty is revealed to be partially inspired by her mother's career as a social worker, although the challenge of a career transition and the status equated with a judgeship also compel her career change. As the final section of this chapter explores, *Judging Amy* depicts Amy's and her mother's struggles against and within imperfect systems of law and government in a much more complex manner than *Providence*'s portrayals of Sydney's medical accomplishments and even the latitude allowed Rene to effect social change. Amy leaves a world of power lunches and salary bonuses and enters a career that exposes heartbreaking realities and makes her responsible for deciding cases of great consequence to those appearing before her.

Lydia's decision to attend college, as a primary narrative catalyst in *That's Life,* is similar to Sydney's, Rene's, and Amy's pursuit of meaningful occupations. A marriage proposal from her longtime boyfriend creates the crisis that necessitates Lydia's life- and status-changing decision. The reality that she could become a wife (and mother) leads her to reevaluate her job hopping, which most recently placed her as a bartender. Lydia's struggles reflect a significant working-class reality that is generally absent from U.S. television. She negotiates among a more limited set of choices and options than those of Sydney, Amy, and Rene. As in the new reality faced by Amy, the narrative uses the difficulties arising from her decision to seek a more fulfilling life to provide challenges she is occasionally unable to surmount.

In *Once and Again,* Lily too faces a reevaluation of her career and the balance between work and family established before her separation. The financial instability of being single (although she continues to rely on her ex-husband for mortgage payments and other support) necessitates that she leave her casual work as part owner of a small bookstore with her sister. Rather than the move from corporate drudgery to the fulfillment of helping others, Lily attempts to reenter the professional world after fifteen years spent mainly as a stay-at-home mom. She receives many rebukes as she realizes that she is no longer perceived to be qualified for the employment she seeks and ultimately accepts a job as an assistant/receptionist for a young female entrepreneur (easily twenty years her junior) who runs a Web magazine. The series depicts her work as a means to a necessary end, similar to the status of Lorelai's work in *Gilmore Girls.* As the manager of the town inn, Lorelai earns a living to support herself and Rory but initially is unable to pursue her dream of opening her own bed and breakfast because of her lack of capital and education.[8]

Many of the family dramas employ the recurrent narrative strategy of new employment to correspond with the various other life reconfigurations faced by female protagonists. To some extent, these career changes provide a narrative obstacle around which the series can explore a multitude of stories. The acknowledgment of a bifurcation between work that is highly rewarded financially (and consequently of great status in a capitalistic society) and work that is personally fulfilling on an emotional or humanitarian level is also significant. Again, given the ways women's career options have been circumscribed, even in narratives superficially offering them gains, this repeated story of professional women forgoing financial status for more emotionally fulfilling work indicates something significant about societal expectations of women's work and roles. Each of the series depicts the protagonist as capable of succeeding in traditionally male-dominated occupations. Rather than a backlash or undercutting of the women's career gains, the career-change decisions are constructed as a commentary on the superficiality of capitalistic values.

The depiction of working women who eschew corrupt or limiting spaces radically shifts the common motif of a decade earlier. The 1980s offered many stories about women proving that they could succeed alongside men; such women adopted the trappings of the power suit and win-at-all-costs mentality depicted as standard within male-dominated corporate cultures (*Baby Boom, L.A. Law*). The protagonists in late 1990s dramas do not flee the corporate world because they are less able than their male or female counterparts but because they have found the system to be bankrupt and choose to evaluate their success by an alternative measure.

This discourse of corporate life as unfulfilling is not unique to female-centered dramas; the NBC series *Ed* (2000–2004) enacts a similar return home (to idyllic small-town Indiana) and redefinition of career for its lead male character. The WB series *Everwood* (2002–) also uses this story and emphasizes that the protagonist's pursuit of a career as a brain surgeon led to his failure as a father and husband. The death of his wife in the pilot leads Andy Brown to exile himself from his New York career and retreat to idyllic small-town Everwood, Colorado, where he attempts to connect with his children and opens a free clinic. Other series debuting alongside these protagonist-centered family dramas and idealizing corporate culture and its excesses (*Bull, The $treet, Titans*) failed to attract audiences, perhaps indicating that the majority of audience members were not eager to embrace corporate heroes even before the U.S. economy sputtered in late 2000 and the Enron scandal disenchanted Americans with corporate behavior. Although the new careers Sydney, Amy, and Rene seek are not as financially rewarding as those they left, they remain in professional roles that in no way indicate a containment of female work within a pink-collar ghetto. Sydney and Rene retain their status as doctor and lawyer, while Amy continues to face challenges that result from entering a field still dominated by old-boys'-club dealings.

The branding of these series as stories for women is also important in evaluating the significance of narratives about characters' decisions to abandon male-dominated spaces and corporate cultures. The varied dramatic stories appearing in the late 1990s indicate a revised cultural context from the 1980s, and the critical strategies used to assess the containment of female characters must be revised as well. If only one of these series had aired in the mid 1980s alongside female depictions (or absences) in series such as *The Cosby Show, Magnum, P.I.,* and *thirtysomething,* a reading of Sydney, Amy, or Rene as enacting a martyring of women's professional abilities or a suppression of women's gains would be much more compelling than the understandings available in the late 1990s and beginning of the twenty-first century. Rather than indicating that women are unable to perform in corporate worlds still dominated by men, these 1990s series offer utopian escape for their characters and a validation for any viewer who struggles over questions about what one's work ultimately contributes to one's community. The shifts to "fulfilling" work are utopian, however, in that none of the shows depicts the characters suffering a change in economic status because of her new career. To the degree that producers and network executives seek television narratives that attract audiences, the moral high ground exhibited in the career choices of the lead characters makes them all the more compelling and heroic.

This analysis of motifs focuses on illustrating similarities among the series, yet it should not be construed as evidence that the protagonist-centered family dramas construct redundant or formulaic characterizations or stories. Their development cycles suggest that these series developed independently rather than as high-concept recombinations (*St. Elsewhere* as *Hill Street Blues* set in a hospital, for example). The recurrence of these motifs may result from an awareness of certain cultural concerns and angst arising in the broader social sphere these series represent. The story of going home is not new, but it previously has been set in comedic settings with humor arising from conflicts in perspective between those who stayed and those who left and returned. In contrast, these dramatic series offer a sophisticated and detailed portrayal of the emotional pain of reconciling various perceptions of self with static notions held by parents and siblings. Nor do the mythic settings populated by quirky and idealized communities provide innovation, as television audiences once enraptured with *Northern Exposure* and *Twin Peaks* can testify. Still, the construction of these spaces in multiple dramatic series dominated by a single protagonist evokes notions of newness and differentiation. Despite the formulaic similarities outlined to this point, the most noteworthy accomplishment of these protagonist-centered family dramas is their use of nearly identical tools to tell remarkably divergent stories. A comparison of *Providence* and *Judging Amy* indicates their variation in politics, perspectives, and ultimately the stories told about women's lives despite their superficial similarity.

Different Stories from Similar Roots

Providence and *Judging Amy* exemplify the protagonist-centered family drama, each subtly varying the conventions of dramatic style in a manner that makes the series strikingly different from one another. Disparate narrative emphases (the family in *Providence* and the protagonist in *Judging Amy*) account for much of the variation in stories, narrative crises, and solutions. Despite the many similarities among protagonist-centered family dramas, particularly between *Providence* and *Judging Amy,* their divergences are crucial to the narrative options available in each. Viewers familiar with *Any Day Now* may recognize that it provides a valuable counterpoint to the contrast between *Providence* and *Judging Amy* in its focus on two protagonists—it emphasizes family stories in plotlines about Mary Elizabeth and protagonist-centered stories about Rene.

Providence concentrates on Sydney, but narratives exploring her handling of her roles as daughter and sister (and as a replacement for her mother) ultimately define her characterization and the stories the series tells, thereby displacing the centrality of her identity in some ways. The common episode construction assigns her two plotlines: one focusing on her personal life, and the other on an aspect of her professional obligations, often a medical crisis that it seems only she can solve. Each episode includes at least one additional primary plot and a secondary plot that alternatively explore the lives of the other residents of the Hansen home: her sister Joanie, brother Robbie, and father Jim. Consequently, the cumulative text of the series explores her family and their struggles with regular connection of Sydney's individual storylines to the family. The emphasis on home and family prescribes certain solutions to the problems encountered because the central narrative question becomes whether the family unit can be maintained. Similar to the domestic sitcom, the family unit serves to contain problems and limit the scope of possible solutions.[9] In terms of gender issues, institutional critique and structural social change never appear as options in this version of the protagonist-centered family drama because of its emphasis on the individual as a component of the family.

Like Sydney, Amy returns to her childhood home, but with a six-year-old daughter and in the process of a divorce. Also similar to *Providence, Judging Amy* features competing primary plots about an aspect of Amy's professional life as a family-court judge and a dilemma within her family. Amy's surviving parent, her mother Maxine (Tyne Daly), works away from home as a social worker with the Department of Children and Families (DCF), and the narrative describes her as a local legend for her work. Amy and Lauren are the primary residents of her mother's home, although her brothers Vincent and Peter and Amy's cousin Kyle maintain a presence in family affairs. The series uses an episode construction similar to *Providence,* providing Amy with a personal and professional plot, Maxine often with a separate storyline, and one of the brothers or Kyle also advances a narrative.[10] Unlike Sydney's "personal" storylines, which often introduce a romantic suitor, Amy's personal stories almost always focus on her family—particularly her balancing of her roles as mother and judge.

Key narrative differences allow the shows to explore conflict with discrepant emphases and outcomes. Some of these differences are subtle and appear incidental, while others clearly result from intentional narrative constructions. The introduction of conflict and the process of its abatement serve as primary narrative requirements of drama, and examining both series' construction of social and familial conflict, as well as the avenues allowed for its resolution, reveals important differences between them. The remainder of this section considers two areas that illustrate the disparate narratives explored by these series and what this means in terms of their identity and ideology. The variant stories about Sydney and Amy negotiating social structures relative to the "power" afforded their characters delimit the expansive gulf between two series with exceptional formal similarity and even characters with striking physical resemblance. The portrayal of family and relationships in each character's life demarcates an additional distinction between them.

That two series built on nearly identical frameworks can tell such different stories is valuable on two levels. Within analysis of the protagonist-centered family dramas, these two series indicate the range of stories that can be explored within a familial context. At the broader level of female-centered dramas in the late 1990s, the variation within this type as well as their variation from other types provides further evidence of the ample range of stories about women's lives told at this time. The range of stories these series offer further aids in deconstructing gender stereotypes by making them uninhabitable.

Unstoppable Individualism or Struggling within Flawed Structures: The Status of Systems and Institutions

Sydney and Amy work in careers that are part of expansive social systems (the U.S. health-care industry and legal system, respectively), but the characters occupy discrepant levels of empowerment because of creative decisions rather than an inherent disparity in their jobs. *Providence* adopts the noble-doctor tradition by drawing Sydney as an individual who is not bound by a system that limits her abilities. This romantic view places the sole responsibility for life and death in the hands of the doctor. When Syd struggles with a case, it is because of something originating within her, as when she questions her abilities as a family doctor[11] or experiences difficulty overcoming the effects of a bout of encephalitis.[12] Similarly, medical successes are attributed to her unwavering devotion and willingness to surmount any obstacle to help her patients, whether she must challenge the Immigration and Naturalization Service to prevent the deportation of a boy with a cleft palate[13] or defy the diagnosis of the Centers for Disease Control to save a friend who apparently suffers from the Ebola virus.[14] The common trajectory of Sydney's medical storylines depict her as the patient's only hope, chart her unrelenting search to solve the problem (she often succeeds because she follows her "instincts"), and provide her with a victory in the end by saving the patient or making the critical diagnosis.

The narrative organization confines most of these plotlines to individual episodes; however, an interesting exception reinforces the narrative reliance on Sydney as an exceptional individual. Although she conquers the bureaucracy and policy of U.S. immigration, she meets a seemingly insurmountable foe in the form of a pharmaceutical company who will not release a dose of a trial drug for a dying infant.[15] By the episode's end she obtains the necessary dose, but only through the aid of a young congressman who recently established an office next to the clinic. The narrative arranges for the prototypic *Providence* ending: Sydney rushes to the company to pick up the medication and hurries into the hospital to administer the dose. In a break from convention, however, she arrives too late; the infant has died (the death of an infant or child is especially unusual on this series).

This apparent "failure" prepares a three-episode story arc in which Syd challenges the pharmaceutical company after they cancel testing of this drug because it cures an affliction suffered by too few to return a profit and is not cost-efficient. Subsequent episodes reveal her failure to save the infant as the catalyst to provoke the larger battle of an individual taking on an enormous corporate entity. Her friend calls congressional hearings, and although Syd eventually succeeds in getting the drug released, her romantic involvement with the married congressman instigates a subplot that takes precedence. The fact that she triumphs despite the enormous resources of the pharmaceutical giant and its connections to the politicians to whom she appeals is exemplary of *Providence*'s depiction of Sydney and her abilities.

In contrast, *Judging Amy* regularly explores the failure of government agencies to aid children and families and often depicts the irresolvable double-binds institutional regulations impose on those trying to intervene. Amy's career as a family-court judge, in concert with the issues that develop in relation to her mother's social work, allow a regular interrogation of public systems of law and justice in which the individual plays a much less significant role in comparison with the possibilities for personal healing afforded to Sydney as a lone physician. Situations painted in myriad shades of ethical and legal gray often complicate *Judging Amy*'s stories in contrast to the clearly defined ethical dichotomies offered by *Providence*. Amy and Maxine fail because of flaws in the system and their own limitations, which ultimately leads the series to contemplate disparate perspectives through characters of substantial complexity.

Judging Amy does not establish a clear narrative formula, and thus it is difficult to identify prototypic episodes or handling of issues. Because many episodes present situations that Amy and Maxine cannot completely or even partially assuage, *Judging Amy* tends to tell stories that examine how its characters handle the situations and dilemmas that they face. Most episodes explore the psychological effects of confronting ambiguous and contradictory systems of law, justice, and public service. The professional and familial often blend as stories depict the effect of personal events on the characters' professional judgment. When Vincent is shot in a robbery, Amy struggles with the sentencing of a fifteen-year-old boy found guilty of shooting a ten-year-old bystander.[16] Maxine experiences overwhelming anger because of her helplessness to prevent many of the atrocities she sees children suffer and protect her own children.[17] Amy makes a ruling that seems inconsistent with the law she cites and her precedents in supporting the rights of a fetus over that of its mother in the aftermath of Peter and his wife having their adopted son revoked by his biological mother.[18] *Judging Amy*'s narrative weaves together personal and professional events to develop psychologically complex characters who evolve and are full of contradictions.

Amy and Maxine lack the self-determination afforded by *Providence*'s individualism and instead must find ways to persevere even when they are unable to act and a family member impugns the system for which they work. In "Dog Days," Amy cannot rule in favor of an older sibling who brings a case against her cult-involved parents to prevent them from marrying off her eleven-year-old sister because the prosecution lacks support for their case.[19] Elsewhere in the courthouse, a prosecutor forces Maxine to testify against a teenage girl once in her care who shot and killed her sexually abusive stepfather, undermining Maxine's sense of who she serves. While Amy and Maxine struggle with their limited roles in a system that seems especially flawed, Vincent, now working as an investigative reporter for the Hartford newspaper, writes an exposé of the foster-care system, which he indicts as a "noble failure," further calling into question the work performed by his mother and sister.

The consequence of the series' divergent strategies for placing their protagonists in public space results in very different stories despite the many structural similarities between them. Sydney and Amy are ultimately disparate types of characters, which likely affects the audiences drawn to the series and how viewers identify with or relate to the characters. Sydney is unquestionably a heroic character who inspires emulation. The series provides escapist television with a fictional universe in which the heroine's great individual powers allow her to save the day by episode's end. Although there is a weekly threat of disease or death that she must defeat—and often a threat to the family as well—the formulaic structure reassures repeat viewers who

know convention dictates that all will be resolved and uncertainty elimi-
nated. In contrast, *Judging Amy* depicts Amy and Maxine as flawed characters who are unable to inspire the same comfortable knowledge that children will be safe from their abusers and the wrongs of the world will be
repaired by the end of the hour. Because of the characters' complex psychology, viewers often see them behave inappropriately as they try to reconcile competing demands, institutional regulations, and inadequate resources. Viewers of *Judging Amy* encounter complicated tales about enduring
trials in a manner that is more likely to provoke than reassure.

The discrepancy between the medical and legal professions does not account for Sydney's ability to triumph as an individual in contrast to Amy's
system-generated limitations. Many stories from late 1990s medical franchises
such as *E.R., Chicago Hope,* and *City of Angels* depict doctors who are con-
strained by hospital policies and especially the stranglehold of health-insur-
ance companies. Likewise, *Judging Amy* could allow Amy a much more activist judicial role that would permit her the individual triumphs achieved by
Sydney. These series choose to tell distinct stories built from specific ideological frameworks for the articulation and negotiation of dramatic conflicts.
This variance in perspective provides an exceptionally powerful tool in constructing the brand, or identity, of the shows. Ultimately, the specific ontol-
ogy of each series overwhelms the structural similarities until the resemblance
disappears.

The Drama *of Family Drama:*
External Threats versus Internal Negotiation

As indicated by the episode structure of *Providence* and *Judging Amy,* the series place stories about the characters' pursuit of partnership and their roles
as family members on par with their professional struggles and dilemmas.
The narrative strategies used to explore the personal lives of Sydney and Amy
are as important as the depiction of their professional lives in establishing the
narrative identity and ideological valence of each series. Unsurprisingly, the
series construct and resolve family crises in disparate ways and afford Sydney's and Amy's romantic lives a different degree of importance. Exploring
these discrepancies provides further evidence of the divergent stories the series tell and expands my argument about their variant ideological identities.

Prototypic family stories in *Providence* introduce a threat to the family
that is resolved by the episode's end. Many crises are not explicitly threats to
the family as a whole but result from one character's mistake that threatens
his or her personal status, thereby affecting the family indirectly. Storylines

involving Syd's brother Robbie regularly fulfill this role, as he repeatedly finds himself in minor legal scrapes. The individual's failure to abide by norms of appropriate behavior potentially undermines the stability of the family unit when Robbie develops a gambling problem,[20] is caught in a game-show scandal,[21] or accepts bets on a children's hockey league;[22] or when Joanie spirals into an alcoholic depression after a miscarriage.[23] Disease also threatens family members when Hannah appears to have tuberculosis,[24] Syd lapses into a coma caused by encephalitis,[25] or health officials quarantine the Hansen home to limit an Ebola outbreak.[26]

Providence also frequently features physical or psychological threats to the family in narratives in which the family unit as it resides in Providence is placed in jeopardy of disruption. Such a story occurs when a multinational corporation offers Joanie a distribution deal for her secret chowder recipe but requires her to relocate to Japan.[27] This scenario repeats when the Hansen's millionaire maternal grandfather offers each child a job and a large sum of money on the condition that they relocate to three distant cities.[28] Even their deceased mother's past threatens the family when Syd recalls a repressed memory that suggests she had an affair,[29] or when a man who was engaged to her returns and claims to be Syd's father.[30] Threats to the family also result from personal-relationship crises, which are depicted as an area of primary narrative importance for the members of the Hansen family. Throughout the series, a variety of suitors for Sydney, Joanie, Robbie, and occasionally the widower Jim circulate through the revolving front door of the Hansen home.[31] The inevitable failure of these relationships often leaves the characters distressed and compromises their ability to fulfill family roles.

The emphasis on and depiction of Sydney's repeated failed romances figures prominently in the cumulative text. Romantic involvement functions as her Achilles' heel, and relationship failures often confound her weekly medical miracles. At times, the series attempts to characterize Syd as lacking the ability to relate with family, friends, or romantic partners—a limitation explicitly juxtaposed against her significant intellectual abilities and professional success. Although this dichotomy may have been part of the original characterization, subsequent episodes (and perhaps the casting) undermined this tension, eliminating its narrative importance. *Providence* concludes its cumulative narrative with Sydney's wedding and decision to follow her husband to a new job in Chicago. Her achievement of marital union serves as the conclusion of the ongoing story chronicling her inability to maintain a romantic relationship. The final episode also emphasizes Sydney's decision to leave Providence as the conclusion of a chapter of her life. Robbie has married, begun a family, and started a business, and Joanie is completing college and has a new romantic interest. The newfound stability of her siblings suggests that Syd is no longer needed as a surrogate mother. Her departure is clearly most difficult for her father, who has not found a partner to replace his wife. Closing the series with a wedding was not surprising, but the decision to break apart the family provided an abrupt departure. Syd must leave her family to stay with her husband, which forces her to make the type of decision frequently faced by the action heroines. However, unlike a character such as Buffy, she chooses a romantic interest above her family and career.[32]

Despite this final departure, struggle among the members of the Hansen family is curiously absent from the manifestation of discord in relation to the family. Jim offers subtle reprimands to Robbie for his illegal escapades, and Syd and Joanie have moments of rivalry, but for the most part, the relations among the family members lack animosity. The closest expression of familial strife results from Joanie or Robbie occasionally acknowledging that they feel that their lives are not as successful as Sydney's, but this jealousy is buried deeply and does not develop as a narrative force. Challenges to the Hansen family and the ensuing drama result from external triggers. This is not the case for the Gray family, where relational tensions remain just below the surface and are explicitly expressed in nearly every episode. The series portrays the Gray family as facing threats from "within" as a result of the series' emphasis on family as a site of complicated relationships that are grounded in love but threatened by jealousy and personal uncertainties.

The Grays also face external threats. Vincent seems a particular target, as plots make him the victim of a robbery and an explosion.[33] Peter also introduces a painful loss for the family, as episodes over the first two seasons chronicle his and his wife Gillian's difficulty conceiving a child, their care for a pregnant young woman whose child they will adopt, the adoption, and then the woman's legal suit to regain custody. Later seasons explore Gillian's surprise pregnancy, which the family believes will result in a child with severe birth defects. The child defies expectations and is born healthy, but Gillian spends five weeks in a coma after giving birth, a complication that leads her to reevaluate her life and separate from Peter. These examples prove the exception, as the majority of narrative time spent examining family in this series focuses on the characters' relationships. A family dinner in the pilot episode sets the general tone for the series. Amy and Maxine are finishing dinner preparations in the kitchen after Amy has had a challenging first day in her new job as judge:

> Amy: You called the cops on me.
> Maxine: Randy is not like a cop. He's like a friend. With a badge and a gun. I
>   was concerned. I'm sorry. It won't happen again.
> Amy: Well, that's good to hear.

(Camera cuts to others around the table.)

Peter: How do you like Hartford, Lauren? It's better than New York, isn't it?

Lauren: No.

Peter: Sure, it is. You didn't have a big front yard like this in Manhattan.

Vincent: That's the great thing about Uncle Peter. He gives you the question and the answer.

Gillian: They can always visit the city. It's not that far.

Peter: There's nothing in Manhattan you can't find right here in Hartford.

Vincent: Exactly. Crime, poverty, unemployment.

Peter: You'd know about unemployment.

Vincent: I have a job.

Peter: Well, the point is that Amy and Lauren were both stressed out in the city. They're obviously happier in Connecticut.

Lauren (to Amy): Why are they talking about us like we're not here?

Amy: Because it's a family tradition, sweetie.

Maxine: I wanna hear about Amy's first day in court. Who was there from the attorney general's office?

Amy: Some guy named Dobbs.

Maxine: He's a punk. Who was there from DCF?

Amy: Lena Railsback.

Maxine: Lena? She's the absolute best.

Amy: I'm not sure all her bases were covered on this one.

Maxine: Sure they were.

Amy: I didn't see you in the courtroom.

Maxine: I know Lena. She's thorough.

Amy: Well, she failed to locate the father.

Maxine: If she can't find him, he can't be found.

Amy: You can't just make an assumption like that.

Maxine: Excuse me, Miss five-minutes-on-the-bench.

Amy: How dare you say that to me?

Maxine: You're a corporate lawyer. Suddenly you're the expert?

Amy: Well, I didn't win the judgeship in a raffle.

Maxine: Well, not far from it.

Amy: Excuse me?

Peter: A friend from Harvard put your name in. That's the next best thing.

Amy: The Bar Association approached me. I didn't go looking for this job, and then I spent six months of my life working my ass off trying to qualify.

Peter: Wow, six whole months.

Maxine: Stop fighting. I wanna eat.

Amy: And, besides, in order to have friends from Harvard, you have to get in to Harvard. Don't you?

Vincent (to Lauren): This is what we call middle-class angst.

(Telephone rings)

Lauren: That's Daddy! Hello? Daddy, I knew it was you.

Maxine: How's the in vitro going, Gillian? Did it take this time?

Gillian: Excuse me. (Leaves the table).

Peter: Mother. (Follows Gillian).

Maxine: Well, she's never been shy about it before. I know more about her
ovaries than I do my own.

Lauren: Mommy, Daddy wants to talk to you.

Amy: Hi. How are you? Uh, you know . . . first day.

Maxine: Lauren, come taste this chicken.

Amy: No. It was . . . it was weird . . . all those people lookin' at me and expectin'
me to know stuff. Wednesday? Uh, I thought we talked about the weekend.
No. No, Michael. I don't think it's a good idea. Because I have my swearing-
in thing. I . . . why do you wanna be there?

Lauren: Mom, he's invited.

Amy: I'm gonna call you later . . . OK? (Returns to table, glares at Maxine, walks
out of the room)

Lauren: Mom, can he still come? (Follows Amy)

Vincent (to Maxine): You sure can clear a room.

Maxine: It hasn't worked on you yet.[34]

The series establishes many of the primary sites of disagreement and causes
of personal insecurity among the characters in less than three and a half minutes of screen time. Peter reveals his feelings of inadequacy in not accom-
plishing the educational or career achievements attained by Amy and Vincent and his insecurity about never having left Hartford. The family's lack of
understanding of what it means to be a writer surfaces, as they believe that
since Vincent does not rise, dress, go off to work, and return indicates that he
does not work. Amy's need for validation conflicts with Maxine's desire for
the same. Maxine's disappointment that Amy has not explained the collapse
of her marriage leads her to create a venue for seeing Michael, also undermining Amy's need for self-determination. The scene emphasizes the importance of getting pregnant to Gillian, as well as Maxine's disregard for scientific solutions and discussion of intimate details. The episode does not
resolve these anxieties, but they keep returning throughout the series as the
siblings struggle to validate their decisions about their lives and the corresponding perceptions the others make of them.

Another important component of the series is its more abstract examination of family, made possible through Maxine's case work and Amy's courtroom stories. These contexts provide space to explore notions of family and
complications of families that come undone, often in tragic situations. This
type of story lacks the underlying safety that exists even during the dining-
room sparring. Here threats to family move from potential to reality, with no

way to adequately repair the damage. Consequently, the institution of family is much less stable in this series than in *Providence* or most others on television.[35] While *Providence* idealizes family, family provides a site of disorder and conflict for Maxine, who routinely encounters abuses of all kinds occurring within the walls of family homes, and for Amy, who hears the most egregious situations and must offer remedy. The series regularly indicates that family only provides safe haven for a few, rather than as a norm, and that even the Gray family struggles through discord and troubled times. This articulation remains distinct from dystopian family situation comedies such as *Married . . . with Children* or *Roseanne*. *Judging Amy* makes family as important as the saccharine families of *The Brady Bunch*, *The Cosby Show*, and *Providence* but tells stories about the complex relationships that occur in these spaces, simultaneously challenging cultural notions of a strong family life as the solution to all problems and questioning the ability of the institution to assuage social needs.

Stories about romantic relationships in *Judging Amy* lack the emphasis evident in *Providence*. *Judging Amy* explores romantic relationships in a way that affords the characters greater psychological depth. An extended plot arc following the loss of their adopted child depicts how different means of coping with tragedy strain Gillian and Peter's marriage. As Vincent's relationship with his girlfriend Carole becomes more serious, episodes depict the characters negotiating the effects of their disparate family experiences on their behavior. Maxine's budding relationship with a wealthy tycoon challenges the independence she established as a widow and leads to complications with his children. The series perhaps gives the least emphasis (particularly in the first three seasons) to developing a relationship for Amy. Instead, the narrative makes an effort to allow her character to become comfortable with being single by leaving her little time to contemplate romantic companionship because of the demands of her job, Lauren, and her other family members.[36]

The depiction of family life and relationship crises in *Providence* and *Judging Amy* further underscores the exceptional disparity between these series. The established conventions of the series make *Providence* a safe place despite the regular threats to health, jobs, and the presence of the characters within the family home. In comparison with *Judging Amy*, the threats depicted in *Providence* ultimately seem superficial. The relations among the Gray family are much more fragile, as this series establishes a narrative space in which the viewer can imagine a character suffering a hurt that leads to estrangement. The depiction of the Gray family and its connection with the cases of familial dysfunction reviewed by Amy and Maxine make the concept of family a site of examination rather than an assumed haven.

I include an assessment of the varied importance of romantic relationships for the protagonists in this section because of the series' divergent emphases and because stories about romantic companionship have provided a site of containment for many previous "strong woman" characters. Previous narratives have allowed female characters atypical professional empowerment and then "punished" them by portraying them as unable to find fulfillment because of the lack of a romantic partner. It is clear that the depiction of Sydney's dating life falls much more within this convention than Amy's (although Syd "succeeds" in the end). The lack of emphasis on romantic companionship for Amy (manifest as her lack of concern about or attention to dating) is unusual when compared with *Providence* and the history of similar television characters.

* * *

The analysis throughout this book illustrates the inadequacy of relying on conventional tools of analysis and precedents of female "containment." The discrepancy in stories told by series such as *Providence* and *Judging Amy* (in a telescape that contains many other series with similarities and variation) indicates a narrative environment unlike those existing previously, which requires reevaluation of the significance of how containment motifs in previous stories might have alternative meanings in an era of a multiplicity of stories. I did not intend to create a hierarchy of "better" or "more feminist" narratives, although readers may have made such an evaluation independently. Rather, the difference itself is noteworthy; the simultaneous existence of these series and the other protagonist-centered family dramas allows female audiences with distinct and varied narrative preferences an abundance of stories.

The comparison of these series also illustrates the problem of using simplistic analytical constructs such as role models. Who is the better role model, Sydney or Amy? Although the narrative of *Providence* enables Sydney with more heroic achievement, it is difficult to assert that she is a "better" or more feminist character. *Judging Amy* depicts Amy as fallible and imperfect, a characterization that provides the series with much of its dramatic depth but complicates attempts to envision her as a role model. Fallibility was certainly a characteristic disproportionately shared by the few female characters occupying professional careers previously in television history; however, the context considered here illustrates that individual series no longer carry the weight of representing the entirety of female experience. The larger sociocultural, institutional, and textual contexts of these series indicate the need for more nuanced assessments of the significance of female characters and the stories told about their lives.

Female audience members have choices previously unavailable, and many vote with their remote controls weekly. Among the many female-centered series airing on broadcast and cable networks at the beginning of the twenty-first century, *Providence* and *Judging Amy* are the overwhelming favorites of U.S. audiences based on ratings and audience shares. Television audiences have fragmented so extensively that it is possible that entirely different audiences view these series; the analysis in the second section of this chapter certainly suggests they appeal to very different narrative preferences.

Overall, this chapter indicates a great deal about the narrative strategies used to hail female audiences and both the commonalities and the disparities among the stories network executives perceive female audiences to desire. The subtle variation in common motifs of mythic spaces, returning home, and reinventing careers at first appears to indicate exceptional standardization among protagonist-centered family dramas despite the multitude available. Close analysis of *Providence* and *Judging Amy* illustrates the fallacy of this superficial assessment and attests to the different narrative ends achieved by writers and producers who appear to start from the same fount. Examination of the protagonist-centered family drama reveals that many different stories and types of stories about female characters and families (defined in many different ways) now circulate. The recurrent motifs are noteworthy, as other series based on these successes are likely to populate network schedules in coming seasons. The use of these motifs for varied ends and the continued production of distinctive and differentiated stories about female characters and families marks the vitality of these stories in the cultural imagination.

5.   Of Female Cops and Docs: The Reformulation of Workplace Dramas and Other Trends in Mixed-Sex Ensembles

One of the first representational issues targeted by feminist criticism was television's limited depiction of women as workers outside of the home. The single-woman character dates to television's early years; however, depictions of women in the workforce after marriage or in lieu of homemaking and motherhood did not appear in a significant manner until the 1970s, and even then often enforced hegemonic American gender roles. Dramatic franchise series about male detectives, doctors, and lawyers have long told stories about the duties of work, but women rarely had a space in these worlds. Few stories about the work women do outside the home have been featured by television narratives, and until recently, stories about career women have primarily chronicled their struggle and difficulty with balancing careers, motherhood, marriage, and traditional constructs of femininity.

Second-wave feminism's emphasis on seeking equality for women in the public sphere made creating career opportunities for women the central activist project, and the results endure as one of the movement's greatest legacies. Like the changing American workplace, U.S. television series increasingly incorporated working women into their casts, with marked change beginning in the 1970s and early 1980s. As explored in the introduction, depictions of female characters pursuing professional careers developed for self-serving reasons when advertisers realized the consumption power of real-world working women.[1] Consequently, the stories about working women that did emerge in dramatic series focused on one particular type of work—that of the career woman. Dramatic stories about working women continued to ignore the work done by poor and most middle-class women, just as the working class has been nearly absent from U.S. television throughout its history.

Television depictions of career women have drawn attention as apparently feminist by definition because of characters' access to spaces outside of the home.[2] The careers of characters in *The Mary Tyler Moore Show, Murphy Brown, Cagney and Lacey,* and even *Charlie's Angels* were seen as progressive because their pursuit of careers indicated cultural importance, regardless of other, less feminist narrative and representational aspects. In the 1980s, female characters began more frequently appearing in roles with narrative significance, as they moved from secretary and nurse to detective and doctor.[3] Embodying career roles, however, still did not lead to many stories about women and their work.[4]

As stories about working women increased in the 1980s, two narrative trends developed that effectively contained the exploration of new stories about women in career roles. As women pursued a liberal feminist agenda that required assimilation into male-dominated workplaces, television series featured stories that suggested women are ill-suited for professional roles or could not be both mothers and career women. The career opportunities afforded these characters led to repeated stories about women's difficulty participating in the workforce, a reasonable story in moderation, as many real women likely had such experiences, but not as a primary type of story repeated across many series. The underlying message of these stories often suggested that women should concede their careers; *Baby Boom, L.A. Law,* and *thirtysomething* provide examples of such characters grappling with new gender scripts and modes of femininity.[5]

In contrast, other series presented stories that simply assumed women could balance work in the public sphere and at home with no difficulty. Networks depicted female characters who traversed the boundary between work and home, many of whom were primarily included in narratives set in the home. Such characterizations contributed to creating the "superwoman" who breezed through occupational demands (always off camera) and "second shift" duties at home (*The Cosby Show, Family Ties, Growing Pains*). These series rarely told stories about women doing work, despite attempting to associate themselves with the progressive trend of depicting women as qualified to work outside the home.

Even series that represented women as able workers and avoided narratives about the challenges they faced in the workplace had difficulty constructing stories that resonated with audiences. Despite the narrative importance of her role and the occupational power of her character, Joyce Davenport (Veronica Hamel) of *Hill Street Blues* presented a narrowly defined "career-woman femininity" that some female viewers found alienating, contradicting producers' efforts to offer empowered characters.[6] The tough veneer worn by Davenport and her contemporaries—a revised femininity donned to survive sexist public spaces—further indicates the challenges in characterization and storytelling strategy that emerged as series began integrating women into the workplace.

The newness of the type, the network-era institutional context, and the conservative political era of backlash in which these series aired led each character to bear a tremendous representational burden. The paucity of working-women characters and the dominance of role-model frameworks for analysis led these characters to serve as bellwethers for understanding and communicating cultural shifts. Many of these shows could have told a greater diversity of stories about women in the workplace, but the attention to these characters as indicative of the success of feminist efforts provided a narrative straightjacket.

By the late 1990s, however, depictions of female characters' choices in work and motherhood derived new meaning. The new multiplicity and diversity of female characters required new critical models for assessing representations. Where the depiction of Amy Gray's struggle in balancing work and life as a single mother might have been interpreted as a cautionary tale in the 1980s, by the 1990s her situation had gained social acceptance, and *Judging Amy* circulated among a broad range of other stories about women, work, and family. This makes it possible to assess this story as a service to those women with whom her struggles resonate, rather than as a conservative attempt to send her back to a failed marriage or into the domestic sphere. The "diversity" of female representations remains limited to those who are white, conventionally attractive, and for the most part, upper-middle-class, but the breadth of female characters at the center of narratives requires that critics account for the changed cultural context and representational environment. Despite various cultural and institutional changes, employment in a professional career remains a crucial component of female representations that critics consider progressive.[7]

Workplace dramas tell stories distinctive from those featured in other narrative types regardless of the universal presence of careers among the characters in the female-centered dramas at the turn of the twenty-first century. The heroines in action dramas often perform jobs that are secondary to their main capacity as warriors, but regardless of the nontraditional nature of this "employment," the heroines' saving-the-world activities primarily circumscribe them as nondomestic or as workers. Similarly, careers provide a defining feature of the comedic drama's new-woman characters, although the stories rarely emphasize the characters facing challenges because of their professional status. *Ally McBeal* and *Sex and the City* (despite their varying narrative occupation of "work" spaces) use storylines resulting from the characters' professions, such as the cases Ally works on and the stories Carrie writes, to probe issues related to their personal lives. Protagonist-centered family dramas often depict the characters struggling to balance professional activities and their personal lives, and many also focus on characters performing career tasks. The workplace cannot become of primary importance, however, because of the narrative equilibrium these series seek between stories of the protagonists' professional duties and their roles as daughter, mother, or sister. Mixed-sex workplace ensembles and series with mostly female casts, such as *Strong Medicine* and *The Division*, provide distinctive narratives that explore stories about public spaces and a diverse range of female characters.

Narrative and Thematic Attributes of Workplace Dramas

The predominant types of dramatic series throughout U.S. broadcast history—the police/detective procedural, the law drama, and medical series—reappear with unfailing consistency because of the sorts of stories their settings allow them to explore. These occupations are well-suited for the episodic nature of television storytelling, as workers in these professions constantly interact with new individuals with new problems, generating new stories. Although *E.R.* may only bear slight resemblance to *Ben Casey* or *NYPD Blue* to *Naked City,* the regular recurrence and gradual evolution of these series reveals much about changes in U.S. culture, from our understanding of diseases and cures to our varying faith in systems of law and order. The central place that workplace dramas occupy in American television storytelling has made them a crucial space for the integration of women; their unfailing repetition and recombination enables critics to trace the gradual progress of female characters into positions of narrative importance.

The predecessors of the characters in *Strong Medicine* and *The Division*, like the women of the second-wave generation, did not find themselves in workspaces accepting of women pursuing careers. Stories about female characters in ensemble narratives often focused on their struggle to infiltrate male spaces and be seen as equals in their colleagues' eyes. These stories emphasize female characters' difficulty balancing their careers with romantic partnership and child rearing or depict male characters questioning their abilities because they are women. Significantly, such stories persist; recent examples depicting complications for female workers include Jamie Ross (Carey Lowell) resigning her assistant district attorney position on *Law and Order* because her ex-husband threatens to challenge her custody of their child because of the number of hours she works, or the surgeon Kate Austin (Christine Lahti) encountering a similar situation on *Chicago Hope* and losing custody of her daughter. The final season of *Homicide: Life on the Street* depicts the challenges Detective Rene Sheppard (Michael Michele) experiences in gaining the respect of other detectives because she was once a beauty-pageant winner and is still an exceptionally attractive woman. Her partner and colleagues are skeptical of her ability to handle the physical aspects of her job.[8]

As part of the shifts in recurring narratives explored through workplace dramas, it is worth noting that some series also emphasize the effect of family demands on male characters—a challenge traditionally faced only by female characters. Harvey Lacey of *Cagney and Lacey* provided an early example of a trend that has since expanded to primary male characters. Early seasons of *E.R.* reversed the situation in which narratives punished women for having demanding careers with repercussions in their family life when Dr. Mark Greene's (Anthony Edwards) marriage ends in divorce because he is unable to devote time to the relationship. His wife later remarries and moves away, which leaves Greene with limited access to his daughter, again because of his career. Dr. Peter Benton (Eriq La Salle) faces a similar challenge in trying to share custody of his infant son with the child's mother. The child's deafness exacerbates Benton's struggle, and the series often depicts the impossibility of balancing the demands of work with the needs of his child. He ultimately resigns from his hectic schedule as an emergency surgeon to gain custody of his son following the death of the child's mother; Detective Rey Curtis (Benjamin Bratt) leaves his job entirely to care for his chronically ill wife and their children on *Law and Order*. Although not emphasized here, the changes in the stories told by late 1990s dramas about women also affect the stories told about men. These series alter previous norms so that female characters increasingly appear as able careerists, and male characters come to realize the family/work double-bind that has long troubled women.

Even ensemble workplace series such as *Law and Order, Homicide,* and *E.R.* do not tell uniform stories about women in the workplace. The professional roles of women appear more naturalized, so that many characters appear as doctors, lawyers, and detectives who are women, rather than as *women* doctors, lawyers, and detectives. This naturalization of women into historically male-dominated careers illustrates an expansion in the range of narratives. The de-emphasis on gender helps series move beyond stories confined to debating the ability of female characters to balance work and home. For example, *Law and Order* and *E.R.* do not depict their doctors, lawyers, and lieutenants as *women* performing jobs so much as they are *people* performing jobs. The shift from highlighting gender when a woman occupies a professional role indicates an acceptance of women in these positions.

The development of "reconfigured" workplace dramas provides the most notable innovation for workplace series in the late 1990s. *Strong Medicine* (2000–2006) and *The Division* (2001–4) both air on Lifetime and move beyond incorporating women into traditionally male spaces to allow them to dominate these spaces in rank and number.[9] Neither series primarily explores stories about women who struggle in their careers because they are women. They also offer the broadest depiction of women as a group composed of individuals with varied needs, experiences, and privileges.[10]

In addition to these reconfigured workspaces, some mixed-sex ensemble series have integrated female characters so that they are no longer exceptional. This development was evident in a variety of series by the early 1990s: doctors in *E.R.;* detectives in *NYPD Blue, Law and Order: Special Victims Unit,* and *Homicide: Life on the Street;* and lawyers in *Law and Order* and *Family Law.* The characters in these mixed-sex ensembles are similar to those in *Strong Medicine* and *The Division;* however, the overwhelmingly female composition of the latter series and their location on a network that specifically targets female audiences enable them to explore stories about women on a weekly basis. Such stories may only receive attention once or twice a season in the mixed-sex ensemble series.

A Space of Their Own: Lifetime's Female-Dominated Workplaces

I have emphasized commonalities by delimiting the characteristics of the type and exploring how prevailing motifs, themes, and elements recur across the series to indicate the similarities and differences of the stories told within each and among all of the narrative types. The workplace dramas require less explanation as a dramatic form; they are defined by their institutional setting, the presence of female characters in professional careers, and their focus on telling stories about the lives of women. In this chapter I examine each series separately and note the different narrative strategies they use to tell stories about women who work in spaces accepting of their presence. *Strong Medicine* and *The Division* provide an unprecedented opportunity for storytelling, although they pursue the objective of reaching female audience members through disparate means. Their variation indicates the diversity possible among series with similar composition and demographic targets and also suggests the breadth of stories workplace dramas can explore.

Strong Medicine

Strong Medicine was the first of Lifetime's female-centered workplace dramas. It focuses on two doctors, Luisa (Lu) Delgado (Rosa Blasi) and Dana

Stowe (Janine Turner).[11] The pilot episode depicts Lu operating a street-front clinic for women and "those they love and care for" in inner-city Philadelphia. This is the neighborhood in which she grew up; the community helped her to pay for medical school, and she now serves them with the aid of a grant. On the other side of town, Dana works at the prestigious Rittenhouse Hospital as one of the nation's top women's health experts. She serves a very different clientele with similar needs. A variety of narrative complications result in Lu losing her clinic and Rittenhouse opening a women's clinic that both doctors must share. The first season emphasizes the differences between the doctors, their outlooks on medicine, and the options afforded to their patients. The series explores this area in subsequent seasons, but it becomes a less primary narrative focus. Janine Turner left the series during the third season, and her character was replaced by Dr. Andy Campbell (Patricia Richardson). Andy spent her career as a military doctor prior to joining Rittenhouse, which allows her to remain distinctive from Lu while creating different interpersonal and professional conflicts than those between Lu and Dana. Andy was appointed U.S. surgeon general in the final episode of the fifth season, and the series altered its form by replacing her with a male doctor, Dylan West (Rick Schroder) at the beginning of the sixth season.

Strong Medicine distinguishes itself from more general hospital franchise series through its focus on two female physicians and the problems that arise in a clinic for women. The series resembles medical dramas such as *E.R.* or *Chicago Hope* in its visual style, episode organization, and narrative emphases. Lu and Dana face dilemmas about how to best treat patients and obligations to a bottom-line-oriented hospital director, and the series occasionally explores the issues they face in their personal lives. Neither doctor is married, but Lu has an adolescent son, and Dana develops a romantic relationship with a male resident, which introduces narrative complications. Andy's marriage provides the focus of stories told about her in her first season. She is married to a man who was laid off and then struggles with his role as house husband and in accepting the duty of raising the couple's young teenage daughters, which eventually leads to uncontrolled anger and domestic violence against Andy. She forces him out of the house pending anger-management therapy; his refusal to seek help results in their divorce.

Strong Medicine also differs considerably from *Heartbeat,* a similarly constructed series ABC attempted in 1988.[12] *Heartbeat* featured containment narratives in which female doctors had to choose either personal or professional lives, a tension that is embodied by the lead character, Dr. Joanne Springsteen (Kate Mulgrew). The different social contexts of the late 1980s and the early 2000s allow the concept of a women's clinic run by women doctors to have a different level of distinction. In *Strong Medicine,* Rittenhouse's mission to serve women across the socioeconomic spectrum receives narrative emphasis in a way that suggests that the notion of a women's clinic or the predominance of female doctors no longer seems exceptional. In *Heartbeat,* the creation of a women's clinic managed by female doctors functions as a point of narrative tension.

Three narrative aspects make the stories *Strong Medicine* tells particularly distinctive: the centrality of women's stories in the case of doctors and patients, the emphasis on episodic stories about patients over those of the doctors, and the hybrid entertainment and educative function of the narratives. The series explores conventional stories about its doctors, as Lu, Dana, and Andy struggle with moral dilemmas in caring for their patients.[13] Such storylines allow the series to interrogate the causes of the doctors' ambivalence about certain treatments in dealing with matters that affect the lives of their female patients, their patients' partners, and children. Narratives do not query the doctors' abilities, a common plot in medical dramas.

The emphasis on the doctors' struggles to resolve life-threatening predicaments suggests their centrality to *Strong Medicine*'s narratives, but Dana and Lu serve mainly as conduits through which the series tells the female patients' stories. This narrative strategy distinguishes the series from a medical drama such as *E.R.,* which foregrounds the doctors and hospital workers. Emphasizing patients' stories means that the series is organized episodically, as new patients enter in the opening scene of each episode and provide a "disease-of-the-week" crisis that must be alleviated by the end. By the third season, the series began emphasizing the personal lives of the two doctors more regularly, slightly decreasing the focus on patients' stories. Even with this readjustment, patients' stories and situations are more developed than is common among coterminous medical series.

Strong Medicine's narrative emphasis on patients enables the third feature of the series: educating viewers through fictional storytelling. In each episode, the doctors cite statistics, health concerns, and discuss good health practices in an explicitly educative manner that clearly links storytelling with education about women's health issues. Most episodes begin with Lu facilitating a women's support group, to whom she explains new developments in women's health care and preventative protocols. Because the series is based in a women's clinic, it explores disorders that disproportionately affect women in a way that introduces lesser-known ailments, their symptoms, and the importance of medical treatment. The series often addresses the subordinate status of women's medicine and the inadequacy of medical models that consider women as smaller versions of men. The official *Strong Medicine* Web page on Lifetime's site reinforces the explicit educative function of the television narratives. Information about the series such as cast biographies and episode guides are secondary to various medical resources, including a link to women's health resources, an expanded description of the disease of the week, links to groups discussing women's health issues, and an "ask the expert" column.

A noteworthy difference in storytelling emerged when Lifetime debuted its *Women Docs* (2001–2) series, a reality show designed to anchor the spin-off Lifetime Real Women network. Each week this series presents a day-in-the-life glimpse of four women doctors, with a new location and new group of doctors in each episode. In contrast to *Strong Medicine,* these stories focus on the doctors and their lives. The dilemmas faced by Lu and Dana are somewhat mirrored in the real doctors' decisions regarding medical protocol, although their quandaries are rarely as ethically complex as those explored in the fictional series. The series focuses on doctors rather than patients for practical reasons, primarily issues of privacy. The combination of these two series on Lifetime aids the network in establishing a brand that centers upon women and presents programming that seeks to serve entertainment and educative functions.

Paradoxically, the "real" depiction of medicine, *Women Docs,* does not pursue the educative agenda clearly established in the fictional *Strong Medicine. Women Docs* emphasizes personalities, with new "characters" each week, and it explores the doctors' personal lives in greater depth than *Strong Medicine.* Audiences hear about the difficulty of balancing home and professional life; the doctors express guilt about the hours they spend away from their children, admit the difficulty of maintaining balance in a career that often requires eighty hours of work per week, and acknowledge their sense of accomplishment in the work they do. Various doctors also have addressed the effects of having few female classmates and colleagues on their feelings about their work and have told stories of being mistaken for nurses because they are women. Having the challenges of the workplace articulated by "real" women provides a different narrative effect than when fictional texts address similar issues, and this alters the viewer's relationship to these ideas. The doctors' challenges evoke a sympathetic response and ally the audience with their struggles. Although the "stories" told in *Women Docs* resonate with the challenges fictional characters faced in 1980s series, it is difficult to find evidence of a containment strategy. Where networks targeted the 1980s ensemble dramas to mixed-sex audiences, Lifetime's female niche makes this televisual space one of women talking with women, which allows the stories about work-related struggles to function more as stories told in confidence than as containment.

Despite the conventions of *Strong Medicine* and its clear attempts to fit within yet vary from the medical drama franchise, the series enables some of the most radically distinct stories of any of the series that air contemporaneously. General medical dramas have not introduced topics such as bleeding fibroids, the dilemmas of becoming a surrogate mother, or the disparate medical opportunities available to poor and upper-class women within the cultural arena, but these stories are possible for *Strong Medicine* because of its narrative construction and Lifetime's niche focus. The stories it tells provide multiple points of distinction. The women's clinic allows for repeated and sustained stories about less-common women's health issues. The emphasis on patients' stories shifts the typical identification point for viewers from the all-knowing physician and provides an opportunity to explore the difficulties poor women face in the absence of universal health care. Its most noteworthy accomplishment, allowing patients a voice—particularly those who are working-class and underprivileged—expands stories available to female audiences and is feminist in nature, providing a service for women beyond narrative entertainment. Lifetime's ability to augment the *Strong Medicine* stories with those of real *Women Docs* allows the network to also tell developed stories about the experiences of female physicians in a narrative space that is supportive rather than threatening.

The Division

In contrast to *Strong Medicine*'s emphasis on patients to introduce narratives, *The Division* uses its regular cast of characters to explore the intricacies of women's lives. Many of the victims of the crimes they investigate are women, but the series does not develop these episodic characters with the depth afforded to the patients of *Strong Medicine*. The victims serve as catalysts for storylines about the detectives or for providing greater character depth, a conventional narrative organization among contemporary workplace dramas. *The Division*'s large cast, five detectives and their female captain, aids its internal focus.[14] Its emphasis on the personal lives of recurring characters affords it a more developed serial component than *Strong Medicine*.

The cast has shifted slightly over the course of the series. Captain Katelyn McCafferty (Bonnie Bedelia) commands the San Francisco unit. She is a divorced white woman with a complicated relationship with her adult daughter who resents Kate's commitment to her career. Kate belongs to the generation that first integrated the police force, and she understands her status as a woman in a police organization differently than the detectives. Detective Jinny Exstead (Nancy McKeon) is a talented cop, a single white woman from a law-enforcement family, but she begins the series on an alcoholic spiral of destruction. Detective Magda Ramirez (Lisa Vidal), a Latina single mother, partners with Exstead after beginning the series with a married male partner who requests a transfer after she rebukes his romantic advances. Detective C. D. DeLorenzo (Tracey Needham) finds herself with a new partner, Angela Reide (Lela Rochon Fuqua), in the first season, after her previous partner (with whom she was having an affair) killed himself. Reide, an African American, advanced through the ranks quickly and has little street experience. After Rochon Fuqua leaves the series, DeLorenzo partners with Nate Basso (Jon Hamm), the only regular male character on the series. Raina Washington (Taraji Henson), an African American raised by white lesbian mothers, begins the series as a uniformed officer assigned to the squad room and later becomes a detective. Stacy Newland (Amy Jo Johnson), a young white woman from a privileged background, replaces her as a uniformed officer in the fourth season.

The factors complicating the characters' personal lives provide much of their differentiation, as the series depicts all of them as able officers. Many of the detectives have complicated personal and family relationships, and much of the weekly story focuses on them discussing personal crises with their partners while going through the motions of police work. Many of these stories create ongoing difficulties for the characters that span multiple episodes and even seasons. For example, the father of Ramirez's child returns after an eight-year absence and desires to create a traditional family. The couple eventually marries, but her husband's constant traveling leads her to have an affair, and he leaves again after she confesses. Her storyline also chronicles her son's fight with leukemia and her complicated relationship with her sister. Similarly, Exstead begins the series as a recklessly promiscuous drunk and requires an intervention by the force and her family at the end of the first season. She goes to rehab but becomes addicted to painkillers after she returns. She marries a man she meets in rehab and divorces him a few months later. She marries again after apparently overcoming her addictions and becoming pregnant. Meanwhile, her family life is complicated by history (her mother committed suicide when she was a child). One of her brothers is gay and struggles to come out to the family and police force; her other brother is killed in the line of duty; and she learns that her father (a retired officer) had a wife and child she and her brothers never knew about. This sample of two characters' storylines suggests the types of stories the series focuses on and its emphasis on the detectives and nonpolice matters.

Ongoing work-related stories filled with this type of melodrama are less frequent, although each episode features the detectives solving a crime. A long plotline chronicles difficult dealings between McCafferty and a sexist police chief and then her pursuit of his job after he is killed, and Exstead's future on the force is uncertain in the early seasons in which she battles addictions and various internal review boards threaten her employment. Each episode of *The Division* features a homicide the characters must solve, which requires some narrative time spent tracking down leads and interrogating suspects, but narratives about solving crimes are emphasized much less than in a series such as *Homicide: Life on the Street* or *Law and Order*. *NYPD Blue* provides a better comparison, particularly in later seasons in which the personal lives of Sipowicz, Simone, Russell, and Sorenson dominate the narrative, although crime solving is more central than in *The Division*. *The Division* creates a workplace environment dominated by female characters and then emphasizes intimate aspects of their lives and personality that bear little relation to their professional duties. The series depicts discussions of crime solving and their personal lives much more than it attends to their doing—plot action is minimal, and standard cop-show fare such as chase scenes or action sequences are negligible (which may also be a budgetary factor related to airing on a basic cable network).

The stories told by and about the female workplace ensemble in *The Division* focus on working women coping with their jobs and the problems they encounter. These problems rarely result from the fact that they are women; the crises are presented as problems working people commonly face, and the narratives depict the characters enduring these struggles. The disparity in the types of stories told by *Strong Medicine, The Division,* and even *Women Docs* indicates the inadequacy of workplace settings as a predictor of story type. *The Division* offers little innovation, tells few original stories, and mainly provides a different version of the cop series by exploring interpersonal relationships among officers more than the work they perform. Like *Strong Medicine, The Division* attends more to diversity among women than any of the other dramas. While *Strong Medicine* emphasizes stories about class difference, *The Division* is notable for the ethnic diversity of its cast—a diversity the series attends to in storylines rather than allowing it to exist only as window dressing. The series also introduces stories about other socially subordinated groups through the families of the detectives. Washington was raised by a white lesbian couple; McCafferty's daughter and Exstead's brother are gay, and the series uses them to explore stories about prejudice, discrimination, and closeting. Basso's sister has Down's syndrome, and the series includes multiple stories about her and her group home. Because the detectives all have the same job, class is not a central issue in this series; *The Division* constructs the differences among the characters as related to their variant demographic features.

The Division immediately evokes comparisons with *Cagney and Lacey*, a groundbreaking series that preceded it by nearly twenty years. The series are very different and indicate the changes in American culture and the television industry. Where Christine and Mary Beth often retreated to the women's room for conferences, the squad room of *The Division* features more women than men, and the series rarely draws attention to the characters' status as women or outsiders. Julie d'Acci's comprehensive study of *Cagney and Lacey* examines CBS's creative interference to make it acceptable to mainstream audiences, including the recasting of Christine Cagney for the more conventionally feminine Sharon Gless and the network's mandate that she be glamorous and linked to upper-class family wealth.[15] In contrast, *The Division* depicts the characters and their duties with a grittier tone (although not as gritty as *Hill Street Blues*) and makes the differences among the women more complex than those of class and marital status. The writers and producers clearly expend little time balancing the femininity of their characters with dominant norms, which CBS constantly required of *Cagney and Lacey*. The arrival and relative success of *Strong Medicine* and *The Division* suggest noteworthy gains, as their workplace settings dominated by female characters make stories about professional women and those they encounter a primary narrative focus that mixed-sex ensemble workplace series can feature only on occasion.

Notable Stories in Mixed-Sex Ensembles

In addition to the reconfigured workplaces of *Strong Medicine* and *The Division*, a few mixed-sex workplace series require mention. Each provides some distinction particularly relevant to the topic of telling stories about women, whether through characterization or in their ability to explore stories pertinent to contemporary gender issues and politics. Female characters engaged in professional careers proliferated in mixed-sex workplace dramas in the late 1990s and early 2000s; there are far too many to explore the varied significance of each. I address these four series because of their distinction (or lack of distinction, in one case). The possibility of disagreement with my selection, arising because of the plurality of representations, is a significant departure from the uniform agreement of previous eras that was possible only because of the paucity of representations and stories.

These series are distinct from many of the others considered in this book because they are less clearly intended for female viewers or do not emphasize the telling of women's stories. These series circulate widely, are closely related to the stories told by *Strong Medicine* and *The Division*, and suggest possibilities for the representation of women in workplaces even when female characters do not dominate these spaces. The multiplicity of female characters in *Strong Medicine* and *The Division* allows these series to reflect vast differences among women, this diversity is less evident in mixed-sex workplace series, which remain dominated by a fairly monolithic view of femininity and female perspectives.

Family Law

The CBS series *Family Law* (1999–2002) came the closest to bringing a female-centered ensemble to a generally targeted broadcast network. This series debuted alongside *Judging Amy* and *Once and Again* and originally seemed part of the female-centered trend emerging in the late 1990s. It begins from a similar narrative premise as *The Trials of Rosie O'Neill:* Lynn Holt's (Kathleen Quinlan) husband and law partner leaves their marriage and takes the couple's legal clients with him. Lynn opens a new firm that specializes in family law and subleases office space to three other lawyers, with whom she forms a partnership in the second season. *Family Law* focuses on the stories of the families who come to Holt's firm for representation, although the lawyers and their legal maneuvering remains central to the narrative. The series explores situations similar to the court cases in *Judging Amy,* such as dilemmas of family, child crime, and custody in a society complicated by divorce and crimes perpetrated by and against children. One of the original four characters and two of six in the second season are male, which allows the series to create a primarily female workspace, but one that affords more space to men than *Strong Medicine* or *The Division.* The series' home on CBS, however, makes its stories more widely circulated: *Family Law* drew four to five times the number of viewers as the Lifetime series.

Family Law ambivalently depicts the legal structure governing families and children. Viewers' sympathy frequently aligns with losing interests, which also corresponds with *Judging Amy*'s complex and pessimistic portrayal of justice. This creates a tone similar to that of *Strong Medicine,* where patients often die, and the episodic resolution frequently denies a happy ending. These narratives challenge viewers. The stories provide persuasive evidence on both sides of an issue, as in an episode that puts a face on teen male violence, gives him a mother who loves him, and also depicts the families of his victims. Such ambivalence is certainly not unique to series with an atypical number of female characters; *Law and Order* also features such stories. The centrality of a multiplicity of female characters enables the series to explore women's varied perspectives and beliefs in an attempt to understand and negotiate complicated social problems. The female characters in *Family Law* often clash because of disparate ideological positions, despite the uniformity of upper-middle-class, white, female characters (at least in the first season).

Among the broad array of female-centered dramas appearing in the late 1990s, *Family Law* most closely replicates the reconfigured workplace drama on a mainstream, general-interest broadcast network. As the analysis of *Strong Medicine* and *The Division* illustrates, this type of series provides important innovations to working-woman characters by allowing them self-determined spaces. *Family Law* offers audiences not specified as female a narrative that examines issues through multiple viewpoints and emphasizes a diversity of female perspectives. The emergence of reconfigured workplaces on Lifetime indicates a preliminary adjustment in the stories told about working women on television, but for such stories to move to a general-interest broadcaster suggests further gains.

Third Watch

NBC's *Third Watch* (1999–2005), a series about a group of police officers, emergency crews, and firefighters who work third shift, provides one of the most unusual and noteworthy representations of and distinctive stories about a female worker. Officer Faith Yokus (Molly Price) is a New York City beat cop, the primary provider for her family, and she is partnered with a racist and sexist male officer. The series' depiction of less-glamorous civil service roles is atypical in 1990s television; *Third Watch* lacks lawyers or detectives in expensive suits and is populated with "anyman" and "anywoman" characters who did not go to college and refer to their workplaces as jobs rather than careers. Yokus is one of three women in the series (one each in the police, fire, and emergency teams throughout most seasons), and she is characterized with rich depth. After a first season of narratives organized by the action of the teams responding to emergencies, *Third Watch* began its second season by focusing on one character in each episode, which allowed previously lacking characterization. In the second season, the series explored Faith's character in two episodes in which it told dramatic stories about a working-class woman—a type of story long absent from U.S. television screens.[16]

With the exception of *Any Day Now*'s Mary Elizabeth, the female characters discussed throughout this book are all privileged with at least upper-middle-class lifestyles that are signified by a lack of attention to financial matters and the depiction of characters' material goods, a representation common on U.S. television.[17] Working-class stories with female characters have emerged occasionally, but only comedic series have survived more than a few airings (*Roseanne, Grace Under Fire*). Even dramatic workplace series that emphasize a character with a working-class background (such as *Strong Medicine*) predominately offer stories about her career or focus on her transition into a new class status rather than highlighting working-class struggles. Stories linked to Faith's class status expose narratives otherwise unavailable and give voice to the realities faced by many of television's viewers.

Faith's family's survival depends on her paycheck, denying her the dilemma of whether or not she should work. Her husband is the children's primary caregiver by default; he is laid off early in the series and struggles to find work. Later, he has a nearly fatal heart attack that necessitates more home rest, again exacerbating the family's reliance on Faith's income. Her class status requires that she confront issues through a different lens than her upper-class counterparts. In the second-season episodes that focus on Faith, she faces an unwanted pregnancy and decides to have an abortion, and later she experiences an identity crisis in frustration with the lack of options in her life. Particularly in the abortion episode, *Third Watch* tells the story of a woman negotiating a limited set of possibilities and an economic reality that leaves little "choice" at all.[18] Faith elects not to tell her husband about the pregnancy because he would want to have the child, and she knows they can barely afford their life with two children. Rather than the typical depiction of an unwanted pregnancy (which often saves the woman from making a decision by having her miscarry or not really be pregnant after all), *Third Watch* portrays a woman who has neither options nor a support system during the crisis. Her partner refuses to consider abortion as an option, which necessitates that she lie to him and tell him she lost the baby due to an injury sustained in the line of duty. The episode closes with Faith alone in a sterile and impersonal clinic. She keeps the decision to herself until the truth emerges two seasons later to complicate her relationships with her partner, husband, and daughter. Their anger and distrust further punishes her.

Third Watch anchors its stories and representations of female workers in a gritty realism of struggle rather than a liberal fantasy of achievement and equality. The series depicts women in nontraditional fields where they must deal with sexism and a testosterone-dominated environment. There is no room for impassioned feminist speeches or legal maneuvers to secure equality; the series depicts women coping with challenging realities with few options but to survive. *Third Watch* contributes a vital perspective to the stories told about women in the late 1990s and early twenty-first century. Its acknowledgment of working-class struggles—even when not focused specifically on a female character or gender issue—exposes a set of stories and gender relations that are vital to creating a diversity of stories about women and their lives.

Law and Order: Special Victims Unit

Another workplace ensemble series that deserves specific mention for its contribution to telling stories about or for women is a spinoff of one of television's most successful workplace franchises. Despite its naming and association with the long-running *Law and Order* (1990–), *SVU* (1999–) breaks from its originator's dual police procedural/legal drama form to primarily explore procedural narratives. As was vogue by the 1990s, the series includes female cast members—one of the primary detectives, the assistant district attorney, and the medical examiner assigned to the unit are women. It is principally relevant to this discussion because of its emphasis on crimes against women. It depicts a police division trained to investigate crimes against "special victims," who are most often women and children who suffer sexual crimes. The narratives emphasize the crime and the process of investigation but offer limited examination of the officers' personal lives. *SVU* primarily tells the stories of its victims rather than the detectives. The inordinate number of women victims whose stories are told makes *SVU* worthy of mention in this context.

SVU treads a fine line between drawing awareness to crimes against women and exploiting these crimes. Stories about rape provide one of the most frequently explored topics for this series, although rape stories had established a place in cop, doc, and legal franchises long before *SVU*'s debut.[19] The series offers valuable narratives validating the experience of female victims, depicting systems of support for those who suffer domestic abuse or rape, and reiterating that these crimes are not her fault. However, weekly explorations of gruesome and horrific crimes (the combination of sex and violence that often attracts high ratings) repeatedly victimize women. *SVU* uses an episodic organization that commonly isolates the women's stories to forty-eight minutes of narrative time, which prevents in-depth exploration of the character or her process of recovery.[20] In this way, the series does not so much tell a diversity of stories about women who recover from deplorable crimes so much as it repeatedly tells a variation of their victimization.

Like *Strong Medicine* and *Family Law, SVU* opens a space for stories about situations that predominately affect women. *SVU*'s narratives and storytelling context, however, are distinct from other series discussed in this chapter, as is its contribution to introducing women's stories to the cultural forum. Unlike *Strong Medicine,* which uses stories about female patients to educate audiences about a variety of ailments commonly suffered by women, the crimes depicted in *SVU* serve only a limited educative function. Unfortunately, news coverage often depicts crimes against women, and most women are well aware of their frequent status as victims, which makes *SVU*'s repeated depiction of these stories a less significant contribution. Additionally, *SVU* does not treat social issues in the complex manner accomplished by *Family Law*. Where *Family Law* depicts the judicial system struggling to negotiate children's best interest in custody situations or in establishing a face and context for the crimes increasingly committed by American children, personalizing a rapist or sexual predator is of more questionable utility. *SVU* has provided thought-provoking stories about how those convicted of sex crimes bear an irremovable stigma as an indication of the limitations of the U.S. penal system for rehabilitation or retribution, but this is the exception rather than the norm. Because of its special-victims focus, crimes suffered by women achieve more regular and detailed examination than in "regular" police dramas such as *Law and Order* or *NYPD Blue*. The stories *SVU* tells provide an important contribution to dramatic stories about women; however, a detailed analysis of the series is necessary to thoroughly assess its ideological significance.

The West Wing

The political drama *The West Wing* (1999–) indicates the limitations and possibilities for female characters in mixed-sex ensembles. I include it here to address how mixed-sex workplace narratives of the late 1990s and 2000s continue to undermine female characters, even in contexts that superficially appear supportive of their increased career status.[21] Women occupy two of eight opening-credit cast positions in this series—press secretary C. J. Cregg (Allison Janney) and assistant Donna Moss (Janel Moloney).[22] Although her status provides C. J. with some authority in the workplace, the dominance of men in this space and occasional tertiary-level plot devices often undercut her competency and indicate the subtle ways a series dominated by male voices (in cast and writing) contains the female empowerment it wears as a proud mark of its alleged progressive politics.[23]

The Seattle television columnist John Levesque highlighted a prime example of the subtle narratives that diminish C. J.'s status (in a way that does not motivate the narrative and is consequently unnecessary) and noted that the *The West Wing* auteur Aaron Sorkin's tendency for such depiction emerges in his series *Sports Night* as well.[24] He cites an episode in which C. J., as well as the recurring character Ainsley Hayes (Emily Proctor), sit in wet paint, requiring them to spend the episode (in which C. J. does a live broadcast from the White House) walking around without pants. Other similar embarrassments befall C. J.; perhaps the most significant case is a repeated device of making her the last to know important information (a running joke that makes it impossible to do her job well). In another unnecessary narrative moment, deputy chief of staff Josh Lyman (Bradley Whitford) returns a pair of underwear to his assistant Donna after meeting with a foreign dignitary. Donna met with the dignitary the previous day, and a pair of underwear fell out of her pants, presumably after being caught in the pant leg from a previous wearing. A promotion for the third season provides another example. In an extended opening for the episode that addressed the events of September 11, each of the characters promotes an upcoming plotline. The male characters address the grand jury investigation of the president and his reelection bid, while Donna announces, "And I get a boyfriend."

It is not my intention to create a hierarchy of workplace dramas that tell women's stories, but I use these examples from *The West Wing* to indicate how a series that professes liberal politics and offers female characters narrative space still undercuts and minimizes their professionalism. These devices only can be identified by examining the stories told by the series; the characters' status as single women in career roles provides no suggestion of the ambivalent nature of their narrative construction. This series does offer important representations and discourses: C. J.'s management of the press corps and First Lady Bartlet's (Stockard Channing) commitment to women and women's issues in her occasionally depicted duties provide significant perspectives of female work. Additionally, the series regularized the role of Amy Gardner (Mary-Louise Parker) in the fourth season, who was originally introduced as the director of a NOW-like organization and openly identified as a feminist.

This characterization and the stories surrounding Amy relative to the other female characters further indicate the complexity of any one series' contribution to stories told about women. In their rhetorical analysis of the series, Trevor Parry-Giles and Shawn Parry-Giles note other moments that both value and contain the female characters.[25] *The West Wing* illustrates the difficulty of assessing the progressive or regressive nature of stories told about women and how crucial it is to utilize an appropriate unit of analysis. This series can be seen in radically divergent ways, depending on which episode one focuses upon, and this illustrates the need to consider the entirety of the series. Additionally, the programming context must be considered to understand the significance of its contradictory gender politics.

* * *

Unquestionably, many other workplace series could be mentioned here. Another author may have attended to the stories told by 1990s series such as *Law and Order, NYPD Blue* (ABC, 1993–2004), *The X-Files* (FOX, 1993–2002), *E.R.* (NBC, 1994–), or *The Practice* (ABC, 1997–2004). As some of the top rated dramas of this era, these series offered significant contributions to television storytelling at the end of the century. Many of them depict a deliberately crafted female competence, but the host of contemporaries illustrates that such depictions are not exceptional. More to the point, these series offer little innovation to the telling of stories about women, either about the central female characters or those they encounter during their work as lawyers, detectives, and doctors. The series I mention here offer some specific contribution: *Family Law* nearly brings a reconfigured, female-centered workspace to a mainstream broadcast network; *Third Watch* offers a rare working-class character in dramatic stories about women as workers; *SVU* emphasizes stories about the crimes women suffer to indicate some of the ways that they remain structurally subordinated; and *The West Wing* serves as a caveat about assuming professional characters necessarily yield politically progressive or feminist representations and stories.

The workplace drama remains a crucial site for assessing dominant social scripts and for charting the status of female audiences. Many of the narratives discussed here indicate an increased acceptance of female characters in workplace dramas in comparison with 1980s dramas, while the emergence of workplaces dominated by women on Lifetime suggests the most unmistakable gain. The fact that depictions of professional women are now less openly contested by narrative circumstances may indicate a need for feminist critics to reassess the portrayal of characters with public roles as inherently progressive; the example of *The West Wing* reminds us of the complex nature of representation and discourse and the need for critical interrogation of apparently empowered characterizations.

Like the dramatic types considered in other chapters, the workplace dramas also offer a distinct contribution to the expansion of stories told about female characters in the period following the network era. *Strong Medicine* and *The Division* illustrate the breadth of stories possible, whether through the rarely heard working-class patients of Lu's clinic or the complicated and often melodramatic interpersonal relationships of *The Division*'s detectives. Workplace series possess such a voluminous place in television history precisely because so many stories can be told through their framework. *Strong Medicine* and *The Division* reinvent this time-tested form by placing new emphasis on stories about female characters or situations experienced by women.

Although the pursuit of work outside of the home functions as a structuring presence across all the series considered in this book, the workplace dramas tell different stories about women and work than can be found in any other dramatic form. These two Lifetime series share features similar to aspects of the comedic dramas and protagonist-centered family dramas, but they are foremost about work and the events that transpire in work spaces. This focus provides these series with a broad canvas for exploring the public or work issues affecting women's lives and how they negotiate them. These series have the most natural narrative motivation for exploring gender issues as part of a large systemic structure of power, rather than the containment to the personal realm that limits most other types of series.

Epilogue:
The 2001–2 Season and Beyond

When I began this project at what seemed the height of the female-centered drama trend, I had no idea how long the trend would continue or what forms it would ultimately take. As the broadcast networks announced cancellations and new series in 2002, 2003, 2004, and 2005, far more of the kinds of dramas I have considered appeared on the list of cancellations than the list of new shows. Many of the series that originally indicated the emergence of a programming trend came full circle with concluding episodes in 2002. Ally McBeal, who caused such commotion five years earlier, left Cage/Fish and McBeal for New York as a mature, complicated woman in comparison to the vessel of youthful uncertainty that audiences first met. Felicity graduated from college; Lily (Manning) Sammler (*Once and Again*) reconstructed her family; Rene Jackson (*Any Day Now*) expanded her firm and married a judge, while her friend Mary Elizabeth Sims became a writer, college professor, and grandmother; Lydia DeLuca (*That's Life*) decided on a major; *Dark Angel*'s Max Guevara led a mutant revolt; Xena martyred herself; and Buffy saved the world, with a little help from her friends. None of these descriptions hints at the manifold stories these series told, but their presence—some brief, some longer—was noted and enjoyed by a range of audiences.

The female-centered dramatic form has waned from its peak in 2000, and the most recent seasons of programming suggest an attempt to repackage female characters in narratives that do not resolutely announce themselves as programs for women. Series debuting after the summer of 2001 receive only passing comment in the main text of this book, as they deviate from the more distinct dramatic types to which previous series conformed. On the surface, *Crossing Jordan* (NBC, 2001–) and *Philly* (ABC, 2001–2) appeared to continue the protagonist-centered family drama, but instead they enacted more common workplace-ensemble narratives with a primary female protagonist. Unlike the protagonist-centered family series, *Crossing Jordan, Philly,* and most recently, *Cold Case* (CBS, 2003–) place little emphasis on their characters outside of their professional roles; but unlike the reformulated workplace dramas of chapter 5, these characters interact with few if any other women in their jobs. In comparison with the characters introduced in preceding seasons, there is little that is notable or unconventional about their characters. As a viewer and critic, I was struck by how immensely unlikable the characters Jordan (*Crossing Jordan*) and Kathleen (*Philly*) are. They are flawed, as are many of the characters in the series considered here; but the writers chose to make Jordan and Kathleen particularly unpleasant women.

The 2001–2 season also debuted a number of new dramas featuring central female characters that did not get renewed for a second season. This was the fate of *Philly,* which was unwisely scheduled against *Judging Amy* (by far the most watched female-centered drama). Two midseason series, *The American Embassy* (FOX, 2002) and *The Court* (ABC, 2002), had barely introduced their characters before they were pulled after less than five episodes. Both series had the potential to develop distinct stories given more time, but notably, like the other new series, they were much more akin to mainstream ensemble dramas than the female-centered types discussed here.[1]

Alias (ABC, 2001–6) clearly emerged as the most-difficult-to-place 2001 addition. I initially expected the series to continue the action drama type but found many significant deviations. Like Nikita, Sydney Bristow possesses no superhuman powers and exists in an ordinary world, although one of spies and intrigue. The narrative form initially blends episodic and serial organization unusually, perhaps best described as episodic with weekly cliffhanger endings. Its story winds a complicated and enigmatic web, and the series reinvents itself and its characters with some regularity. The relative absence of female colleagues and counterparts distinguishes *Alias* from many of the series considered in chapter 2, again making it most comparable to *La Femme Nikita*. However, *La Femme Nikita*'s prescience as a series debuting before *Buffy the Vampire Slayer, Charmed, Dark Angel,* and *Witchblade* affords it greater significance than *Alias'* reembodiment of the form five years later. In fact, *Alias* redeploys many features of *Charlie's Angels,* albeit with a single protagonist.[2] The series plays heavily with spectacle and masquerade, and male advisors often determine Sydney's missions (particularly in early seasons). The series fetishizes Sydney in a manner unlike the other action heroines, making her very much an object to be looked at (her cover costumes often repeat the undercover-prostitute gig common in the past), yet it emphasizes overwrought familial and interpersonal relationships to allow Sydney the melodramatic character depth common among the action dramas. *Alias* failed to draw a sizable audience (perhaps because it isolates Sydney from a community of other female characters), although it was popular among many critics because of its variation in narrative form and spectacular locales and stunts. Had it not been a moderately performing series for ABC during an exceptionally poor year (the network's audience size was down 25 percent for the year), *Alias* too may have been a one-season series.

The 2001–2 season appeared to continue the female-centered drama trend, but all of the series debuting this season decreased the narrative centrality of the primary female character. This reduced role was only apparent when watching the series; promotion spots, series naming, and opening sequences often suggested they were akin to those considered throughout this book. They attempted to trade on the status and popularity of other female-centered series while not fulfilling their narrative commitment. Additionally, although I have emphasized a singular female protagonist as a determining characteristic of the female-centered drama, I had not realized the necessity of a community of female characters for telling many of these stories until I compared the series I have been writing about with many emerging after 2000. *Alias, Crossing Jordan, Philly, The Court, The American Embassy, Cold Case, Tru Calling,* and *Karen Sisco* clearly establish a central female protagonist, but they also isolate her from other women and favor overwhelmingly male-dominated settings. This hints of a "mainstreaming" strategy utilized by the Big Four networks to make the series attractive to female audiences but not hail primarily female audiences so emphatically. The failure of these series in attracting audiences when compared with those more genuinely about female characters suggests the complexity of designing programs to attract audiences and that audiences desire more than an isolated female character. This narrative shift also helps explain why many of these shows lasted only one season.

New dramas in the 2001–2 season generally fared poorly, with high-profile series such as *Citizen Baines* (CBS, 2001), starring James Cromwell, and *The Education of Max Bickford* (CBS, 2001–2), starring Richard Dreyfuss, also failing. It is particularly noteworthy that these two shows, as well as the ratings success *The Guardian* (2001–4), attempted to follow the female-centered drama narrative structure while centering a male protagonist. Yet *Citizen Baines* and *Max Bickford* included multiple female characters or used settings that enabled the exploration of stories about women. Three adult daughters surround the central character, Senator Baines, with each daughter receiving an independent plotline in most episodes. Max Bickford also occupies an overwhelmingly female environment, as a professor at a women's college. His central relationships include his daughter Nell, his colleague and former lover Andrea, his friend and the college president Judith, his friend Steve, who appeared in the pilot as Erica after undergoing sex-change surgery, his secretary Lorraine, and the countless students who introduce narrative complications. The academic setting also allowed the introduction of what might be considered "female-centered themes," with stories about the value of all-female education, the status of contemporary feminism, women's deliberation of egg donation, and feminist debates on pornography all explored in the single season. These shows clearly incorporate characters and premises that allow for the introduction of stories particularly relevant to women regardless of their male protagonists. In fact, *The Education of Max Bickford* presented a greater number of and more developed female characters than *Crossing Jordan* and told stories exploring women's lives and feminist issues in a much more substantive way. Despite the commercial failure of these series, the incorporation of such strategies into more general dramatic narratives further suggests the long-term effects of female-centered dramas.

The 2002–3 season brought even fewer series and indicated that using a larger female ensemble would not ensure success either. FOX only allowed David E. Kelley's universally panned *Girls Club* a handful of outings. While there was a glimmer of potential in plotlines dealing with gender dynamics, the series clearly lacked the heart and central ethos that led audiences to care about the characters in *Ally McBeal*. The WB's *Birds of Prey* attempted the multiple-protagonist action drama but failed to find an audience. Narratively, CBS's *Presidio Med* provided the medical equivalent of *Family Law* with a female-dominated hospital setting. The series crafted some beautiful episodes and exhibited a talented female cast who offered graceful and intelligent portrayals, but it also failed to find a sizable audience.

The 2003–4 season was bizarrely saturated with dramatic series in which otherworldly voices spoke to young female characters. Dead people speak to Tru Davies in *Tru Calling,* inanimate objects talk to Jaye Tyler on *Wonderfalls,* God speaks to Joan Girardi on *Joan of Arcadia,* and Jess Mastriani sees where kidnappers hold their victims in her dreams on Lifetime's *MISSING.* The uniformity of brunette women under the age of twenty-five hearing so many extraworldly voices strikes me as more curious than the supernatural nature of their concepts. In describing the genesis of the concepts for their series, the creators repeatedly deferred to the zeitgeist of post–September 11 culture, yet no one addressed why writers chose for all these various forces to speak to women. In addition to these shows, a series built around Elmore Leonard's character Karen Sisco from *Out of Sight* perpetuated the female-centered dra-

matic form in a manner similar to *Crossing Jordan* and *Philly.* Ten years earlier, Karen Sisco would have been an innovation on television screens, but by
2003 there was little original about her tough veneer and career as a federal
marshal. *Cold Case* provides a more successful variation of a female-centered
workplace narrative but tells few stories about women and rarely offers a
glimpse of its protagonist outside of work.

The 2004 season offered the fewest new additions since the trend began,
with only *Desperate Housewives* (ABC) and *Veronica Mars* (UPN) fitting the
genre. Few would have forecast that *Desperate Housewives* would become the
popular culture phenomenon of the year. This series complements many of
those discussed here by returning female characters without careers and with
husbands and children to the center of its narratives. Although the series has
earned much acclaim, it is difficult to place relative to the narratives discussed here. It offers wholly different stories than those featured in the categories that organize this book. The series has also challenged feminist critics. Like *Ally McBeal*, its tone is highly uncertain, including as much comedy
as drama. It is often unclear where viewer sympathies are meant to lie, as the
female characters are all fairly unlikable. Rather, disidentification seems the
central viewer relationship in the show's uncertain satire.

The Inside (FOX) and *The Closer* (TNT) debuted in the summer of 2005,
and both center upon a female law-enforcement officer or criminal profiler.
Each opened with unsettling crimes that featured a tortured and sadistically
killed female victim. *The Inside* (originally developed for 2004–5 as a story
about a young officer who goes undercover in a high school) treads this ter-
ritory nearly every week, often using its young female lead to either go undercover as bait or depicting her foolishly working alone, only to be caught
and needing to be rescued. It was stunning to see such a retrograde narrative
after the innovation of the dramas discussed here, but over-the-top depictions of violence against women were featured in a number of pilots for the
2005–6 season (*Bones* [FOX], *Close to Home* [CBS], *Killer Instincts* [FOX],
Criminal Minds [CBS], *Night Stalker* [ABC]), some of which appeared to continue the female-centered-drama trend (*Bones, Close to Home*). It seemed as
though the creative community believed that narratives featuring horrific vi-
olations of women could be forgiven if there was a female character heading
up the investigation or prosecution. The development of these shows followed
a year of substantial legislative rhetoric about and FCC fines for sexual imagery. With networks fearful of programming sexual content, they turned instead to violence and the nearly naked, mangled corpses that occupy the
screens of *CSI, CSI: Miami, CSI: New York*, and *Crossing Jordan*, which had
not been named in the crackdown on exposed flesh. Regardless of the spe-

cific causes, the new shows offer an important reminder of the complicated process of shifting cultural norms and dominant ideology.

The presence of female-centered dramatic series on network schedules and the narrative and thematic organizations that dominate these series will likely shift cyclically, although it seems reasonable to suspect that U.S. television will not return to the nearly complete absence of these forms that characterized most of its history. The drop in the gross abundance of these series offers little cause for concern, as schedules from 1997 through 2002 were arguably oversaturated with female-centered dramas, and the reduction indicates an incorporation into convention likely to yield a presence but not an overabundance of multiple series.

Conclusion:
U.S. Feminist Television Criticism
in the Post-Network Era

People said, "The network's not gonna go for it—there's no male epicenter," but I think [execs] are finally realizing there's an audience for shows where women do something other than function in relation to men.

—Amy Brenneman, actor/executive producer, *Judging Amy*

Innovation only becomes possible when people are willing to contest "conventional wisdom" or hegemonic norms. The broadcast television industry is an insular community, and by the time executives achieve decision-making positions, they have been fully schooled in the conventional wisdom upon which the industry operates. It is likely that a network executive told Barney Rosenzweig the same thing about *The Trials of Rosie O'Neill* in the early 1990s that executives advised Amy Brenneman of *Judging Amy;* and in the previous case the conventional wisdom prevailed. Many fail in the process of discerning when a change occurs or when the time is right for something new. The potential return on being the first "new thing" when audiences are looking for something innovative partially explains why networks risk scheduling unconventional series.[1]

Many if not all of the series discussed in these pages challenged network executives' beliefs about the indispensable male epicenter. The networks repeated the experiment of female-centered dramatic series with enough success to refute one barrier of conventional wisdom, at least for a few years. It is easy to see the significance of the late 1990s in changing the range of representations and stories available for female characters and audiences; table 1 continues to amaze me. But what is the significance of the programming environment in place from 1997–2002, both as a distinct moment and in terms of its legacy? What contributions did these shows make to the television audiences who viewed them as they aired, to television scholars who have attempted to make sense of them, and to future narrative storytelling about women?

While there was no grand plan or conspiratorial overthrow of the conventions of the dramatic genre in an effort to provide a greater diversity of dramatic female characters, the context of reception and circulation changed in an extraordinary way that must be reflected in critical assessments. This rupture in programming norms underscores the need for feminist media scholars to reconsider foundational frameworks and their consequences. We must consider how the radical change in programming context affects conventional assumptions and recognize that the old tools can still be used, but we must first consider their validity in this context and make appropriate adjustments. The substantial change in the programming environment requires conversation, deliberation, and reconsideration of our models and their consequences. Chapters 2 through 5 indicate the expansive range of stories told about women by various dramas and types. The multiplicity of characters in these series requires a reassessment of what individual characters mean, as these manifold dramas—in concert with three distinctly branded women's cable networks—disrupt the previous embodiment of traditional representational types such as the new woman, working woman, and mother to make conventional stereotypes or representations of women uninhabitable.

Scholars applying a cultural studies framework might argue that the dominance of the role-model framework of feminist analysis has needed to be balanced with methods providing greater complexity for some time, but the multiplicity of narratives and networks chronicled in this book should make clear that the late 1990s ruptured established industry truths about women in dramatic series. Adherence to the role-model framework yields narrow conversations; it is unequipped to assess the nuances of narrative complexity. Some questions still might be best answered through its methods and assumptions, but the role-model framework excessively dominates U.S. studies of gender and television. My primary critique is not of individual research so much as the pervasive reach of the role-model framework into policy, journalism, and even critical and cultural analyses. The presence of a previously unimaginable multiplicity of stories about women decreases the utility of this model, particularly when other frameworks remain obscured by its centrality.

Women are now fortunate enough to be characterized in disparate and complex ways, a shift that requires sophisticated analytical tools and methods. The role-model framework lacks tools for examining how narratives construct conflicted characters and how they use characters' moments of weakness and exasperation to tell stories rather than advocating the containment of women's gains. Admittedly, the flaws exhibited by the characters—the imperfections characteristic of humans rather than role models—provide much of the richness of contemporary characterizations. Amy Gray (*Judging Amy*) cannot balance her career and offer her child the same things that Lauren claims "everyone else's mother" does. Lily Manning (*Once and Again*) makes questionable decisions while pursuing a postdivorce relationship as she reexperiences dating in her forties. Ally McBeal admits uncertainty about how her life has turned out and is disappointed about personal unfulfillment despite professional success. Many of these dramatic characters are expertly drawn to evolve, have irrational responses, and defy our expectations, as people often do. Maybe new female characters will succumb to traditional behavior or impose dominant norms this week, but the complicated lives depicted indicate more about contemporary female reality than a flawless role model might.

The whole notion of the positive representation or idealized role model needs deconstruction, as anointing role models becomes much more difficult in a programming context populated by so many characters. In response to the overwhelming historical portrayal of women as wives and mothers who did not work outside of the home, single, childless, working women became the ultimate counterpoint. By the 1970s, new women began to have a place in the public sphere, but narratives contained these gains with inordinate attention to dating and marriage, which further reinforced an emphasis on work or professional life as emblematic of "positive" representations. The dramas of the late 1990s present a different problem. The pendulum of representation has swung to the opposite extreme, and while these series tell a wide range of stories, the basic demographic similarity of the characters is disconcerting. The prevalence of single characters who work outside the home suggests that the television creative and executive communities are also aware of the terms by which the role-model framework determines "positive" characters, a status they seek. The uniformity with which women in all the series discussed in this book work outside of the home and in most cases are unmarried establishes a new construct of what women should be rather than increasing the uninhabitability of confining gender roles. Is it impossible for a dramatic character to have a meaningful, committed, romantic relationship? Are women who do not work outside of the home now stigmatized? Are feminist depictions and married characters mutually exclusive? As a colleague noted, the most stable relationship among the series I consider is one whose romantic dimensions are unstated (*Xena: Warrior Princess*), an absence that speaks volumes.[2] Regardless of the terms of the old rules and frameworks, such uniformity should inspire concern and debate.

I encountered two of the key book-length studies of U.S. feminism and television early in my graduate career—Julie d'Acci's *Defining Women* and Bonnie J. Dow's *Prime-Time Feminism,* books that notably emerged from different areas of the field. These works inspired me, and at one point this project bore closer resemblance to the focused feminist analyses they offer. Feminist critics may wish I had followed their lead more closely—indeed, there are days when I wish I had, too. However, the change in the institutional context between the germination of this project and the final drafting of this book made it impossible for me, as a feminist approaching the topic as a media scholar, to write such a book. Whether because of confusion created by the contradictory texts of series such as *Ally McBeal* or uncertainty about how to weigh individual texts amidst such a multiplicity of stories, most of my attempts to argue that any of these series are feminist or antifeminist are fraught with such schizophrenia as to make them unintelligible. The intricacy required to acknowledge the contradictory valences within an individual episode would have yielded a book on any one of these shows. This book would ultimately have argued that both feminist and antifeminist attributes could be identified within the series, a scholarly contribution that did not seem of great utility.

The coterminous emergence of various postfeminist and third-wave developments in feminist theory and the coming of age of the post–Baby Boom generation of women required complex adjustments in critical frameworks. In addition to the institutional shifts I address here, feminist media scholars are divided on the use of the term "postfeminism" and its relation to feminism. Elsewhere I have advocated the complex understanding of postfeminism articulated by Australian, British, and New Zealander counterparts, rather than the use of this term in much popular journalism as synonymous with "antifeminist," or characteristic of texts that suggest feminism is obsolete.[3] Critics such as Bonnie J. Dow, Tania Modleski, and Elspeth Probyn rightly identify discourses of containment in 1980s and early 1990s media texts, but their naming of this discourse as "postfeminism" does not transfer well into the mid and late 1990s, when the valence of narratives about women and work shifted again. The theorization of postfeminism by scholars outside of the U.S. makes the term more multidimensional and usefully acknowledges conceptual and contextual shifts, while remaining politicized. The U.S. institutional context, the sociocultural context of a generation raised since the height of second-wave feminism, and the theoretical context, including developments in feminist theory, all contribute to the rupture that makes it vital to reconsider models of program analysis and underlying theoretical frameworks.

Further Implications of the End of the Network Era

The multichannel transition is still in the process of establishing new standards, practices, and conventional wisdom. Michael Curtin and Thomas Streeter have repeatedly considered how the dynamics of industrial practice are changing as a result of the culture industries' conglomerated ownership structures and their need to employ dual and somewhat contradictory strategies of producing products with mass appeal and sharply defined edge.[4] For nearly all of television history, only the former strategy proved viable. The success of narrowcasting requires reconsideration of the standards of television criticism in the same way that industry executives have had to rethink and adjust their conventional practices. The competitive dynamics of the U.S. television industry continue to change daily with new merger announcements, technological applications, programming schedules, and regulation revisions. Some trends and practices have lasted over fifty years, while exceptional cases and short-lived norms are more common. This commercial industry responds to multiple stimuli and markets: advertisers, viewers, conglomerated owners, federal regulators, independent interest groups, and the dictates of the economy. All of these interested parties prevent the television industry from remaining static.

The development of diverse dramatic series centering upon female characters corresponds to perception of the value of female audiences among advertisers and network executives. The U.S. television industry now includes conglomerates and networks deploying mass-appeal strategies and more clearly narrowcast endeavors. The conglomerated media empire Viacom, for example, makes use of economies of scope (producing as wide a range of commodities as possible) by featuring a mass-interest exhibition outlet with CBS and outlets with increasingly demarcated edge such as UPN, Nickelodeon, MTV, VH1, VH1 Classic, and so on. But there are no absolutes; one of the series most clearly constructed to appeal to a female audience that succeeds in drawing one of the largest female audiences in size and percentage of female viewers (*Judging Amy*) aired on CBS, the most generally branded outlet.

The appearance of so many female-centered dramas might be understood simply as a marketing strategy to draw upscale female audiences to networks and their advertisers. Indeed, every programming shift in the U.S. system of commercial television can be understood as a marketing strategy to some extent, or as a ploy to enhance profits; this was clear, for example, when Lee Heffernan used the parlance of the industry to say that her network "sells women." The research of Kathryn Montgomery on the outcome of various advocacy efforts seeking to change media content confirmed that those groups whose campaigns were most compatible with the economic goals of the industry achieved the greatest success.[5] Reaching professional women continues to be a primary goal of many advertisers, and those women seek programming that resonates with their experiences. The fact that series featuring complex female dramatic characters also deliver demographically valuable audiences does not diminish their significance. In many ways, this is a necessary aspect of a commercial television industry. If a show does not draw a substantial audience, it will be canceled.

My argument is not that the multichannel transition initiated a shift to a more feminist-oriented or socially concerned entertainment industry. The proliferation of female-centered dramas in the late 1990s made good business sense. The cause does not render the effect meaningless for critical scholars studying hegemonic struggles in popular culture. Evidence of a changed institutional realm should inspire us to revisit the questions we ask, the environment we study, and the contributions we believe mediated texts may make. As a scholar who concedes that U.S. media will be dominated by a commercial system for my lifetime (which is not to say I don't dream of funding for a vibrant public system alongside it), I am curious about the ways in which business interests and feminist aims can coexist symbiotically. The multichannel transition has illustrated new possibilities for program content, and as Laybourne's enterprise with Oxygen may indicate, feminists may see at least limited gains as a result of efforts to exploit the buying power of feminist and more politically progressive audience members and consumers.

The enhanced viability of narrowcasting as a competitive strategy enabled by the post-network era has contributed to altering the status of female audiences and the type and plentitude of narrative texts available, but we cannot uncritically embrace narrowcasting as revolutionary for many other groups who have long been sought through limited and stereotypical depictions. Even with renewed industrial attention to the underrepresentation of ethnic-minority groups, little gain has been achieved. While women's networks have multiplied, BET remains the only cable network to demarcate an African American edge, and Latino/a television images and stories remain limited to Spanish-speaking networks.[6] On broadcast networks, series with diverse and multiple nonwhite characters remain limited to comedies, and one could query whether a diversity of characters exists or merely a multiplicity of the same types. The "black sitcom" as it emerged on FOX in the early 1990s and The WB and UPN later in the decade appeared to be an example of how narrowcasting may benefit nondominant ethnic groups, but by 2002, television programmers retreated. In this area of programming, the emergent trend has been a reassertion of domestic sitcoms with black casts that are clearly designed to appeal to black and white audiences, the antithesis of programming exhibiting edge. The post-network era has been touted as the potential solution to the underrepresentation of gay and lesbian characters, and Viacom's launch of a "gay-themed" network suggests unprecedented possibility. Whether or not the network materializes is a less crucial question than how advertisers will regard it, whether viewers will visit it, and whether multiple systems operators will include it among their offerings. Both of these cases reassert how significant the new competitive environment has been for women relative to other groups. The multichannel transition does not eliminate the discrepant allocation of power among different groups; power is reallocated, but some audiences enjoy far more benefits than others.

The next decade will likely introduce changes to the institution of broadcasting that render it a far distant version of the network era and even remove it from this transitional configuration. Digital technology has enabled the industry to change faster than corporate money makers, viewers, regulators, and content providers can maintain, and the dissemination of DVRs and on-demand services such as Mag Rack threaten the viability of an advertiser-based system. Regardless of whether these changes occur in 2005 or 2015, the relationship between a specific industrial context and the texts it produces remains fixed. Media scholars and activists must adjust as quickly as the technologies and industries to keep pace with institutional adjustments affecting textual content.

Changes in audience size and demographic features challenge established theoretical approaches to the study of television. The ubiquity of television texts and the representations they offer to millions of homes and a wide range of viewers drives my fascination with this medium. Although the multichannel transition initiated many changes that resulted in programming that addresses a greater diversity of audiences, it also eroded the pervasiveness and affordability of television texts. Most of the female-centered dramas reach no more than five million households each week, which is not a reflection of the subgenre but increasingly true of most programs. The network-era norm of "free" programming also has been altered, with nearly 85 percent of viewers paying a minimum of thirty dollars a month for "basic" cable tiers, with fees easily reaching close to one hundred dollars monthly for additional access to more extensive tiers and premium cable networks. The economics of niche cable networks and upstart broadcasters may make programs serving small audiences viable, but the series also circulate among a much smaller audience than when theorists such as Horace Newcomb and Paul Hirsch analyzed television as a cultural forum.[7] I am not yet ready to argue that industrial conditions invalidate foundational assumptions such as the "cultural forum" or Todd Gitlin's oppositional argument of its hegemonic process, but we must reconsider network-era theories and reassess what "television" is when audiences split their attention across six broadcasters and countless cable networks.[8]

Questions of validity and significance become more problematic in research design as a result of audience erosion. By the early 1990s it was already difficult to argue for the significance of a single-text study (of book length), especially if only employing a textual methodology. The proliferation of programming characteristic of the multichannel transition diminishes the significance of any one show, particularly those on cable networks, but more comprehensive studies remain informative. Throughout the 2001–2 television season, the medium continued to enact its cultural-forum function for a society attempting to make sense of the 9/11 disaster. Critics could not look to only one show to see this function occurring. *The West Wing, Third Watch, Family Law, The Education of Max Bickford, Boston Public, The Practice, Law and Order, 7th Heaven, American Family, The District, The Division, NYPD Blue,* and likely some series I missed all offered episodes with narratives considering post–September 11 anxiety and the arbitrary erosion of the civil rights of Muslims, or those thought to be Muslims, in America. The plurality of series enacting these stories and the audience size of any of these series makes analysis of one "9/11 episode" incomplete in seeking to address how "television" explored these events and their aftermath. To continue to invoke the cultural-forum foundation, we must apply it as it operates—across many series—to better account for fractionalized audiences.

The advance provided by a narrowcast industrial environment is not without consequences that severely undermine the assumptions of television scholars in some cases. The benefits of such competition still outweigh these consequences, as successful risks taken by niche networks likely trickle down to the decisions made by networks that circulate programming to a larger audience. Broadcast networks likely would not have taken the risk of programming *Providence, Judging Amy,* and *That's Life* without the success of *Ally McBeal, Any Day Now,* and *Sex and the City.* As the debate over the effects of conglomeration also indicates, television scholarship must continue to adapt macro frameworks explaining the function of ideology and commerce in the creation of television texts to the changing relationships among producers, distributors, advertisers, and audiences. Specific case studies illuminate the intricate negotiations that industry-scale models omit. As media scholars continue to publish research, more examples of institutional processes become available to either verify or disprove theoretical models created without application. Scholars must be increasingly wary of adopting perspectives and assumptions about television that were produced in a network broadcast era for this environment in which television continues its transition to a narrowcast medium. These models and approaches still offer great utility, but we must attend to their increasing limitations.

In many ways the research presented here marks a starting point from which future studies examining gender roles and representations or the effects of changing industrial practices on programming can expand. The late 1990s provided an intersection of a range of factors, including cultural concerns, a specific competitive environment, and various perspectives on gender and feminism. The confluence of these factors can be seen in the plurality of female-centered dramas at this time, as well as in the intricate stories told by each series. These series mark a moment in the ongoing cultural and representational negotiation of women's roles in society, but in their entirety, they clearly disrupt the legacy of such forms. Television texts continue to provide the forum for the most widely shared storytelling in U.S. culture, depicting cultural anxieties, fears, hopes, and questions in a constantly evolving manner. Understanding how shifts in these depictions correspond to changes in cultural attitudes and theoretical frameworks helps explain the cultural negotiation of beliefs about gender roles and attitudes toward other aspects of identity.

A Replay TV advertisement from 2000 features a young woman explaining her use of the DVR device: "If I had my own channel I would only put on shows that depict strong, independent women so I could see how they do their hair." A key absence in this study is detailed audience research that may better illuminate why female audiences choose various shows and the pleasures they take from them. Regardless of what I argue, audiences could be tuning in only to see the latest variation in hairstyles. My narrative and institutional analysis provides a launching point for studies that may better explain why certain series survived and others failed, beyond the narrative and industrial-based estimations I provide. Audience research could reveal a great deal, especially because of the variation among these series. I most enjoy some of the series that I am most critical of from a feminist perspective, and such contradictions must be explored. In the limited audience research I reported elsewhere on *Any Day Now*, I found that audiences engage the intricate themes of identity in complicated ways and as negotiated by their own subjectivity (as well as many discussions of Rene's hairstyles).[9]

Well-deployed audience research can contribute a great deal to text-based hypotheses, providing the only way to know what audiences make of this diverse array of dramatic texts. Audiences are a confounding variable whose behavior cannot be predicted. At the same time as these various dramas aired and Oxygen and WE battled with Lifetime to bring new stories to television audiences, SoapNet's rapid growth in distribution and viewership provided the biggest story in terms of female audiences. SoapNet is watched by well over twice the audience viewing Oxygen and by fifteen thousand more homes than WE, even though it reaches half as many homes as the other networks.[10] Comparatively, its business model is highly profitable, as it repurposes daily programs from ABC and airs various soap archives that had no previous second-run value. So while we may be on a precipice of innovation, audiences pursue interests in a manner contrary to programmers' and executives' expectations.

The longevity of *Touched by an Angel* provides another such case. The series began its run in 1994, predating the series I study here, and it continued to compete alongside them and outlasted many. *Touched by an Angel* is distinct from many of the series I consider and has much more in common with previous series such as *Dr. Quinn, Medicine Woman,* and *Murder, She Wrote;* but it also places female characters at its fore and particularly hails a female audience. The series drew consistent and sizable audiences despite the limited innovation of its narratives. Female angels, vampire slayers, spies, doctors, judges, and genetically engineered mutant hybrids all surpassed the barriers required to become U.S. television characters, and various segments of predominantly female audiences tuned in to watch their adventures. The impossibility of understanding why some characters and contexts catch on while others fail is underscored by the short careers of many network programmers; they aim to please a fickle, unpredictable audience.

At a family gathering I overheard an aunt mention that she only watches a soap that she time-shifts for evening viewing and *Touched by an Angel* on Sunday nights. My mother is a fan of *Providence* but refuses to watch *Judging Amy.* My preference is the opposite, but we both enjoy *Gilmore Girls.* The range of female-centered dramas that greeted audiences in the late 1990s and early twenty-first century began to address the diverse needs and pleasures of female audiences. Many of the series went beyond the edginess of primarily hailing female audiences to address particular tastes and pleasures of subgroups within the female audience. Some groups were overserved because of their attractiveness to advertisers, and all but Lifetime offered little range in the demographics of their characters, despite the range of stories explored. There is much new ground these dramas could explore—lesbian characters, partnered characters, characters without rewarding careers, and stay-at-home parents remain relatively absent. Female audiences face more options than in previous eras, but this diversity must be approached with caution. We must carefully sort the gains from the retractions and apply complicated theoretical models that account for cultural and industrial contexts in assessing programs and their ideological contributions (and, of course, how the characters wear their hair).

Notes

Introduction

1. See, for example, Collins, "Ally McBeal."

2. Bellafante, "Feminism."

3. *The Profiler* and *Sabrina the Teenage Witch* premiered in 1996. Although these series vary from the action-heroine format, they also bear some similarity due to the lead characters' supernatural powers.

4. Other series premiering during this time, such as *Felicity, Family Law,* and *Popular,* are related but ultimately more accurately classified as ensemble series. They originated as female-centered dramas but went through a process of textual negotiation in an attempt to reach a larger audience, which resulted in a format more consistent with the ensemble dramatic series.

5. Higgins, "Lifetime Hits No. 1."

6. Prikios, "HBO."

7. This similarity cannot be underestimated, but it is also true of nearly all shows airing on U.S. commercial networks. I do not note this to excuse this limited demographic portrayal but in recognition of a specific industrial context that circumscribes the range of stories likely to be told on television. I wholeheartedly affirm critiques of the limited depiction of "reality" presented by U.S. television content and its skewed picture of a nearly uniform upper-middle-class, white, heterosexual world. At the same time, I understand why this has been and will likely continue to be the tendency of a commercially based television system. As much as I would prefer an alternative, it is important to seriously engage the narratives and images presented by this system because they circulate widely, and television remains the central storyteller in U.S. culture. While I and many other critics would like to see a greater demographic diversity of women on television, we miss an opportunity to explore what else of significance can be found in these series if we categorically disavow existing content based on these attributes alone.

8. I begin with 1970 for the sake of expediency. There is clearly an important history before second-wave feminism as well; however, it has less bearing on the late 1990s environ-

ment. See, for example, d'Acci, "Nobody's Woman?"; and Luckett, "A Moral Crisis in Prime Time."

9. d'Acci, *Defining Women;* Rabinovitz, "Ms.-Representation"; Byars and Meehan, "Once in a Lifetime."

10. d'Acci, *Defining Women,* 67.

11. Rabinovitz, "Ms.-Representation," 145.

12. Ibid., 146.

13. Ibid.

14. See Lotz, "Postfeminist Television Criticism," 107.

15. Byars and Meehan, "Once in a Lifetime," 18.

16. See also d'Acci, *Defining Women,* 65–73.

17. Byars and Meehan, "Once in a Lifetime," 19.

18. d'Acci, *Defining Women,* 68–69.

19. Byars and Meehan, "Once in a Lifetime," 20.

20. Ibid., 21; Arthurs, "*Sex and the City* and Consumer Culture."

21. This change is emphasized in Staiger, *Blockbuster TV.*

22. NOW produced earlier studies as well. See National Organization for Women, *Facts on Women and Media.* I encourage readers to explore the findings and methodology of the reports. The 2000–2002 reports are available on NOW's website, <www.NOW.org>.

23. In the 2002 survey, the study assigned letter grades rather than numbers.

24. See Zoonen, *Feminist Media Studies,* for an overview.

25. The essays collected in Tuchman, Daniels, and Benet, *Hearth and Home,* reflect the norms of this early work.

26. Janus, "Research on Sex-Roles in the Mass Media"; Tuchman, "Women's Depictions by the Mass Media"; Waldman, "There's More to a Positive Image Than Meets the Eye." A later article by Marjorie Ferguson makes a slightly different criticism; she addresses concerns about the assumption of early scholarship that increasing the number of women in media industries and their power would positively affect women's representations. See Ferguson, "Images of Power and the Feminist Fallacy." As feminist theory delineated the difference between sex and gender, the primary terms in this research shifted, although much else about the research method and theoretical assumptions remains the same.

27. Lisa Parks presents a parallel critique of the legacy of quantitative studies of television violence and also seeks to identify ways in which critical television scholarship might participate in cultural debates. See Parks, "Brave New *Buffy.*"

28. Employment possibilities were also a concern, an emphasis Ferguson critiques as misplaced. More recent research continuing this approach includes Seggar, "Imagery of Women in Television Drama"; Reep and Dambrot, "Television's Professional Women"; Davis, "Portrayals of Women in Prime-Time Network Television"; Atkin, Moorman, and Lin, "Ready for Prime Time"; Vest, "Prime-Time Pilots"; Vande Berg and Streckfuss, "Prime-Time Television's Portrayal of Women and the World of Work"; Elasmar, Hasegawa, and Brain, "The Portrayal of Women in U.S. Prime Time Television"; Lauzen and Dozier, "Making a Difference in Prime Time"; Lauzen, Dozier, and Hicks, "Prime-time Players and Powerful Prose."

29. I am indebted to Sharon Marie Ross for this insight. See Lotz and Ross, "Bridging Media-Specific Approaches."

30. Haskell, *From Reverence to Rape;* Rosen, *Popcorn Venus.*

31. See Kaplan, *Regarding Television;* Mellencamp, *Logics of Television;* Mellencamp, "Situation Comedy, Feminism, and Freud."

32. See Caughie, *Television Drama,* 21–24, for a more elaborate discussion of the British negotiations.

33. Brunsdon, *"Crossroads";* Hobson, *Crossroads;* Brown, "The Politics of Soaps"; Brunsdon, *The Feminist, the Housewife, and the Soap Opera.*

34. Ang, *Watching Dallas;* Brunsdon and Morley, *Everyday Television;* Gillespie, *Television, Ethnicity, and Cultural Change;* Gray, *Video Playtime.*

35. Jhally, *Stuart Hall.*

36. Ibid.

37. National Organization for Women, "Watch Out, Listen Up!"

38. See deMoraes, "NOW's Bewildering Picks and Pans"; Fazzone, "NOW's Strange Taste in TV."

39. Ross, "Super(Natural) Women."

40. The mass communication language of effects has been so dominant because of the comparatively plentiful governmental and interest-group funding available for this method. In self-funding its initiative, however, NOW was free to deviate from the methods commonly supported by many funding agencies. NOW's initiative has not attracted journalists' attention in the same way as the media-content initiatives of ethnic minority groups such as the NAACP, likely because of the contradictions in the survey's rankings and analysis, although the very different histories of gender and ethnic equality cannot be discounted either.

41. Sharkey, "Women Get More Cybillized"; Collins, "A Woman's Work Is Never Shown"; and Schwarzbaum, "We're Gonna Make It after All," reflect the influence of the role-model framework. Theroux, "TV Women Have Come a Long Way," provides a notable contrast. Examples of rhetorical or literary criticism include Dow, *Prime-Time Feminism;* Cloud, "Concordance, Complexity, and Conservatism"; Cloud, "Hegemony or Concordance?"; Projansky and Vande Berg, "Sabrina, the Teenage . . ."; and Inness, *Tough Girls.*

42. Dow, *Prime-Time Feminism;* Inness, *Tough Girls;* Helford, *Fantasy Girls;* Wilcox and Lavery, *Fighting the Forces;* Inness, *Action Chicks;* Akass and McCabe, *Reading "Sex and the City."* In contrast, Meyers, *Mediated Women,* mainly includes work by communication researchers that transcends the role-model framework (although only a fraction of the chapters consider television).

43. In framing *Mediated Women,* Meyers struggles in her attempt to move discussions within communication beyond the role-model framework. She describes the status of women's representations as "fractured" to acknowledge the new variance in the roles allowed to women in media. But lacking the cultural studies framework, she is left to assert that this diversity is "more confusing than liberating." Meyers, "Fracturing Women," 12.

44. Brunsdon, "Feminism, Post-feminism, Martha, Martha, and Nigella," 112. In her review of soap opera research, Brunsdon notes similar changes in contexts and argues that they require an evolution in research methods (*The Feminist, the Housewife, and the Soap Opera*). Concerns about the limitations of role-model analysis are evident in Macdonald, *Representing Women.*

45. Two new journals, *Television and New Media* and *Feminist Media Studies,* which began publishing in 2000 and 2001, respectively, remedy this to some degree.

46. Brunsdon, d'Acci, and Spigel, *Feminist Television Criticism.*

47. For a more expansive discussion of these varied feminist approaches, see Lotz and Ross, "Bridging Media-Specific Approaches."

48. See, for example, essays in the following anthologies: Brown, *Television and Women's Culture;* Spigel and Mann, *Private Screenings;* Baehr and Gray, *Turning It On;* Brunsdon, d'Acci, and Spigel, *Feminist Television Criticism;* d'Acci, "Lifetime"; and Haralovich and Rabinovitz, *Television, History, and American Culture.* See also Brunsdon, *Screen Tastes;* Brunsdon, *The Feminist, the Housewife, and the Soap Opera;* d'Acci, *Defining Women;* Feuer, *Seeing through the Eighties;* Haralovich, "Sit-coms and Suburbs"; Rabinovitz, "Sitcoms and Single Moms"; Rabinovitz, "Ms.-Representation"; Rowe, *Unruly Woman;* Spigel, *Make Room for TV;* Spigel, "From Domestic Space to Outer Space"; and White, *Tele-advising.*

49. See Lotz and Ross, "Bridging Media-Specific Approaches."

50. Although the number of series could be raised to twenty-two if one considered series that generally fit the form, but not my categories.

51. Feminist viewpoints on pornography illustrate one such issue.

52. Bellafante, "Feminism."

53. I do not mean to suggest academic and activist as mutually exclusive categories of feminism, but rather to acknowledge that both exist.

54. Dow, *Prime-Time Feminism;* Rabinovitz, "Sitcoms and Single Moms"; Rabinovitz, "Ms.-Representation"; d'Acci, *Defining Women;* Deming, "*Kate and Allie*"; Rowe, *Unruly Woman;* Mayne, "*L.A. Law* and Prime-Time Feminism"; Clark, "*Cagney and Lacey*"; Thomas, *Fans Feminisms and "Quality" Media.*

55. hooks, *Ain't I a Woman,* 194.

56. Brooks, *Postfeminisms,* 4.

57. Ibid.

58. Dow, *Prime-Time Feminism;* Press, *Women Watching Television;* Modleski, *Feminism without Women;* Vavrus, *Postfeminist News;* and Projansky, *Watching Rape.*

59. See Lotz, "Postfeminist Television Criticism."

60. The cultural studies approach to institutions differs from traditional political economy and more descriptive business histories that have established a place in mass communication scholarship. Recent work by Paul du Gay, David Hesmondhalgh, and others has offered a significant contribution to demarcating the distinction of the study of institutions within cultural studies as well as theorization of the place of production within the "circuit of culture." The cultural studies approach to institutions distinguishes itself from business history by incorporating critical analysis in its examination of industries and differentiates itself from traditional political economy by acknowledging that the creation of content is determined by more than only economic factors. Cultural studies does not presuppose economic determinism but views the creation and dissemination of cultural texts as complex, contradictory, and resulting from factors that cannot be reduced to a simple economic base; yet it still acknowledges the significant role of economic and business factors. It conceives of questions about texts, audiences, and social contexts as carefully integrated and critical to informing analysis of the production process. See du Gay, *Production of Culture/Cultures of Production;* du Gay et al., *Doing Cultural Studies;* Hesmondhalgh, *Culture Industries;* Grossberg, "Cultural Studies vs. Po-

litical Economy"; Kellner, "Overcoming the Divide"; and Johnson, "What Is Cultural Studies Anyway?"

61. In 1985, Loews chairman Laurence Tisch took control of CBS, and Capital Cities Communications (Cap Cities) acquired ABC. General Electric bought RCA, NBC's parent company, in 1986. The new corporate owners of the broadcast networks brought changes to traditional network operations as they sought to create lean, profit-maximizing institutions. A second round of corporate owners altered network ownership for CBS with a buyout first by Westinghouse in 1995 and then Viacom in 1999, and Cap Cities/ABC merged with Disney in 1995. See Auletta, *Three Blind Mice.*

62. Rupert Murdoch succeeded where DuMont, United Network, Paramount, and Metromedia failed and launched the Fox Broadcasting Company as a fourth broadcast network in the fall of 1986. Although only programming one night per week and reaching only 75 percent of viewers at first, FOX grew into a fourth network force by 1989, when it turned a profit and first won a nightly ratings race. Additional broadcast competitors continued to adjust the competitive balance, with The WB and UPN first offering programming to a limited viewing audience on two nights per week in 1995. See Block, *Outfoxed.*

63. See Byars and Meehan, "Once in a Lifetime," 23.

64. Stevens, *International Television and Video Almanac;* Initiative Media, "Today in National Television."

65. Byars and Meehan, "Once in a Lifetime," 23.

66. Stevens, *International Television and Video Almanac,* 10.

67. Ibid.

68. Caldwell, *Televisuality,* 11.

69. Dempsey, "Cable Aud's Now Bigger that B'Cast."

70. Higgins and Romano, "Cheaper by the Thousand." Advertisers also perceive broadcast advertising time to be scarce because of the few networks, while cable advertising slots are more plentiful. However, advertising is not based on buying an advertisement, but rather pricing is based on advertisers purchasing the exposure of their message to a predetermined audience size (it costs X dollars to reach a hundred thousand viewers). Consequently, there is not more advertising available; rather, it is spread across a greater number of outlets. Broadcasters cannot offer audiences as large as during the network era, but they still provide the best option for many advertisers seeking the largest possible general audience or those with time-specific products, such as a film premiere. Advertisers with less need for expansive and general exposure did gain from the success of cable and may now choose among increased outlets. Those marketing niche goods can target their advertising with cable buys, often at less cost than required by a broadcast campaign.

71. Owen and Wildman, *Video Economics,* 151.

72. Curtin, "Feminine Desire in the Age of Satellite Television"; Curtin and Streeter, "Media."

73. Curtin, "Feminine Desire in the Age of Satellite Television," 63.

74. Caldwell, *Televisuality,* 9.

75. USA had programmed other original series (*Cover Me, The War Next Door, Manhattan, AZ*), but until the 2002 success of *Monk* and *The Dead Zone,* it had the most success with female-focused series. See Higgins, "Herzog Heads Home."

76. The WB lost *Buffy the Vampire Slayer* to UPN in a bidding war at the end of its fifth season, but the series remained on an upstart network.

77. "The Facts," Oxygen Home Page, <http://www.oxygen.com/corporate/html/ox_vi _fact.htm>, October 11, 1999.

78. Scholars have identified women's programs in various ways and offered manifold criteria for determining their components, although no clear or consistent standard exists. Some have applied categories developed for other media. In examining the original films aired by the Lifetime network, Heather Lyn Hundley uses the distinctions of female, feminine, and feminist literature developed by Elaine Showalter in relation to British women novelists. These variations are useful for Hundley's study of films; however, the ongoing nature of narrative television series renders these distinctions less functional for series television. Showalter's categorizations rely on a contained narrative, and the female protagonists in the dramatic series I explore evolve significantly week to week and season to season, as they face crises and situations that often allow them inconsistent and contradictory stances. See Hundley, "Defining Feminine Programming and Co-opting Liberal Feminism"; Showalter, *Literature of Their Own.*

After reviewing early scholarship, John Fiske demarcates a category of "feminine television" to distinguish the features of programs designed to attract female audiences. He lists key attributes, including disrupted narratives, serial organization that defers resolution and emphasizes process, distinct themes of sexuality and empowerment, narrative and visual excess consistent with melodrama, a multitude of characters who create an environment conducive for polysemy, and decentered subjects that deny a unified reading position (*Television Culture,* 179–97). Soap operas utilize nearly all of these attributes, although many of these narrative features have steadily infiltrated prime-time genres that were once episodic and more likely to fit Fiske's category of "masculine television." Fiske's choice of identifying narrative features dominant in soap operas as "feminine" raises issues of primacy, as in the relationship among narrative forms, the gendering of tastes, and sex-specification of audiences. Julie d'Acci's work expands the definition beyond common soap-opera attributes in her determination of narrative attributes common among "women's programs." She notes multiple factors, including the sex/gender of the protagonist, the sex/gender of the target audience, certain narrative structures and textual operations (many consistent with those described by Fiske), and the manner through which programs constitute the masculinity and femininity of their spectators. Similarly, Annette Kuhn considers the "construction of narratives motivated by female desire and processes of spectator identification governed by female point of view" as another description of the defining features of the "women's picture" as a textual system (Kuhn, "Women's Genres," 145).

Understanding a concept like "women's programming" as composed of a variety of factors is critical to developing units of analysis that do not essentialize gender distinctions, because correlation among types of programming and audience preferences are culturally constructed rather than biologically determined. d'Acci addresses the problems of conflating notions of "female," "feminine," and "feminist" with the sex specification of audiences by troubling the association of narrative forms predominately enjoyed by those of a certain sex specification with particular generic attributes. Concerns about how cultures gender narrative preferences and then assign them varying cultural capital led feminist scholars to interrogate descriptions of programming as "feminine television," or even as "women's" programs or genres. Surveys of female audiences, their interpretations, and preferences illustrate the diversity of tastes and pleasures experienced by female audiences to a degree to which text-based theory cannot adequately account. See Press, *Women Watching Television,* for variation based on class and generation.

79. I use "female" instead of "women" because at least one series begins with a teen-aged girl rather than a woman as its narrative center. In accord with the growing body of youth and girl studies, I acknowledge a difference between women's and girls' experience; however, this book primarily considers shows that center upon adult women characters, and I do not intend for my use of "female" to indicate a conflation of girl and woman. Concurrent with the series I consider here, a rise in girl-centered series has also occurred, particularly on Nickelodeon, with *Clarissa Explains It All, The Mystery Files of Shelby Woo, Caitlin's Way,* and *Tania,* and Disney's *That's So Raven, Even Stevens,* and *Lizzie McGuire.* Both networks have also developed a number of cartoon series featuring central girl characters as well. These shows indicate an important development, but they are part of a different legacy than the series I consider here.

80. Significantly, the gender composition of the audience varies considerably in different types of female-centered dramas.

81. This distinction excludes workplace ensemble series such as *Family Law* and serial ensembles such as *Felicity.* Many ensemble series primarily develop as "franchise" series built around topics such as medicine, law, and police work, which provide their organizational theme, while the protagonist functions as the focus of the female-centered dramas. See Turow, *Playing Doctor.*

82. Tudor, "Genre," 7.

83. Mittell, "A Cultural Approach to Television Genre Theory."

84. Rabinovitz, "Sitcoms and Single Moms," 3; Mellencamp, "Situation Comedy, Feminism, and Freud"; Rowe, *Unruly Woman;* Dow, *Prime-Time Feminism.*

85. In the late 1990s, audiences mainly found serial dramas on upstart networks that targeted teens and young adults (*Dawson's Creek*). The high-profile failure of Aaron Spelling's *Titans* (NBC) in 2000 further indicates the decreased status this form possesses in the competitive environment I examine. Indeed, Lifetime continues to receive its highest ratings with original movies, and broadcast networks also have occasional successes, particularly when the films feature major or otherwise retired female stars. For example, the reunion of Mary Tyler Moore and Valerie Harper in *Mary and Rhoda* (ABC, February 7, 2000), or the gathering of Elizabeth Taylor, Shirley MacLaine, Debbie Reynolds, and Joan Collins in *These Old Broads* (ABC, February 12, 2001). For feminist scholarship on soap operas, see Brunsdon, *The Feminist, the Housewife, and the Soap Opera;* for perspectives on the made-for-television movie, see Feuer, *Seeing through the Eighties;* and Schulze, "The Made-for-TV Movie."

86. See, for example, Pennington, "Now, It's 'Wham, Bam'—and from the Ma'am"; and Tomashoff, "Actresses Are Beginning to Get a Bigger Cut of the Action."

87. Such hybrid narratives with extensive serial features are the hallmark of *Xena: Warrior Princess* and *Buffy the Vampire Slayer.*

88. As Byars and Meehan argue ("Once in a Lifetime"), networks originally sought for dramas such as *Cagney and Lacey* and *St. Elsewhere* to include women in positions of power to draw a broader cross-section of the audience (more women).

89. See Meehan, "Conceptualizing Culture as Commodity."

90. Gough-Yates, *Understanding Women's Magazines,* 39.

91. A point also made by Gough-Yates (ibid.).

Chapter 1

Kathy Haesele quoted in Shawna Malcom, "Women on the Verge," *Entertainment Weekly,* September 3, 1999.

1. A network brand can also develop unintentionally and be a negative association, as indicated by Lifetime's more derogatory reputation as a "victim's network" because of its staple "women in crisis" films. See McAdams, "Opportunity of a Lifetime," 28.

2. See Popcorn and Marigold, *EVEolution;* Quinlan, *Just Ask a Woman;* Barletta, *Marketing to Women.*

3. Meehan and Byars, "Telefeminism," 35–36.

4. As late as 1992, advertiser-created programming comprised 10 percent of Lifetime's schedule and was on the rise. Bronstein, "Mission Accomplished?" Lifetime's first surge in viewership resulted from acquisition of syndication rights to the CBS series *Cagney and Lacey.*

5. Meehan and Byars, "Telefeminism," 36–38.

6. Ibid., 43.

7. Ibid., 45.

8. "Original" indicates that these series were produced for a first run on Lifetime, as opposed to narrative series bought in syndication. Lifetime attempted weekly original series as early as 1989, with its continuation of *The Days and Nights of Molly Dodd,* then with series such as *Confessions of Crime, The Hidden Room,* and *Veronica Clare* in 1991, but these performed dismally in comparison with Lifetime's original films. See Wilson, "Upscale Feminine Angst"; Johnson, "Lifetime's Feminine Psychographic Space and the *Mystery Loves Company* Series."

9. Basic cable networks paid more than five billion dollars for their 1998–99 programming, two billion more than they paid two years earlier. Dempsey, "Cable Casts Broadcast-size Coin over New Programs."

10. Petrozzello, "Only on Cable."

11. *Any Day Now, Maggie,* and *Oh Baby* are the series that aired. Ibid., 42.

12. Freeman, "Falling Under a Spell(ing)." By the end of the 1998–99 season, Lifetime dismantled the evening of original series, moving its two half-hour comedies (*Maggie* and *Oh Baby*) to Saturday nights, while leaving *Any Day Now* in its Tuesday time slot. The 1999–2000 television season brought additional changes, as Lifetime moved *Any Day Now* to Sunday, canceled one of the comedies, and added a comedic-interview program and a one-hour reality show. By 2000–2001, Lifetime canceled the remaining sitcom and premiered two additional dramas, *Strong Medicine* and *The Division.*

13. See Hundley, "Defining Feminine Programming and Co-opting Liberal Feminism"; Byars and Meehan, "Once in a Lifetime"; Meehan and Byars, "Telefeminism."

14. Burgi, "Channel Change."

15. Dempsey, "LMN Landing on Cox."

16. Larson, "Broadband Babies"; McAdams, "Too Big to Ignore," 98.

17. Moss, "Lifetime Adding More Movies, Hoping for Lift."

18. Alexander, "Opportunity of a Lifetime."

19. Black also had extensive marketing experience; she worked on home video sales for Disney and on the "softer side of Sears" advertising campaign by DDB Needham. Ibid.

20. McAdams, "Opportunity of a Lifetime," 23.

21. Ibid.

22. Lee Heffernan, personal communication with the author, May 27, 2003.

23. McAdams, "Opportunity of a Lifetime," 26.

24. Higgins, "Top 25 Networks."

25. Ibid.

26. Ross, "Turner Explores Cable Network Aimed at Women."

27. Because of the size of the Time Warner/Turner media enterprise, the proposed Women's Network was well-positioned in terms of distribution and programming. It likely would have received distribution through Time Warner Cable, which possessed a subscription base of 12.6 million homes. Additionally, programming was slated to use many of the female-focused magazines owned by Time Warner, including *People, In Style, Sports Illustrated for Women,* and *Parenting,* as well as drawing on a partnership with the publishing giant Conde Nast, whose titles include *Vogue, House and Garden,* and *Vanity Fair.* See Haddad, "Cable Targets Women for Two New Channels."

28. Coleman, "Fuzzy Vision Doomed Channel?"

29. Petrozzello, "TCI, Laybourne to Launch Oxygen."

30. Moss, "Laybourne Preps New Women's Net."

31. Winfrey had second thoughts about giving up the licensing rights and renegotiated her ownership stake with Oxygen in 2002 to retain *The Oprah Winfrey Show* library. Instead she produces an original series for the network, *Oprah after the Show.* Winfrey also hosted the Oxygen series *Oprah Goes Online* early in the network's history. See Petrozzello, "The A-Team"; deMoraes, "Enriched Oxygen."

32. "Vulcan Ventures Makes $100 Million Investment in Oxygen Media"; McAdams, "Laybourne Waits to Exhale."

33. Prior to its cable launch, Oxygen operated a number of online properties, including Thrive, a healthy-living site; Moms Online, a parenting site; Oprah Online; ka-Ching, which provided information on small business, personal finance, and careers; and O_2 live, a site featuring live chats with "influential" women. As part of its integrated media approach, Oxygen pledged 5.3 million dollars to Oxygen/Markle Pulse, a joint venture between Oxygen and the Markle Foundation to "survey women's opinions on issues and seek to get more women online." The Markle Foundation invested 4.5 million dollars in the venture. "Oxygen Media and Markle to Fund Women's Research Initiative."

34. "Geraldine Laybourne."

35. Rutenberg, "Poor Showing for Oxygen in Ratings."

36. Larson, "Oxygen Finding Its Way."

37. See Penley, Parks, and Everett, "Log On."

38. Stanley, "The Oxygen TV Channel Is Bowing to Tastes."

39. Rather than the derelict duo of Patsy and Edina played against the straight Saffy, the *Good Girls Don't* duo embodies an opposition, with Jane presenting Patsy and Edina's unruliness contrasted against Marjorie's traditional femininity. The series also regularly incorporates more characters (including regular male characters), unlike *Absolutely Fabulous.*

40. Granger, "Rainbow Woos Ops with 'Romance' Tales."

41. Moss, "Romance Ups Original Productions."

42. Donohue, "Romance Execs Plan to Relaunch an 'Oasis.'"

43. Moss, "Romance Ups Original Productions," 130.

44. Berkowitz, "Johnson & Johnson Signs Ad Deal with WE Network."

45. Umstead, "WE Facelift Completes Changeover."

46. WE Upfront Sales Kit.

47. Romano, "BET Is about to Get a Real Rival."

48. By 2003–4, networks such as TNT, TBS, and USA had rebranded themselves with more specific identities and returned to their status as top cable networks.

49. Lee Heffernan, personal communication with the author, May 27, 2003.

50. Anna Gough-Yates looks at similar issues during a similar time of adjustment in the women's target market in her book on the British magazine industry. Many useful parallels can be drawn between the case studies. Gough-Yates, *Understanding Women's Magazines.*

51. Curtin, "Feminine Desire in the Age of Satellite Television."

52. Although networks commission all kinds of proprietary research about how viewers perceive network brands and their priorities in viewing them, much of this work must be replicated by academic researchers who do not have a stake in the outcome before we can draw a more comprehensive picture of how viewers manage their viewing options in an era of so many programming providers.

53. Romano, "Wish You Were Younger?" According to Lifetime, their median viewer age is 47.4. The discrepancy likely results from different time periods, as cable's primetime audience tends to be older than the daytime audience.

54. Lee Heffernan, personal communication with the author, May 27, 2003.

55. Many advertisers value affluent customers, with ratings in households with income greater than fifty thousand dollars providing an important audience attribute.

56. All data from author's interviews with network executives. Lifetime: Tim Brooks, May 12, 2003, New York; Tricia Melton, May 13, 2003, New York. Oxygen: Deborah Breece and Sarah Barasch, May 8, 2003, New York. WE: Lee Heffernan, May 27, 2003, telephone interview.

57. Meehan and Byars, "Telefeminism."

58. I include the quoted jargon because it drives home the transaction that occurs. In selling time, networks establish a cost-per-thousand rate so that advertisers can compare prices across different networks. Heffernan is explaining that the cost-per-thousand rate for female audience members is now typically higher than the rate for a mixed-gender audience. Advertisers have long sought audiences composed of women because of their buying responsibilities. In the mid-1990s case of Lifetime that Meehan and Byars write about, it is likely that the emergent nature of cable led the network to be hesitant to only target women because cable audiences were generally very small, and it was more important to increase gross ratings to illustrate cable's viability.

59. Kahle and Chiagouris, *Values, Lifestyles, and Psychographics.*

60. A version of a VALS survey is available at <www.sric-bi.com/vals/surveynew .shtml>.

61. "Syndicated" indicates standard surveys (such as VALS) that are the property of

specific agencies that are hired to apply the standard survey for a specific company. The other type of survey would involve those developed specifically to survey a particular market or product use.

62. See Surmanek, *Media Planning.*

63. Morgan and Levy, "Targeting to Psychographic Segments."

64. Quoted in Benzel, "Three Phases of Eve."

65. Quoted in ibid.

66. At Lifetime I spoke with Tricia Melton, vice president of marketing, and Tim Brooks, senior vice president of research. Melton had only been with Lifetime for eight weeks and had previously worked for Oxygen. Brooks has worked at Lifetime since 2000 and previously worked for USA; he is frequently quoted in the trade press as an expert on the broadcast and cable industries.

67. Lifetime Upfront Sales Kit. Information about each initiative also appears on the network's Web site: <www.lifetimetv.com/community/olc/index.html>.

68. Lifetime Real Women is distributed to less than ten million households. At this point, the network is not differentiating its programming as much as it is likely to once it becomes more widely available. LRW repurposes a great deal of Lifetime and LMN content, likely to keep programming costs down until wider distribution can be secured.

69. At Oxygen, I spoke with Deborah Beece, president of programming, and Sarah Barasch, vice president of research. Beece had worked for Oxygen since its launch and had previously worked at TVLand. Barasch came from MTV and noted that many other staffers had come from MTV as well.

70. In my interview with WE's senior vice president of marketing, Lee Heffernan, she also reflected on her five-year experience in marketing at Lifetime. Heffernan referenced quantitative and qualitative focus-group studies by the network of viewers' responses to their films. She noted that they found that many women used the films as educational devices (particularly women in C and D counties), that many women believed the films were based on real stories, and that viewing Lifetime made them feel better about themselves and the struggles in their own lives. This type of audience research provides an important component for understanding what audiences do with texts.

71. See Rowe, *The Unruly Woman.*

72. WE Upfront Sales Kit. I spoke with Lee Heffernan, senior vice president of marketing at WE. Before joining WE in late 2001, Heffernan spent five years in marketing at Lifetime, which provides her with a broad and comparative view of women's cable networks and their brand specificity.

73. Ibid.

74. Ibid.

75. Ibid.

76. deMoraes, "The Unthinking Women's Network."

77. Although WE's rebranding comes chronologically close to Oxygen's launch, Oxygen established its brand in the press well before its launch, which would have allowed WE executives to anticipate the new network's identity.

78. Also noted by Jensen, "Zeroing in on What Women Watch."

79. This has been more of an occasional feature than a regular series.

80. This comparison is useful to illustrate superficial differences across types of pro-

grams, but these shows meant different things to their respective networks. Lifetime has produced hundreds of *Intimate Portraits,* while *Who Does She Think She Is?* and *Cool Women* were both short-lived examples of the early histories of their networks. The relationship of the "style" shows to the network brand also varies significantly by network.

Chapter 2

James Schamus quoted in Richard Corliss and Jeanne McDowell, "Go Ahead, Make Her Day," *Time,* March 26, 2001, 64–67.

1. See Levine, "Wallowing in Sex," 194–304, for a thorough production history of *Wonder Woman* and a detailed analysis of the contradictory ways *Charlie's Angels* constructed and contained its characters as sex symbols and in relation to feminism.

2. See ibid.; Gough-Yates, "Angels in Chains?"; and Douglas, *Where the Girls Are.*

3. Inness, *Tough Girls,* 32.

4. I define them as commercially successful because they drew audiences large enough to air for more than one season. *Charlie's Angels* differs in significant ways from the other two series because of the characters' lack of superhuman ability and because of the narratives of friendship enabled by multiple lead female characters. I would not classify *Charlie's Angels* as a gender-reversal narrative, and the scholarship of Douglas, Gough-Yates, and Levine attends to the ambivalent feminist potential of these series.

5. Fiske, *Television Culture,* 179–223.

6. *Alias* debuted during the editing of this chapter. This series incorporates some of the themes and tools prominent among the series I examine here, yet it deviates in significant ways as well. The contributions of series debuting in 2001 and after are addressed in the epilogue.

7. In comparison with their action-drama contemporaries, series about tough female law enforcement officers, such as *The Profiler* and *The Huntress,* provide ordinary stories. I also considered excluding *La Femme Nikita* for this reason; I ultimately included it because many of its textual components correlate with the other action dramas, despite its "normalcy." *The Profiler* and *The Huntress* feature female protagonists in unusual roles (crime-scene profiler and bounty hunter, respectively), but other series illustrate that much more empowerment and conventional "career" deviation was possible for female characters by the late 1990s. It is difficult to include these series in an analysis of those that offer characters superhuman abilities or place them in otherworldly settings because of the range of narratives such abilities and environments enable.

V.I.P., Cleopatra 2525, Relic Hunter, Sheena, Queen of the Jungle, Queen of Swords, and *She Spies* are better classified as adventure series than action dramas. Adventure series focus on plot advancement and spectacle in contrast to characterization and psychological motivation. Perhaps a comparison can be drawn between adventure series and kiddie westerns (such as *The Lone Ranger*), as distinguished from action dramas and adult westerns (such as *Gunsmoke*), to illustrate this disparity. See MacDonald, *Who Shot the Sheriff?* Although the series originate from a similar premise and take place in comparable contexts, action dramas and adult westerns develop stories motivated by complex characterization, while adventure series and kiddie westerns emphasize the spectacle of chases and fight scenes. Additionally, these adventure series inordinately emphasize the heroine's sexuality. The containment of action drama heroines through hegemonic constructions of female sexuality also develops as a complicated point of analysis for these shows, but the inclusion of more complex narrative aspects helps them transcend singular definition as sexualized entities that the adventure series' heroines are less able to surmount. As a result of their various narrative priorities, action dramas explore very different stories than adventure series featuring female heroines.

The more comedically oriented series focusing on heroines who are girls tell stories that are circumscribed by their younger target audience and episodic closure. These series also indicate important innovation, particularly in their telling of stories about girls and teens, but their characters possess little of the psychological depth afforded to the heroines of action dramas. That supernaturally empowered heroines appear in such a variety of narrative forms targeted to such a varied audience indicates the transformational nature of the programming at this time.

I exclude other similar series because they utilize an ensemble of characters and place their stories in entirely different worlds, rather than incorporating limited aspects of science fiction (*Farscape, Lexx, Black Scorpion, Babylon 5, Star Trek: Voyager, Star Trek: Deep Space Nine*). Although many of these shows feature important female characters, they construct narratives for an ensemble rather than focusing on one or more female protagonists. Consequently, the science fiction series do not tell stories about female characters in the consistent and recurrent manner that is common among the series emphasized throughout this book. Labeling these series as "science fiction" may appear nebulous, as I do consider series that exhibit limited characteristics of science fiction (most commonly through the supernatural empowerment of the heroines and the series' depiction of the contemporary world as inhabited by demons), but exclude those series that set their stories in worlds entirely different from the contemporary world. The inclusion of *Dark Angel* and *Xena: Warrior Princess* results from a judgment call. Although *Dark Angel* is set in a future, postapocalyptic Seattle, the series remains bound by many contemporary limitations: the stories do not show a future enabled by fantastic technology but serve more as a warning. *Xena*'s mythological setting makes it unusual among those considered here, but it has more in common with the action dramas than science fiction series perhaps because of the fantastic limitations of going back in time instead of into the future.

8. Lowry, "A Guy's Weakness for Strong Women"; Sims, "High-Heeled and Dangerous."

9. See, for example, Beale, "Attack of the Sexy-Tough Women"; Tomashoff, "Actresses Are Beginning to Get a Bigger Cut of the Action"; Pennington, "Now, It's 'Wham, Bam'— and from the Ma'am"; Millman, "Chicks Who Kick"; and Holston, "Tough Babes in Tubeland."

10. See Tomashoff, "Actresses Are Beginning to Get a Bigger Cut of the Action"; Beale, "Attack of the Sexy-Tough Women"; Pennington, "Now, It's 'Wham, Bam'—and from the Ma'am"; Millman, "*Alias*"; Pozner, "Thwack! Pow! Yikes!"; and Tung, "Embodying an Image."

11. Modleski, *Loving with a Vengeance;* Brunsdon, *The Feminist, the Housewife, and the Soap Opera;* Fiske, *Television Culture,* 179–223.

12. In most series these duties are shared among a group; only Max of *Dark Angel* and Sara of *Witchblade* regularly fight alone.

13. My analysis takes into account the full run of *Xena: Warrior Princess, La Femme Nikita, Dark Angel, Buffy the Vampire Slayer,* and *Witchblade* and the first five seasons of *Charmed.*

14. *Buffy the Vampire Slayer* and *Xena: Warrior Princess* (the series with the longest runs) became more serial as they developed each season. Seasons three through seven of *Buffy* feature a climax at each season's end (although not every episode clearly contributes to the serial narrative), while *Xena* gradually developed complex narrative connections that referenced small details of previous episodes.

15. Buffy regularly requires mystical aid from Willow by the fourth season of *Buffy the Vampire Slayer*.

16. A technique noted in Fiske, *Television Culture*, 194–95. Notably, the series that most emphasize the exceptional individual heroine (*La Femme Nikita, Dark Angel,* and adventure series such as *V.I.P.* and *Sheena*), are those that networks did not intend as women's programs and often draw substantial male audiences. See Tomashoff, "Actresses Are Beginning to Get a Bigger Cut of the Action"; and McDowell, "Babe Tube."

17. In understanding what types of forms appeal to female audiences, it should be noted that *Xena: Warrior Princess* and *Buffy the Vampire Slayer* developed active fan communities. These series differ from the others in a variety of ways, making it impossible to identify their establishment of a community of empowered characters as the primary determinant of fan interest, particularly female fan interest. *La Femme Nikita* also developed a fan base that responded vociferously when USA first canceled the series, leading the network to return the show for more episodes.

18. Susan J. Douglas notes the relationships among the characters as one of the defining attributes of *Charlie's Angels.* See Douglas, *Where the Girls Are,* 291.

19. When Shannen Dougherty, the actress who played Pru, decided to leave the series, her character was killed, and a previously unknown half-sister surfaced to continue the "power of three."

20. Contrarily, David Greven reads the gyneco-centric legacy of *Witchblade* as a dangerous essentialism. See Greven, "Throwing Down the Gauntlet."

21. See Levine, "*Buffy* and the 'New Girl Order.'"

22. See Penley, Lyon, Spigel, and Bergstrom, *Close Encounters;* Barr, *Future Females, the Next Generation;* Russ, *To Write Like a Woman;* and Christopher, "Little Miss Tough Chick of the Universe."

23. The relationship between Nikita and Michael in *La Femme Nikita* fits here as well, as he is first her superior, then a sometimes love interest. This relationship is too complicated to describe in passing, but it is relevant nonetheless. *Alias* also replicates the strategy: Sydney is guided by a male CIA handler and a male SD6 partner; her father and her friend Will provide unofficial guidance as well.

24. This definition of hegemonic masculinity is drawn from Robert Hanke's summary of Nick Trujillo's work. Hanke, "On Masculinity," 186. See also Hanke, "Redesigning Men."

25. See Brown, "The Politics of Soaps." Fiske describes the "good" male as "caring, nurturing, and verbal" and the villainous nature of hegemonic masculinity as characteristic of soap operas in the late 1980s (*Television Culture,* 186). Robert Hanke dates a negotiated version of hegemonic masculinity to the 1980s series *thirtysomething.* See Hanke, "Hegemonic Masculinity in *thirtysomething.*"

26. d'Acci, *Defining Women,* 195–98.

27. See Helford, "Feminism, Queer Studies, and the Sexual Politics of *Xena: Warrior Princess*"; and Jones, "Histories, Fictions, and *Xena: Warrior Princess,*" 416 n.1.

28. *Charmed* establishes the familial connections because the characters are sisters. I

develop an analysis of Xena and Gabrielle's relationship that is friendly to but does not depend upon the lesbian subtext. If one views female relationships on a lesbian continuum, as Adrienne Rich suggests, the same-sex loyalties evident across the series can be understood more effectively than if defining lesbianism solely by a sexual definition. See Rich, "Compulsory Heterosexuality and Lesbian Existence."

29. See Ross, "Super(Natural) Women."

30. In what was originally the finale, the narrative reveals that Nikita has been spying on Section One since her escape at the end of season one and that she was sent to evaluate and then suggest changes for the unit. This means that Nikita's loyalties were to an additional unknown party, "Mr. Jones." In the subsequent fifth-season episodes, added after viewer protest over the cancellation of the series, Nikita learns that the real Mr. Jones who runs the center is her father (whom she never knew). The actual final episode forces Nikita to choose between the life of her father and Michael's son.

31. Rachel Moseley discusses the relationship among work, witchcraft, and feminist empowerment. See Moseley, "Glamorous Witchcraft."

32. I consider The WB series finale of *Buffy the Vampire Slayer* because it served the narrative function of a series finale, despite the well-known rebirth of the character for an additional run on UPN. Sara Crosby argues that the martyring of the heroines contains the challenge to patriarchy their empowerment presents. This is a viable reading, but such endings do not negate the previous hundreds of hours of narrative, and the texts also provide evidence for reading the characters' demise in more sophisticated ways. "And they lived happily ever after" would not necessarily provide a more satisfying conclusion. See Crosby, "The Cruelest Season."

33. Byars and Meehan, "Once in a Lifetime."

34. Quinlan, *Just Ask a Woman.* Quinlan's research is designed to help companies better sell their goods to women, yet the extent of her qualitative discussions with women affords it other important dimensions. I learned about her research from Lee Heffernan, who had worked with Quinlan when Lifetime hired her to develop some research for the network. It is clear that many of the television networks targeting women are aware of the multiple demands stressing women's lives and that they construct network identities as offering escape.

35. I chose these two series because their narrative trajectories were most clearly established at the time I began writing. *Witchblade* and *Dark Angel* are limited by their containment to two seasons. *La Femme Nikita*'s episodic orientation, lack of female relationships, and constantly shifting allegiances make it a less compelling case. And *Charmed* was still in production as of the final writing, which provided some uncertainty to its cumulative narrative.

36. "The Deliverer" (episode 303); "Gabrielle's Hope" (episode 304).

37. "The Debt Part I" (episode 306) and "The Debt Part II" (episode 307).

38. "Maternal Instincts" (episode 311).

39. "The Bitter Suite" (episode 312).

40. "Sacrifice Part I" (episode 321) and "Sacrifice Part II" (episode 322).

41. "Innocence" (episode 214).

42. "Becoming" (episode 222).

43. Beginning in its fourth season, *Sex and the City* explored intimacy among friends with greater emphasis.

44. Beale, "Attack of the Sexy-Tough Women," 52.

Chapter 3

Phyllis Theroux, "TV Women Have Come a Long Way, Baby—Sort Of," *New York Times*, May 17, 1987, sec. 2, 35.

1. Other authors refer to these as stories of "single girls." Some uses of "girl" attempt to reclaim a term once used to subordinate females, but this use obscures studies of girls (those under age eighteen) that also have been subordinated within women's studies. I use "women" instead of "girls" because all the characters in these series are women.

2. Quoted in Alley and Brown, *Women Television Producers*, 25.

3. Luckett, "Sensuous Women and Single Girls"; and Luckett, "A Moral Crisis in Prime Time."

4. See Lotz "Postfeminist Television Criticism."

5. Ann Marie did not marry within the text of the series at Thomas's request, although she seemed likely headed to the altar. The network sought, but Thomas rejected, additional seasons depicting Ann and Don marrying and beginning a family. Alley and Brown, *Women Television Producers*, 25.

6. Dow, *Prime-Time Feminism*, 40–45.

7. For popular criticism, see Shalit, "Canny and Lacy"; Dowd, "Ally McBeal Is a Unisex Role Model"; Jefferson, "You Want to Slap Ally McBeal, but Do You Like Her?" For academic feminist criticism, see Vavrus, Afterword to *Postfeminist News;* Ouellette, "Victims No More"; Dubrofsky, "Ally McBeal as Postfeminist Icon"; Dow, "*Ally McBeal*, Lifestyle Feminism, and the Politics of Personal Happiness"; and Shugart, Waggoner, and Hallstein, "Mediating Third-Wave Feminism."

8. Wilson, "Upscale Feminine Angst," 110–11.

9. Ibid.

10. Perhaps the eventual commercial failure of the series *Cybill* can be explained by its attempts to insert more openly feminist narrative material into the standard sitcom form.

11. Resolving conflict by episode's end is crucial to the sitcom, while ongoing crises often motivate dramas.

12. Arthurs, "*Sex and the City* and Consumer Culture," 86; Ouellette, "Victims No More."

13. See Brooks, *Bobos in Paradise*.

14. Arthurs, "*Sex and the City* and Consumer Culture," 86.

15. See Shalit, "Canny and Lacy," for example.

16. Later seasons reveal that Charlotte does leave work after marrying, but the narrative makes this a decision unpopular with her friends and addresses the decision explicitly rather than depicting it as a nonproblematic assumption.

17. Arthurs, "*Sex and the City* and Consumer Culture," 84.

18. "Love Unlimited" (episode 212).

19. Vavrus, *Postfeminist News*, 172.

20. Ibid., 172–73.

21. This engagement with cultural dialogue about the series is not a unique occasion. In a crossover episode with *The Practice*, Kelley included an exchange between the characters played by Lara Flynn Boyle and Calista Flockhart in which they refer to the popular speculation about their waiflike physiques.

22. Moseley and Read, "'Having it *Ally*'"; Cooper, "Unapologetic Women, 'Comic Men,' and Feminine Spectatorship in David E. Kelley's *Ally McBeal*."

23. Vavrus, *Postfeminist News;* Dubrofsky, "Ally McBeal as Postfeminist Icon"; Kim, "*Sex and the Single Girl* in Postfeminism."

24. Laurie Ouellette also produced a detailed analysis of *Ally McBeal.* Her findings fit awkwardly in this comparison because of her focus on identifying "postvictimization femininity" as characteristic of postfeminism. Diane Negra's exploration of *Sex and the City* offers a sophisticated reading of the ambivalence of the series. By framing it in relation to single-woman stories told in film, she finds the antifeminist readings of the series to be more persuasive than I do. See Ouellette, "Victims No More"; and Negra, "Quality Postfeminism?"

25. The exceptional variety of uses of "feminism" and "postfeminism" suggests another complicated but understandable factor confounding feminist media criticism. Rachael Dubrofsky, L. S. Kim, Mary Vavrus, and Laurie Ouellette all use "postfeminism" in ways slightly different than my use. Helen A. Shugart, Catherine Egley Waggoner, and Lynn O'Brien Hallstein briefly address *Ally McBeal* in relation to third-wave feminism.

26. Moseley and Read make a similar assertion ("'Having It *Ally*'").

27. See d'Acci, "Nobody's Woman?"; Dow, *Prime-Time Feminism;* Luckett, "A Moral Crisis in Prime Time"; Luckett, "Sensuous Women and Single Girls"; Radner, "Introduction"; and Wilson, "Upscale Feminine Angst."

28. For analysis of these series, see Kaler, "*Golden Girls*"; Butler, "Redesigning Discourse"; Dow, *Prime-Time Feminism;* and Haggins, "There's No Place Like Home."

29. Nochimson, "*Ally McBeal*," 29.

30. I explore one episode each of *Sex and the City* and *Ally McBeal* as exemplary of the series' voicing of divergent female perspectives and negotiation of discrepancies according to the demands of narrative structure. For the sake of comparison I have chosen a legal storyline from *Ally McBeal* to contrast with *Sex and the City*'s customary examination of social norms.

31. Although even in *Ally McBeal* judiciary concerns are often explored as moral and ethical rather than strictly legal.

32. "The Baby Shower" (episode 110).

33. The narratives about motherhood in *Sex and the City* do not perpetuate the "new momism" Susan J. Douglas and Meredith W. Michaels find characteristic of many discourses about motherhood in this era. See Douglas and Michaels, *The Mommy Myth.*

34. This varies by season, as the series experienced significant cast changes throughout its run. Here I count those primarily present in seasons two and three: Ally, Renee, Elaine, Nelle, Ling, Georgia, and Judge Jennifer (Whipper) Cone.

35. See, for example, Katz, "*Ally McBeal*"; Bellafante, "Feminism"; Walton, "Feminist Role Model or Ditzy Broad?"; and Shalit, "Canny and Lacy."

36. Although *Ally McBeal*'s female cast includes an African American and an Asian American, as well as a character with a pink-collar instead of professional career, the series does not acknowledge these disparities in its narratives. See Braxton, "Colorblind or Just Plain Blind?"

37. Another likely reason for critics' uncertainty about the feminist potential of *Ally McBeal* results from the series' use of rhetoric and terminology of the feminist movement in narratives that turn these concepts around in a way that requires significant contemplation. Feminist critics may fear audiences will assume the series' message is feminist because it uses a feminist vocabulary, while its meanings are rarely literal.

38. "Just Looking" (episode 209).

39. See Dow, *Prime-Time Feminism;* Rabinovitz, "Sitcoms and Single Moms"; and Rabinovitz, "Ms.-Representation."

40. Dow, *Prime-Time Feminism.*

41. Dow, "*Ally McBeal,* Lifestyle Feminism, and the Politics of Personal Happiness"; Dubrofsky, "Ally McBeal as Postfeminist Icon."

42. Quoted in Heywood, "Hitting a Cultural Nerve"; and Ouellette, "Victims No More," 321.

43. Quoted in Stark, "Ally McBeal."

44. Quoted in Chambers, "How Would Ally Do It?" 58–59.

45. Ibid.

46. See ibid., 59; Heywood, "Hitting a Cultural Nerve"; and Walton, "Feminist Role Model or Ditzy Broad?"

47. Stack, "Fiction Is Not a Feminist Issue"; Chambers, "How Would Ally Do It?"

48. This is the story presented in the pilot episode; Ally and the audience later learn that Billy met Georgia at a conference and chose to transfer to the University of Michigan to be with her.

49. "Happy Birthday, Baby" (episode 119).

50. "Out in the Cold" (episode 309).

51. "In Search of Pygmies" (episode 312).

52. "Pursuit of Loneliness" (episode 313).

53. Downey's drug-related legal problems and the fact that FOX made a late decision not to renew the show provide two crucial institutional factors affecting its final season and how Kelley chose to end the series. Compared with *Sex and the City,* whose writers knew a full season in advance that they would have eighteen episodes to write the story's final chapter, the last season of *Ally McBeal* is considerably influenced by factors limiting storytelling possibilities.

54. See Dow, *Prime-Time Feminism,* for her analysis of this use of motherhood in *Murphy Brown* and *Dr. Quinn, Medicine Woman.*

55. Ally's daughter Maddie is born from an egg Ally had donated. Maddie arrives on Ally's door as a ten-year-old after the deaths of the parents who had raised her.

56. Generally, the female-centered dramas discussed throughout this book counter what Douglas and Michaels identify as the dominant discourse of the new momism evident in *thirtysomething* or the critique of it by dystopic family comedies such as *Roseanne* or *Married . . . with Children.* The ambivalence of characters such as Miranda, Carrie, and Samantha toward motherhood provides an important counterbalance to the more dominant discourse embodied by Charlotte and Ally. Additionally, these shows must be considered relative to the harried and nonidealized depictions of motherhood in protagonist-centered family dramas (*Judging Amy*) and of characters in workplace dramas that have children. See Douglas and Michaels, *The Mommy Myth.*

57. "They Shoot Single People, Don't They?" (episode 204).

58. "Four Women and a Funeral" (episode 205).

59. See, for example, Gitlin, "Prime Time Ideology"; and Dow, *Prime-Time Feminism.*

60. "The Agony and the 'Ex'-tasy" (episode 401).

61. I stress the importance of the cumulative story of the series because the episodic installments of narrative television allow it to be a contradictory and complex form. There

are unquestionably episodes of each series that depict the characters obsessively trying to overcome insecurity about being single. The structure of television programming requires critics to assess how the episodes combine to form a whole story.

62. Probyn, "New Traditionalism and Post-Feminism," 130.

63. "Time and Punishment" (episode 407). This is a particularly rich and complex episode in terms of the issues raised here. This decision is difficult for Charlotte; she does appear uncertain, but much of this also results from her awareness of how her friends will respond. Given her character, this decision is not particularly surprising, yet the episode thoroughly explores how unsupported this once-dominant social script is within certain cultural spaces.

64. Moseley and Read, "'Having it *Ally*,'" 247.

65. See McKenna, "The Queer Insistence of *Ally McBeal*."

Chapter 4

1. "If You Build It, They Will Come."

2. See Bellafante, "Meet the Post-Ally Women."

3. In three of the fourteen weeks, one of the series was preempted with a special, so they only directly competed on eleven occasions.

4. See d'Acci, *Defining Women*, 72.

5. "Pilot" (episode 101).

6. "Welcome to Providence."

7. Ibid. (my emphasis).

8. By the fourth season, she and and her business partner, Sookie, begin renovations on their own inn.

9. See Leibman, *Living Room Lectures;* or Taylor, *Prime-Time Families.*

10. Vincent moves to California at the beginning of the third season and is effectively "replaced" by Kyle, who appears two episodes later and moves into Vincent's old apartment and fulfills Vincent's place in family life. Vincent returned to the series in its final season, and cousin Kyle departed accordingly. Mimi White explores the multiplicity of narratives and narrative spaces commonly included within a single episode of the series. White, "Meanwhile, Back in the Emergency Room."

11. "Runaway Sydney" (episode 105).

12. "Rescue Me" (episode 304).

13. Ibid.

14. "Exposure" (episode 317).

15. "Meet Joe Connelly" (episode 319).

16. "Near Death Experience" (episode 108).

17. "Unnecessary Roughness" (episode 205).

18. "One for the Road" (episode 214).

19. "Dog Days" (episode 207).

20. "Taste of Providence" (episode 109).

21. "Paradise Inn" (episode 223).

22. "Saved by the Bell" (episode 311).

23. "The Invisible Man" (episode 314).

24. "The Apartment" (episode 214).

25. "Paradise Inn" (episode 223).

26. "Exposure" (episode 317).

27. "Saint Syd" (episode 112).

28. "Magician" (episode 318).

29. "Big Night" (episode 309).

30. "Parenthood" (episode 315).

31. Robbie finally marries at the beginning of the fourth season, although his wife's postpartum depression quickly introduces another threat to the family.

32. Syd notes that she can work as a doctor in Chicago. The most recent plot regarding her career had chronicled her move from the free clinic to an emergency room, a transition that is initially difficult, but she decides to move just as she becomes part of the E.R. and acknowledges how much she enjoys the work.

33. "Near Death Experience" (episode 108), and "Blast from the Past" (episode 123).

34. "Pilot" (episode 101) transcript, <http://judgingamy.tripod.com/amy/episode /a101t.htm>, June 7, 2001.

35. The cases examined in *Family Law* offer comparable narratives.

36. A series of episodes in the second season focuses on Amy's struggle to compose a "normal" life, a notion ultimately revealed as an unattainable myth. She develops a relationship with an old friend in the fourth season in a relationship obviously destined for destruction. Amy mistakenly accepts his wedding proposal at the end of the fourth season, but leaves him at the altar early in the fifth season. She then pursues a complicated relationship with a prosecutor whose wife was murdered and whose son dates Lauren. The series effectively builds romantic tension between Amy and a court services officer, Bruce Van Exel, through sporadic storylines, but as of this writing it remains unclear whether this relationship will ever be acknowledged by the characters.

Chapter 5

1. See Rabinovitz, "Ms.-Representation"; and d'Acci, *Defining Women.*

2. Press, *Women Watching Television*, 35.

3. Pepper Anderson of *Police Woman* is notable for her arrival in the 1970s, but as I explore in chapter 2, her exceptionality makes her characterization more exemplary of the action-heroine tradition.

4. Academic explorations of the possibilities for depictions of women in professional roles on 1980s television include Reep and Dambrot, "Television's Professional Women"; Atkin, Moorman, and Lin, "Ready for Prime Time"; and Japp, "Gender and Work in the 1980s."

5. For criticism of the antifeminist tendencies of each of these series, see Desjardins, "*Baby Boom*"; Mayne, "*L.A. Law* and Prime-Time Feminism," 87; Probyn, "New Traditionalism and Post-Feminism"; and Dow, *Prime-Time Feminism.*

6. See Press, *Women Watching Television*, 150–52.

7. This is likely a norm that programming executives also recognize. All of the adult characters in the series explored in this book work outside of the home.

8. Sex is not a similar impediment for the two other female detectives working with Sheppard, suggesting that beauty rather than sex particularly marks her as less able.

9. Lifetime's third attempt at this type of series, *For the People* (2003), did not succeed; it attempted a reconfigured legal series.

10. The particular circumstances of airing on a network targeting female viewers enables these series to explore narratives that would have been less possible in any of the other series discussed in this book (with the exception of *Any Day Now*).

11. The impetus for the series came from the experiences of the actor and director Whoopi Goldberg during her daughter's pregnancy. Goldberg recognized how many stories about women's health and women's needs as patients had not been told through series television and the compelling bravery embodied by doctors and patients.

12. The archival holdings of the Museum of Television and Radio only include the two-hour pilot of *Heartbeat,* so my analysis is based on a small and potentially unrepresentative sample.

13. Examples of such dilemmas include whether to separate conjoined twins who may die to save one and guarantee the death of the other ("Attachments," episode 205); or what to do about a mother who removes her HIV-infected son from medication to allow him a better quality of life ("Misconceptions," episode 103).

14. Season to season, the series experienced cast changes, but its basic formula of four detectives and a captain (with a range of five female characters) remained constant. The first season featured the detectives DeLorenzo, Exstead, Ramirez, and Reide. Reide left after the first season and was replaced by Nate Basso, but a uniformed officer, Raina Washington, was added to the precinct in seasons two and three. In the fourth season, Washington moved up to detective and was replaced by Newland, and DeLorenzo left the series. McCafferty served as the captain for the entire series.

15. d'Acci, *Defining Women.*

16. The closest comparison may be Mary Beth Lacey. However, even she was a detective rather than a beat cop.

17. I struggled with identifying the standard representation as either upper-class or upper-middle-class. I employ the terminology consistent with dominant American ideology to prevent confusion. While it is true that these characters generally do not exhibit opulent wealth, the upper-middle classifier obscures the uniform way American television depicts society as classless and characters without financial woes, a reality more indicative of upper-class than middle-class life.

18. "Faith" (episode 202).

19. See Cuklanz, *Rape on Prime Time;* and Projansky, *Watching Rape.*

20. An exception includes a return celebrity guest appearance by Tracey Pollan in which the police pursue a serial rapist who was not caught in the initial episode ("Closure," episode 110; "Closure II," episode 303).

21. This point is particularly worth making given cultural discourse that asserts the series to be "liberal."

22. Stockard Channing was added to the regular cast in her role as the president's wife in the third season. The series has featured women in a number of recurring roles. Noteworthy are those of Mandy Hampton (Moira Kelly), Ainsley Hayes (Emily Proctor), Joey Lucas (Marlee Matlin), Amy Gardner (Mary-Louise Parker), and Kate Harper (Mary McCormack).

23. This analysis includes the four seasons that Aaron Sorkin was executive producer

and a primary writer for the series, as well as the disastrous fifth season in which the re-placement scribes destroyed the artful complexity of the characters by making them all unlikable. The intelligence and grace of the female characters was particularly absent in post-Sorkin seasons.

24. Levesque, "Sorkin's Treatment of Women Gets More Annoying."

25. Parry-Giles and Parry-Giles, "*The West Wing*'s Prime-Time Presidentiality."

Epilogue

1. Admittedly, the 2001–2 season was somewhat atypical. The September 11, 2001, di-saster pushed the start of the season back and called into question the type of fare audi-ences would desire. Additionally, the weak economy destroyed the advertising market, making it a relatively unprofitable year for the networks. This led to much less experi-mentation with new series for fall 2002 and fewer pilot commitments, actually making the renewal cut easier for mid-range performing series.

2. See Gough-Yates, "Angels in Chains?"

Conclusion

1. See Turow, "Unconventional Programs on Commercial Television."

2. Sharon M. Ross, conversation with the author, June 11, 2002.

3. Lotz, "Postfeminist Television Criticism." See also Brooks, *Postfeminisms*.

4. Curtin and Streeter, "Media."

5. Montgomery, *Target: Prime Time*.

6. TV One launched a few months before the final drafting of this chapter as a com-petitor to BET. TV One is not yet available on my cable system and many others, mak-ing it too early to determine whether the network will provide viable competition.

7. Newcomb and Hirsch, "Television as a Cultural Forum."

8. Gitlin, "Prime Time Ideology."

9. Lotz, "Televising Feminist Discourses."

10. Lafayette, "What Women Want"; Fannin, "What Women Watch"; Romano, "Women's Net Rivals Find Their Niche."

Works Cited

Akass, Kim, and Janet McCabe, eds. *Reading "Sex and the City."* London: I. B. Tauris, 2004.

Alexander, Keith. "Opportunity of a Lifetime: CEO Carole Black Determined to Make Cable Network a Strong Brand Name for Women." *USA Today,* July 29, 1999, 1B.

Alley, Robert S., and Irby B. Brown. *Women Television Producers: Transformation of the Male Medium.* Rochester, N.Y.: University of Rochester Press, 2001.

Ang, Ien. *Watching Dallas: Soap Opera and the Melodramatic Imagination.* Trans. Della Couling. New York: Routledge, 1989.

Arthurs, Jane. "*Sex and the City* and Consumer Culture: Remediating Postfeminist Drama." *Feminist Media Studies* 3.1 (2003): 83–98.

Atkin, David J., Jay Moorman, and Carolyn A. Lin. "Ready for Prime Time: Network Series Devoted to Working Women in the 1980s." *Sex Roles* 25.11–12 (1991): 677–85.

Auletta, Ken. *Three Blind Mice: How the TV Networks Lost Their Way.* New York: Vintage Books, 1992.

Baehr, Helen, and Ann Gray, eds. *Turning It On: A Reader in Women and Media.* New York: St. Martin's Press, 1996.

Barletta, Martha. *Marketing to Women: How to Understand, Reach, and Increase Your Share of the World's Largest Market Segment.* Chicago: Dearborn Trade Publishing, 2003.

Barr, Marleen S., ed. *Future Females, the Next Generation: New Voices and Velocities in Feminist Science Fiction Criticism.* Lanham, Md.: Rowman and Littlefield, 2000.

Beale, Lewis. "Attack of the Sexy-Tough Women: In Movies and TV, Sisters Are Kicking Butt for Themselves." *New York Daily News,* October 19, 2000, 52.

Bellafante, Ginia. "Feminism: It's All About Me!" *Time,* June 29, 1998, 54–60.

———. "Meet the Post-Ally Women." *Time,* February 15, 1999, 70.

Benzel, Jan. "Three Phases of Eve: Mother, Wife, Friend." *New York Times,* August 16, 1998, sec. 13.

Berkowitz, Harry. "Johnson & Johnson Signs Ad Deal with WE Network." *New York Newsday,* March 27, 2001, A42.

Block, Alex Ben. *Outfoxed: Marvin Davis, Barry Diller, Rupert Murdoch, Joan Rivers, and the Inside Story of America's Fourth Television Network.* New York: St. Martin's Press, 1990.

Braxton, Greg. "Colorblind or Just Plain Blind? 'Race Not Being an Issue Makes It an Issue,' Says David E. Kelley of an Unspoken Topic on *Ally McBeal.*" *Los Angeles Times,* February 9, 1999, F1.

Bronstein, Carolyn. "Mission Accomplished? Profits and Programming at the Network for Women." *Camera Obscura* (special issue on "Lifetime: A Cable Network for Women," ed. Julie d'Acci) 33–34 (1994): 213–41.

Brooks, Ann. *Postfeminisms: Feminism, Cultural Theory, and Cultural Forms.* New York: Routledge, 1997.

Brooks, David. *Bobos in Paradise: The New Upper Class and How They Got There.* New York: Simon and Schuster, 2000.

Brown, Mary Ellen. "The Politics of Soaps: Pleasure and Feminine Empowerment." *Australian Journal of Cultural Studies* 4.2 (1987): 1–25.

———, ed. *Television and Women's Culture: The Politics of the Popular.* London: Sage, 1990.

Brunsdon, Charlotte. "*Crossroads:* Notes on Soap Opera." *Screen* 22.4 (1981): 32–37.

———. "Feminism, Post-feminism, Martha, Martha, and Nigella." *Cinema Journal* 44.2(2005): 110–14.

———. *The Feminist, the Housewife, and the Soap Opera.* New York: Oxford University Press, 2000.

———. *Screen Tastes: Soap Opera to Satellite Dishes.* London: Routledge, 1997.

Brunsdon, Charlotte, Julie d'Acci, Lynn Spigel, eds. *Feminist Television Criticism: A Reader.* New York: Oxford University Press, 1997.

Brunsdon, Charlotte, and David Morley. *Everyday Television: Nationwide.* London: British Film Institute, 1978.

Burgi, Michael. "Channel Change." *Mediaweek,* December 1, 1997, 30.

Butler, Jeremy. "Redesigning Discourse: Feminism, the Sitcom, and *Designing Women.*" *Journal of Film and Video* 45.1 (1993): 13–26.

Byars, Jackie, and Eileen R. Meehan. "Once in a Lifetime: Constructing the 'Working Woman' through Cable Narrowcasting." *Camera Obscura* (special issue on "Lifetime: A Cable Network for Women," ed. Julie d'Acci) 33–34 (1994): 12–41.

Caldwell, John Thornton. *Televisuality: Style, Crisis, and Authority in American Television.* New Brunswick, N.J.: Rutgers University Press, 1995.

Caughie, John. *Television Drama: Realism, Modernism, and British Culture.* Oxford: Oxford University Press, 2000.

Chambers, Veronica. "How Would Ally Do It?" *Newsweek,* March 2, 1998, 58–61.

Christopher, Renny. "Little Miss Tough Chick of the Universe: *Farscape*'s Inverted Sexual Dynamics." In *Action Chicks: New Images of Tough Women in Popular Culture.* Ed. Sherrie A. Inness. 257–81. New York: Palgrave Macmillan, 2004.

Clark, Danae. "*Cagney and Lacey:* Feminist Strategies of Detection." In *Television and Women's Culture: The Politics of the Popular.* Ed. Mary Ellen Brown. 117–33. London: Sage, 1990.

Cloud, Dana. "Concordance, Complexity, and Conservatism: Rejoinder to Condit." *Critical Studies in Mass Communication* 14.2 (1997): 193–97.

———. "Hegemony or Concordance? The Rhetoric of Tokenism in 'Oprah' Winfrey's Rags-to-Riches Biography." *Critical Studies in Mass Communication* 13.2 (1996): 115–37.

Coleman, Price. "Fuzzy Vision Doomed Channel?" *Broadcasting and Cable*, August 23, 1999, 40.

Collins, Gail. "A Woman's Work Is Never Shown." *Working Woman* 19.9 (September 1994): 102.

Collins, James. "Ally McBeal." *Time*, November 10, 1997, 117.

Cooper, Brenda. "Unapologetic Women, 'Comic Men,' and Feminine Spectatorship in David E. Kelley's *Ally McBeal*." *Critical Studies in Media Communication* 18.4 (2001): 416–35.

Corliss, Richard, and Jeanne McDowell. "Go Ahead, Make Her Day." *Time*, March 26, 2001, 64–67.

Crosby, Sara. "The Cruelest Season: Female Heroes Snapped into Sacrificial Heroines." In *Action Chicks: New Images of Tough Women in Popular Culture*. Ed. Sherrie A. Inness. 153–80. New York: Palgrave Macmillan, 2004.

Cuklanz, Lisa M. *Rape on Prime Time: Television, Masculinity, and Sexual Violence*. Philadelphia: University of Pennsylvania Press, 2000.

Curtin, Michael. "Feminine Desire in the Age of Satellite Television." *Journal of Communication* 49.2 (1999): 55–70.

Curtin, Michael, and Thomas Streeter. "Media." In *Culture Works: The Political Economy of Culture*. Ed. Richard Maxwell. 225–49. Minneapolis: University of Minnesota Press, 2001.

d'Acci, Julie. *Defining Women: Television and the Case of "Cagney and Lacey."* Chapel Hill: University of North Carolina Press, 1994.

———. "Nobody's Woman? *Honey West* and the New Sexuality." In *The Revolution Wasn't Televised: Sixties Television and Social Conflict*. Ed. Lynn Spigel and Michael Curtin. 72–93. New York: Routledge, 1999.

———, ed. "Lifetime: A Cable Network for Women." Special issue of *Camera Obscura* 33–34 (1994).

Davis, Donald M. "Portrayals of Women in Prime-Time Network Television: Some Demographic Characteristics." *Sex Roles* 23.5–6 (1990): 325–32.

Deming, Robert. "*Kate and Allie*: 'New Women' and the Audience's Television Archive." In *Private Screenings: Television and the Female Consumer*. Ed. Lynn Spigel and Denise Mann. 203–14. Minneapolis: University of Minnesota Press, 1992.

deMoraes, Lisa M. "Enriched Oxygen: Oprah Moving to Prime Time." *Washington Post*, June 11, 2002, C1.

———. "NOW's Bewildering Picks and Pans." *Washington Post*, July 2, 2001, C7

———. "The Unthinking Women's Network." *Washington Post*, January 18, 2001, C7.

Dempsey, John. "Cable Aud's Now Bigger Than B'Cast." *Variety.com*, May 20, 2004 <www.variety.com/story.asp?l=story&a=VR1117905396&c=14> (May 26, 2004).

———. "Cable Casts Broadcast-size Coin over New Programs." *Variety* 371.2 (1998): 37.

———. "LMN Landing on Cox." *Daily Variety*, June 8, 1999, 7.

Desjardins, Mary. "*Baby Boom*: The Comedy of Surrogacy in Film and Television." *Velvet Light Trap* 29 (1992): 20–30.

Donohue, Steve. "Romance Execs Plan to Relaunch an 'Oasis.'" *Multichannel News*, March 6, 2000, 32.

Douglas, Susan J. *Where the Girls Are: Growing Up Female in Mass Media*. New York: Times Books/Random House, 1994.

Douglas, Susan J., and Meredith W. Michaels. *The Mommy Myth: The Idealization of Motherhood and How It Has Undermined Women.* New York: Free Press, 2004.

Dow, Bonnie J. "*Ally McBeal,* Lifestyle Feminism, and the Politics of Personal Happiness." *Communication Review* 5 (2002): 259–64.

———. *Prime-Time Feminism: Television, Media Culture, and the Women's Movement since 1970.* Philadelphia: University of Pennsylvania Press, 1996.

Dowd, Maureen. "Ally McBeal Is a Unisex Role Model." *New York Times,* April 15, 1998, C5.

Dubrofsky, Rachael. "Ally McBeal as Postfeminist Icon: The Aestheticizing and Fetishizing of the Independent Working Woman." *Communication Review* 5 (2002): 265–84.

du Gay, Paul, et al. *Doing Cultural Studies: The Story of the Sony Walkman.* London: Sage, 1997.

du Gay, Paul, ed. *Production of Culture/Cultures of Production.* London: Sage, 1997.

Elasmar, Michael, Kazumi Hasegawa, and Mary Brain. "The Portrayal of Women in U.S. Prime Time Television." *Journal of Broadcasting and Electronic Media* 43.1 (1999): 20–34.

Fannin, Rebecca A. "What Women Watch." *Cable World,* August 5, 2002, 30.

Fazzone, Amanda. "NOW's Strange Taste in TV." *New Republic,* July 30, 2001, 16–17.

Ferguson, Marjorie. "Images of Power and the Feminist Fallacy." *Critical Studies in Mass Communication* 7 (1990): 215–30.

Feuer, Jane. *Seeing through the Eighties: Television and Reaganism.* Durham, N.C.: Duke University Press, 1995.

Fiske, John. *Television Culture.* New York: Routledge, 1987.

Freeman, Michael. "Falling under a Spell(ing)." *Mediaweek,* September 28, 1998, 9.

"Geraldine Laybourne: Chairman and CEO, Oxygen Media." *Electronic Media,* January 11, 1999, 36.

Gillespie, Marie. *Television, Ethnicity, and Cultural Change.* London: Routledge, 1993.

Gitlin, Todd. "Prime Time Ideology: The Hegemonic Process in Television Entertainment." In *Television: The Critical View.* 5th ed. Ed. Horace Newcomb. 516–36. New York: Oxford University Press, 1994.

Gough-Yates, Anna. "Angels in Chains? Feminism, Femininity, and Consumer Culture in *Charlie's Angels.*" In *Action TV: Tough Guys, Smooth Operators, and Foxy Chicks.* Ed. Bill Osgerby and Anna Gough-Yates. 83–99. London: Routledge, 2001.

———. *Understanding Women's Magazines: Publishing, Markets, and Readerships.* New York: Routledge, 2003.

Granger, Rod. "Rainbow Woos Ops with 'Romance' Tales." *Multichannel News,* November 30, 1992, 1.

Gray, Ann. *Video Playtime: The Gendering of a Leisure Technology.* New York: Routledge, 1992.

Greven, David. "Throwing Down the Gauntlet: Defiant Women, Decadent Men, Objects of Power, and *Witchblade.*" In *Action Chicks: New Images of Tough Women in Popular Culture.* Ed. Sherrie A. Inness. 123–52. New York: Palgrave Macmillan, 2004.

Grossberg, Lawrence. "Cultural Studies vs. Political Economy: Is Anybody Else Bored with this Debate?" *Critical Studies in Mass Communication* 12.1 (1995): 72–81.

Haddad, Charles. "Cable Targets Women for Two New Channels." *Austin-American Statesman,* June 27, 1999, 8.

Haggins, Bambi L. "There's No Place Like Home: The American Dream, African-American Identity, and the Situation Comedy." *Velvet Light Trap* 43 (1999): 23–36.

Hanke, Robert. "Hegemonic Masculinity in *thirtysomething*." *Critical Studies in Mass Communication* 7 (1990): 231–48.

———. "On Masculinity: Theorizing Masculinity with/in the Media." *Communication Theory* 8.2 (1998): 183–203.

———. "Redesigning Men: Hegemonic Masculinity in Transition." In *Men, Masculinity, and the Media*. Ed. Steve Craig. 185–98. Newberry Park, Calif.: Sage, 1992.

Haralovich, Mary Beth. "Sit-coms and Suburbs: Positioning the 1950s Homemaker." In *Private Screenings: Television and the Female Consumer*. Ed. Lynn Spigel and Denise Mann. 110–41. Minneapolis: University of Minnesota Press, 1992.

Haralovich, Mary Beth, and Lauren Rabinovitz, eds. *Television, History, and American Culture: Feminist Critical Essays*. Durham, N.C.: Duke University Press, 1999.

Haskell, Molly. *From Reverence to Rape: The Treatment of Women in the Movies*. Chicago: University of Chicago Press, 1973.

Helford, Elyce Rae. "Feminism, Queer Studies, and the Sexual Politics of *Xena: Warrior Princess*." In *Fantasy Girls: Gender in the New Universe of Science Fiction and Fantasy Television*. Ed. Elyce Rae Helford. 135–62. Lanham, Md.: Rowman and Littlefield, 2000.

———, ed. *Fantasy Girls: Gender in the New Universe of Science Fiction and Fantasy Television*. Lanham, Md.: Rowman and Littlefield, 2000.

Hesmondhalgh, David. *The Culture Industries*. Thousand Oaks, Calif.: Sage, 2002.

Heywood, Leslie. "Hitting a Cultural Nerve: Another Season of *Ally McBeal*." *Chronicle of Higher Education*, September 4, 1998, B9.

Higgins, John M. "Herzog Heads Home." *Broadcasting and Cable*, March 12, 2001, 11.

———. "Lifetime Hits No. 1: Women's Network on Top for an Entire Quarter for the First Time." *Broadcasting and Cable*, April 9, 2001, 11.

———. "Top 25 Networks." *Broadcasting and Cable*, December 1, 2003, 34–40.

Higgins, John M., and Allison Romano. "Cheaper by the Thousand." *Broadcasting and Cable*, February 4, 2002, 20–28.

Hobson, Dorothy. *Crossroads: The Drama of a Soap Opera*. London: Metheun, 1982.

Holston, Noel. "Tough Babes in Tubeland." *New York Newsday*, October 26, 2003.

hooks, bell. *Ain't I a Woman: Black Women and Feminism*. Boston: South End Press, 1981.

Hundley, Heather Lyn. "Defining Feminine Programming and Co-opting Liberal Feminism: A Discursive Analysis of Lifetime's Original Movies." Ph.D. dissertation, University of Utah, 1999.

"If You Build It, They Will Come." *Entertainment Weekly*, February 12, 1998, 65.

Initiative Media. "Today in National Television." April 9, 2004. New York: Magna Global.

Inness, Sherrie A. *Tough Girls: Women Warriors and Wonder Women in Popular Culture*. Philadelphia: University of Pennsylvania Press, 1999.

———, ed. *Action Chicks: New Images of Tough Women in Popular Culture*. New York: Palgrave, 2004.

Janus, Noreene. "Research on Sex-Roles in the Mass Media: Toward a Critical Approach." *Insurgent Sociologist* 7 (1977): 19–32.

Japp, Phyllis M. "Gender and Work in the 1980s: Television's Working Women as Displaced Persons." *Women's Studies in Communication* 14 (1991): 49–74.

Jefferson, Margo. "You Want to Slap Ally McBeal, but Do You Like Her?" *New York Times*, March 18, 1998, E2.

Jensen, Elizabeth. "Zeroing in on What Women Watch." *Los Angeles Times,* December 26, 2000, F1.

Jhally, Sut, dir. *Stuart Hall: Representation and the Media.* Northampton, Mass.: Media Education Foundation, 1997.

Johnson, Eithne. "Lifetime's Feminine Psychographic Space and the *Mystery Loves Company* Series." *Camera Obscura* (special issue on "Lifetime: A Cable Network For Women," ed. Julie d'Acci) 33–34 (1994): 42–75.

Johnson, Richard. "What Is Cultural Studies Anyway?" *Social Text* 16 (1986–87): 38–80.

Jones, Sara Gwenillian. "Histories, Fictions, and *Xena: Warrior Princess.*" *Television and New Media* 1.4 (2000): 403–18.

Kahle, Lynn R., and Larry Chiagouris, eds. *Values, Lifestyles, and Psychographics.* Mahwah, N.J.: LEA, 1997.

Kaler, Anne K. "*Golden Girls:* Feminine Archetypal Patterns of the Complete Woman." *Journal of Popular Culture* 24.3 (1990): 49–60.

Kaplan, E. Ann, ed. *Regarding Television: Critical Approaches—An Anthology.* Los Angeles: American Film Institute, 1983.

Katz, Alyssa. "*Ally McBeal.*" *The Nation,* December 15, 1997, 36.

Kellner, Douglas. "Overcoming the Divide: Cultural Studies and Political Economy." In *Cultural Studies in Question.* Ed. Marjorie Ferguson and Peter Golding. 102–20. London: Sage, 1997.

Kim, L. S. "*Sex and the Single Girl* in Postfeminism: The *F* Word on Television." *Television and New Media* 2.4 (2001): 319–34.

Kuhn, Annette. "Women's Genres: Melodrama, Soap Opera, and Theory." In *Feminist Television Criticism: A Reader.* Ed. Charlotte Brunsdon, Julie d'Acci, and Lynn Spigel. 145–54. New York: Oxford University Press, 1997.

Lafayette, Jon. "What Women Want." *Cable World,* February 4, 2002, 5.

Larson, Megan. "Broadband Babies." *Mediaweek,* February 4, 2002, 21–26.

———. "Oxygen Finding Its Way." *Mediaweek,* March 22, 2004, 6.

Lauzen, Martha, and David M. Dozier. "Making a Difference in Prime Time: Women on Screen and behind the Scenes in the 1995–1996 Television Season." *Journal of Broadcasting and Electronic Media* 43.1 (1999): 1–19.

Lauzen, Martha M., David M. Dozier, and Manda V. Hicks. "Prime-Time Players and Powerful Prose: The Role of Women on Screen and behind the Scenes in the 1997–1998 Season." Paper presented at the International Communication Association Annual Conference, San Francisco, May 30, 1999.

Leibman, Nina. *Living Room Lectures: The Fifties Family in Film and Television.* Austin: University of Texas Press, 1988.

Levesque, John. "Sorkin's Treatment of Women Gets More Annoying." *Seattle Post-Intelligencer,* February 12, 2001 <http://seattlepi.nwsource.com/tv/tv/1213.shtml> (March 6, 2001).

Levine, Elana. "*Buffy* and the 'New Girl Order': Defining Feminism and Femininity." In *Red Noise: Television Studies and "Buffy the Vampire Slayer."* Ed. Lisa Parks and Elana Levine. Durham, N.C.: Duke University Press, forthcoming.

———. "Wallowing in Sex: American Television and Everyday Life in the 1970s." Ph.D. dissertation, University of Wisconsin at Madison, 2002.

Lifetime Upfront Sales Kit, 2003.

Lotz, Amanda D. "Postfeminist Television Criticism: Rehabilitating Critical Terms and Identifying Postfeminist Attributes." *Feminist Media Studies* 1.1 (2001): 105–21.

———. "Televising Feminist Discourses: Postfeminist Discourse in the Post-Network Era." Ph.D. dissertation, University of Texas at Austin, 2000.

Lotz, Amanda D., and Sharon Marie Ross. "Bridging Media-Specific Approaches: The Value of Feminist Television Criticism." *Feminist Media Studies* 4.2 (2004): 187–204.

Lowry, Brian. "A Guy's Weakness for Strong Women." *Los Angeles Times,* May 4, 2003, 8.

Luckett, Moya. "A Moral Crisis in Prime Time: *Peyton Place* and the Rise of the Single Girl." In *Television, History, and American Culture: Feminist Critical Essays.* Ed. Mary Beth Haralovich and Lauren Rabinovitz. 75–97. Durham, N.C.: Duke University Press, 1999.

———. "Sensuous Women and Single Girls: Reclaiming the Female Body on 1960s Television." In *Swinging Single: Representing Sexuality in the 1960s.* Ed. Hilary Radner and Moya Luckett. 277–89. Minneapolis: University of Minnesota Press, 1999.

MacDonald, J. Fred. *Who Shot the Sheriff? The Rise and Fall of the Television Western.* Westport, Conn.: Praeger, 1987.

Macdonald, Myra. *Representing Women: Myths of Femininity in the Popular Media.* London: Edward Arnold, 1995.

Malcom, Shawna. "Women on the Verge." *Entertainment Weekly,* September 3, 1999, 34–37.

Mayne, Judith. "*L.A. Law* and Prime-Time Feminism." In *Feminist Television Criticism: A Reader.* Ed. Charlotte Brunsdon, Julie d'Acci, and Lynn Spigel. 84–97. New York: Oxford University Press, 1997.

McAdams, Deborah D. "Laybourne Waits to Exhale: Oxygen Expects to Challenge Lifetime for Its Women TV Franchise Next February." *Broadcasting and Cable,* October 18, 1999, 29.

———. "Opportunity of a Lifetime: Carole Black Girds Lifetime for Its First Direct Challenge." *Broadcasting and Cable,* October 18, 1999, 21–29.

———. "Too Big to Ignore: Television Warms Up to Women with Growing List of Nets." *Broadcasting and Cable,* November 27, 2000, 98.

McDowell, Jeanne. "Babe Tube: Look What Xena Has Wrought." *Time,* November 8, 1999, 133.

McKenna, Susan E. "The Queer Insistence of *Ally McBeal:* Lesbian Chic, Postfeminism, and Lesbian Reception." *Communication Review* 5 (2002): 285–314.

Meehan, Eileen. "Conceptualizing Culture as Commodity: The Problem of Television." In *Television: The Critical View.* 5th ed. Ed. Horace Newcomb. 563–72. New York: Oxford University Press, 1994.

Meehan, Eileen, and Jackie Byars. "Telefeminism: How Lifetime Got Its Groove." *Television and New Media* 1.1 (2000): 33–51.

Mellencamp, Patricia, "Situation Comedy, Feminism, and Freud: Discourses of Gracie and Lucy." In *Feminist Television Criticism: A Reader.* Ed. Charlotte Brunsdon, Julie d'Acci, and Lynn Spigel. New York: Oxford University Press, 1997.

———, ed. *Logics of Television: Essays in Television Criticism.* Bloomington: Indiana University Press, 1990.

Meyers, Marian. "Fracturing Women." In *Mediated Women: Representations in Popular Culture.* Ed. Marian Meyers. 3–22. Cresskill, N.J.: Hampton Press, 1999.

———, ed. *Mediated Women: Representations in Popular Culture.* Cresskill, N.J.: Hampton Press, 1999.

Millman, Joyce. "*Alias:* A Modern Cinderella, No Prince Needed." *New York Times,* November 18, 2001, 34.

———. "Chicks Who Kick." *Boston Phoenix,* October 24, 2003 <www.bostonphoenix.com /boston/arts/tv/documents/03257879.asp> (July 10, 2005).

Mittell, Jason. "A Cultural Approach to Television Genre Theory." *Cinema Journal* 40.3 (2001): 3–24.

Modleski, Tania. *Feminism without Women: Culture and Criticism in a "Postfeminist" Age.* New York: Routledge, 1991.

———. *Loving with a Vengeance: Mass-Produced Fantasies for Women.* London: Metheun, 1982.

Montgomery, Kathryn. *Target: Prime Time: Advocacy Groups and the Struggle over Entertainment Television.* New York: Oxford University Press, 1989.

Morgan, Carol, and Doran Levy. "Targeting to Psychographic Segments." *Brandweek,* October 2, 2002, 18–20.

Moseley, Rachel. "Glamorous Witchcraft: Gender and Magic in Teen Film and Television." *Screen* 43.4 (2002): 403–22.

Moseley, Rachel, and Jacinda Read. "'Having it *Ally*': Popular Television (Post-)Feminism." *Feminist Media Studies* 2.2 (2002): 231–49.

Moss, Linda. "Laybourne Preps New Women's Net." *Multichannel News,* October 19, 1998, 1.

———. "Lifetime Adding More Movies, Hoping for Lift." *Multichannel News,* April 19, 2004, 1.

———. "Romance Ups Original Productions." *Multichannel News,* December 8, 1997, 130.

National Organization for Women. *Facts on Women and Media.* New York: NOW Legal Defense and Education Fund, 1986.

———. "Watch Out, Listen Up! 2002 Feminist Primetime Report." <http://www .nowfoundation.org/watchout3/index.html> (April 16, 2003).

Negra, Diane. "Quality Postfeminism? Sex and the Single Girl on HBO." *Genders* 39 (2004) <http://www.genders.org/g39/g39_negra.html> (July 10, 2005).

Newcomb, Horace, and Paul Hirsch. "Television as a Cultural Forum." In *Television: The Critical View.* 5th ed. Ed. Horace Newcomb. 503–15. New York: Oxford University Press, 1994.

Nochimson, Martha P. "*Ally McBeal:* Brightness Falls from the Air." *Film Quarterly* 53.3 (2000): 25–32.

Ouellette, Laurie. "Victims No More: Postfeminism, Television, and *Ally McBeal.*" *Communication Review* 5 (2002): 315–35.

Owen, Bruce, and Steven S. Wildman. *Video Economics.* Cambridge, Mass.: Harvard University Press, 1992.

"Oxygen Media and Markle to Fund Women's Research Initiative." *Communications Daily,* July 27, 1999.

Parks, Lisa. "Brave New *Buffy:* Rethinking 'TV Violence.'" In *Quality Popular Television.* Ed. Mark Jancovich and James Lyons. 118–33. London: British Film Institute, 2003.

Parry-Giles, Trevor, and Shawn J. Parry-Giles. "*The West Wing*'s Prime-Time Presidentiality: Mimesis and Catharsis in a Postmodern Romance." *Quarterly Journal of Speech* 88.2 (2002): 209–27.

Penley, Constance, Elisabeth Lyon, Lynn Spigel, and Janet Bergstrom, eds. *Close Encounters: Film, Feminism, and Science Fiction.* Minneapolis: University of Minnesota Press, 1991.

Penley, Constance, Lisa Parks, and Anna Everett. "Log On: The Oxygen Media Research Project." In *New Media: Theories and Practices of Digitextuality.* Ed. Anna Everett and John Caldwell. 225–42. New York: Routledge, 2003.

Pennington, Gail. "Now, It's 'Wham, Bam'—and from the Ma'am." *St. Louis Post-Dispatch,* January 28, 2001, F1.

Petrozzello, Donna. "The A-Team: Geraldine Laybourne, Oprah Winfrey, Marcy Carsey, and Women's Cable Programming Venture Oxygen Media." *Broadcasting and Cable,* November 30, 1998, 6.

———. "Only on Cable." *Broadcasting and Cable,* October 26, 1998, 42.

———. "TCI, Laybourne to Launch Oxygen." *Broadcasting and Cable,* October 19, 1998, 88.

Popcorn, Faith, and Lys Marigold. *EVEolution: The Eight Truths of Marketing to Women.* New York: Hyperion, 2000.

Pozner, Jennifer L. "Thwack! Pow! Yikes! Not Your Mother's Heroines." *Sojourner: The Women's Forum* 23.2 (October 1997): 12–13.

Press, Andrea L. *Women Watching Television: Gender, Class, and Generation in the American Television Experience.* Philadelphia: University of Pennsylvania Press, 1991.

Prikios, Karen Anderson. "HBO: Digital to the Max." *Broadcasting and Cable,* March 19, 2001, 72.

Probyn, Elspeth. "New Traditionalism and Post-Feminism: TV Does the Home." In *Feminist Television Criticism: A Reader.* Ed. Charlotte Brunsdon, Julie d'Acci, and Lynn Spigel. 126–38. New York: Oxford University Press, 1997.

Projansky, Sarah. *Watching Rape: Film and Television in Postfeminist Culture.* New York: New York University Press, 2001.

Projansky, Sarah, and Leah R. Vande Berg. "Sabrina, the Teenage . . . : Girls, Witches, Mortals, and the Limitations of Prime-Time Feminism." In *Fantasy Girls: Gender in the New Universe of Science Fiction and Fantasy Television.* Ed. Elyce Rae Helford. 13–40. Lanham, Md.: Rowman and Littlefield, 2000.

Quinlan, Mary Lou. *Just Ask a Woman: Cracking the Code of What Women Want and How They Buy.* Hoboken, N.J.: John Wiley and Sons, 2003.

Rabinovitz, Lauren. "Ms.-Representation: The Politics of Feminist Sitcoms." In *Television, History, and American Culture.* Ed. Mary Beth Haralovich and Lauren Rabinovitz. 144–67. Durham, N.C.: Duke University Press, 1999.

———. "Sitcoms and Single Moms: Representations of Feminism on American TV." *Cinema Journal* 29 (1989): 3–19.

Radner, Hilary. "Introduction: Queering the Girl." In *Swinging Single: Representing Sexuality in the 1960s.* Ed. Hilary Radner and Moya Luckett. 1–35. Minneapolis: University of Minnesota Press, 1999.

Reep, Diana C., and Faye H. Dambrot. "Television's Professional Women: Working with Men in the 1980s." *Journalism Quarterly* 64.2–3 (1987): 376–81.

Rich, Adrienne. "Compulsory Heterosexuality and Lesbian Existence." In *The Lesbian and Gay Studies Reader.* Ed. Henry Abelove, Michele Aina Barale, and David M. Halperin. 227–54. New York: Routledge, 1993.

Romano, Allison. "BET Is About to Get a Real Rival." *Broadcasting and Cable,* January 20, 2003, 46.

———. "Wish You Were Younger? So Do Many Cable Nets." *Broadcasting and Cable,* August 25, 2003, 12.

———. "Women's Net Rivals Find Their Niche" *Broadcasting and Cable,* March 10, 2003, 15.

Rosen, Marjorie. *Popcorn Venus.* New York: Avon, 1973.

Ross, Chuck. "Turner Explores Cable Network Aimed at Women: Time Warner Division Would Flex Muscle to Take on Lifetime, Oxygen." *Advertising Age,* March 15, 1999, 3.

Ross, Sharon Marie. "Super(Natural) Women: Female Heroes, Their Friends, and Their Fans." Ph.D. dissertation, University of Texas at Austin, 2002.

Rowe, Kathleen. *The Unruly Woman: Gender and Genres of Laughter.* Austin: University of Texas Press, 1995.

Russ, Joanna. *To Write Like a Woman: Essays in Feminism and Science Fiction.* Bloomington: Indiana University Press, 1995.

Rutenberg, Jim. "Poor Showing for Oxygen in Ratings." *New York Times,* April 22, 2002, C1.

Schulze, Laurie. "The Made-for-TV Movie: Industrial Practice, Cultural Form, Popular Reception." In *Hollywood in the Age of Television.* Ed. Tino Balio. 351–76. Boston, Unwin Hyman, 1990.

Schwarzbaum, Lisa. "We're Gonna Make It After All." *Working Woman* 20.10 (October 1995): 30–37.

Seggar, John F. "Imagery of Women in Television Drama: 1974." *Journal of Broadcasting* 19.3 (1975): 273–82.

Shalit, Ruth. "Canny and Lacy." *New Republic,* April 6, 1998, 27–33.

Sharkey, Betsy. "Women Get More Cybillized: The Strong, Even Macho Female Lead Is Showing Up in More Places on Prime Time TV." *Mediaweek,* November 3, 1997, 28–30.

Showalter, Elaine. *A Literature of Their Own: British Women Novelists from Bronte to Lessing.* Princeton, N.J.: Princeton University Press, 1977.

Shugart, Helene A., Catherine Egley Waggoner, and D. Lynn O'Brien Hallstein. "Mediating Third-Wave Feminism: Appropriation as Postmodern Practice." *Critical Studies in Media Communication* 18.2 (2001): 194–210.

Sims, Amy C. "High-Heeled and Dangerous." *FOXNews.com,* June 26, 2003 <www.foxnews .com/printer_friendly_story/0,3566,90439,00.html> (July 6, 2003).

Spigel, Lynn. "From Domestic Space to Outer Space: The 1960s Fantastic Family Sit-Com." In *Close Encounters: Film, Feminism, and Science Fiction.* Ed. Constance Penley, Elisabeth Lyon, Lynn Spigel, and Janet Bergstrom. 205–35. Minneapolis: University of Minnesota Press, 1991.

———. *Make Room for TV: Television and the Family Ideal in Postwar America.* Chicago: University of Chicago Press, 1992.

Spigel, Lynn, and Denise Mann, eds. *Private Screenings: Television and the Female Consumer.* Minneapolis: University of Minnesota Press, 1992.

Stack, Teresa. "Fiction Is Not a Feminist Issue." *Pittsburgh Post-Gazette,* July 18, 1998, A13.

Staiger, Janet. *Blockbuster TV: Must-See Sitcoms in the Network Era.* New York: New York University Press, 2000.

Stanley, Alessandra. "The Oxygen TV Channel Is Bowing to Tastes." *New York Times*, February 25, 2002, C1.

Stark, Steven D. "Ally McBeal." *New Republic*, December 29, 1997, 13–15.

Stevens, Tracy, ed. *International Television and Video Almanac*. 45th ed. La Jolla, Calif.: Quigley Publishing, 2000.

Streeter, Thomas. "Media: The Problem of Creativity." Paper presented at the International Communication Association Annual Conference. Washington, D.C., May 26, 2001.

Surmanek, Jim. *Media Planning: A Practical Guide*. 3d ed. Lincolnwood, Ill.: NTC Publishing, 1996.

Taylor, Ella. *Prime-Time Families: Television Culture in Postwar America*. Berkeley: University of California Press, 1989.

Theroux, Phyllis. "TV Women Have Come a Long Way, Baby—Sort Of." *New York Times*, May 17, 1987, sec. 2, 35.

Thomas, Lyn. *Fans Feminisms and "Quality" Media*. London: Routledge, 2002.

Tomashoff, Craig. "Actresses Are Beginning to Get a Bigger Cut of the Action." *Los Angeles Times*, November 20, 2000, F12.

Tuchman, Gaye. "Women's Depictions by the Mass Media." *Signs* 4 (1979): 528–42.

Tuchman, Gaye, Arlene Kaplan Daniels, and James Benet, eds. *Hearth and Home: Images of Women in the Mass Media*. New York: Oxford University Press, 1978.

Tudor, Andrew. "Genre." In *Film Genre Reader II*. Ed. Barry Keith Grant. 3–10. Austin: University of Texas Press, 1995.

Tung, Charlene. "Embodying an Image: Gender, Race, and Sexuality in *La Femme Nikita*." In *Action Chicks: New Images of Tough Women in Popular Culture*. Ed. Sherrie A. Inness. 95–122. New York: Palgrave Macmillan, 2004.

Turow, Joseph. *Playing Doctor: Television, Storytelling, and Medical Power*. New York: Oxford University Press, 1989.

———. "Unconventional Programs on Commercial Television: An Organizational Perspective." In *Mass Communicators in Context*. Ed. D. Charles Whitney and James Ettema. 107–29. Beverly Hills, Calif.: Sage, 1982.

Umstead, R. Thomas. "WE Facelift Completes Changeover." *Multichannel News*, October 29, 2001 <www.tvinsite.com/multichanne_int_page&doc_id&articleID+CA179545> (October 29, 2001).

Vande Berg, Leah R., and Diane Streckfuss. "Prime-Time Television's Portrayal of Women and the World of Work: A Demographic Profile." *Journal of Broadcasting and Electronic Media* 36.2 (1992): 195–207.

Vavrus, Mary. *Postfeminist News: Political Women in Media Culture*. Albany: State University of New York Press, 2002.

Vest, David. "Prime-Time Pilots: A Content Analysis of Changes in Gender Representation." *Journal of Broadcasting and Electronic Media* 36.1 (1992): 25–43.

"Vulcan Ventures Makes $100 Million Investment in Oxygen Media." *PR Newswire*, June 16, 1999.

Waldman, Diane. "There's More to a Positive Image Than Meets the Eye." In *Issues in Feminist Criticism*. Ed. Patricia Erens. 13–18. Bloomington: Indiana University Press, 1990.

Walton, Dawn. "Feminist Role Model or Ditzy Broad?" *Ottawa Citizen,* June 29, 1998, E5.

WE Upfront Sales Kit, 2003.

"Welcome to Providence." <http://members.tripod_cometoprovidence/pro/background .htm> (February 21, 2001).

White, Mimi. "Meanwhile, Back in the Emergency Room . . . : Feminism, Aesthetic Form, and Narrative Politics of *Judging Amy.*" Paper presented at the Console-ing Passions Conference. New Orleans, May 30, 2004.

———. *Tele-advising: Therapeutic Discourse in American Television.* Chapel Hill: University of North Carolina Press, 1992.

Wilcox, Rhonda V., and David Lavery. *Fighting the Forces: What's at Stake in "Buffy the Vampire Slayer."* Lanham, Md.: Rowman and Littlefield, 2002.

Wilson, Pamela. "Upscale Feminine Angst: *Molly Dodd,* the Lifetime Cable Network, and Gender Marketing." *Camera Obscura* (special issue on "Lifetime: A Cable Network for Women," ed. Julie d'Acci) 33–34 (1994): 102–31.

Zoonen, Liesbet van. *Feminist Media Studies.* Thousand Oaks, Calif.: Sage, 1994.

Index

AMANDA D. LOTZ is an assistant professor of communication studies at the University of Michigan. She earned a Ph.D. in Radio-Television-Film and a certificate in women's studies at the University of Texas at Austin in 2000. She has published articles in *Critical Studies in Media Communication, Feminist Media Studies, Communication Theory, Journal of Broadcasting and Electronic Media, Television and New Media, Screen, Journal of Popular Film and Television,* and *Women and Language.* She was named the Coltrin Professor of the Year by the International Radio and Television Society in 2004 for her case study exploring the redefinition of television.

The University of Illinois Press
is a founding member of the
Association of American University Presses.

Composed in 10.5/13 Adobe Minion
with Minion display
by Type One, LLC
for the University of Illinois Press
Manufactured by Thomson-Shore, Inc.

University of Illinois Press
1325 South Oak Street
Champaign, IL 61820-6903
www.press.uillinois.edu